UNCTAD/DITE/3(Vol. VIII)

United Nations Conference on Trade and Development
Division on Investment, Technology and Enterprise Development

International Investment Instruments: A Compendium

Volume VIII

United Nations
New York and Geneva, 2002

Note

UNCTAD serves as the focal point within the United Nations Secretariat for all matters related to foreign direct investment and transnational corporations. In the past, the Programme on Transnational Corporations was carried out by the United Nations Centre on Transnational Corporations (1975-1992) and the Transnational Corporations and Management Division of the United Nations Department of Economic and Social Development (1992-1993). In 1993, the Programme was transferred to the United Nations Conference on Trade and Development. UNCTAD seeks to further the understanding of the nature of transnational corporations and their contribution to development and to create an enabling environment for international investment and enterprise development. UNCTAD's work is carried out through intergovernmental deliberations, technical assistance activities, seminars, workshops and conferences.

The term "country", as used in the boxes added by the UNCTAD secretariat at the beginning of the instruments reproduced in this volume, also refers, as appropriate, to territories or areas; the designations employed and the presentation of the material do not imply the expression of any opinion whatsoever on the part of the Secretariat of the United Nations concerning the legal status of any country, territory, city or area or of its authorities, or concerning the delimitation of its frontiers or boundaries. Moreover, the country or geographical terminology used in the boxes may occasionally depart from standard United Nations practice when this is made necessary by the nomenclature used at the time of negotiation, signature, ratification or accession of a given international instrument.

To preserve the integrity of the texts of the instruments reproduced in this volume, references to the sources of the instruments that are not contained in their original text are identified as "note added by the editor".

The texts of the instruments included in this volume are reproduced as they were written in one of their original languages or as an official translation thereof. When an obvious linguistic mistake has been found, the word "sic" has been added in brackets.

The materials contained in this volume have been reprinted with special permission of the relevant institutions. For those materials under copyright protection, all rights are reserved by the copyright holders.

It should be further noted that this collection of instruments has been prepared for documentation purposes only, and its contents do not engage the responsibility of UNCTAD.

UNCTAD/DITE/3 Vol. VIII

UNITED NATIONS PUBLICATION

Sales No. E.02.II.D.15

ISBN 92-1-112564-2

Copyright © 2002, United Nations
All rights reserved

K
3828
.A1
I5
2002
v. 8

OCT 2 4 2002

PREFACE

International Investment Instruments: A Compendium contains a collection of international instruments relating to foreign direct investment (FDI) and transnational corporations (TNCs). The collection is presented in nine volumes. The first three volumes were published in 1996. *Volumes IV* and *V* were published in 2000 followed by *Volume VI* in 2001. *Volumes VII, VIII and IX* bring the collection up to date. Most of the instruments reproduced in these volumes were adopted in the 1990s, the rest were adopted between 2000 and 2002.

The collection has been prepared to make the texts of international investment instruments conveniently available to interested policy-makers, scholars and business executives. The need for such a collection has increased in recent years as bilateral, regional, interregional and multilateral instruments dealing with various aspects of FDI have proliferated, and as new investment instruments are being negotiated or discussed at all levels.

While by necessity selective, the present collection seeks to provide a faithful record of the evolution and present status of intergovernmental cooperation concerning FDI and TNCs. Although the emphasis of the collection is on relatively recent documents (the majority of the instruments reproduced date from after 1990), it was deemed useful to include important older instruments as well, with a view towards providing some indications of the historical development of international concerns over FDI in the decades since the end of the Second World War.

The core of this collection consists of legally binding international instruments, mainly multilateral conventions, regional agreements, and bilateral treaties that have entered into force. In addition, a number of "soft law" documents, such as guidelines, declarations and resolutions adopted by intergovernmental bodies, have been included since these instruments also play a role in the elaboration of an international framework for FDI. In an effort to enhance the understanding of the efforts behind the elaboration of this framework, certain draft instruments that never entered into force, or texts of instruments on which the negotiations were not concluded, are also included; prototypes of bilateral investment treaties are reproduced as well. Included also are a number of influential documents prepared by business, consumer and labour organizations, as well as by other non-governmental organizations. It is clear from the foregoing that no implications concerning the legal status or the legal effect of an instrument can be drawn from its inclusion in this collection.

In view of the great diversity of the instruments in this *Compendium* -- in terms of subject matter, approach, legal form and extent of participation of States -- the simplest possible method of presentation was deemed the most appropriate. Thus, the relevant instruments are distributed among the *nine volumes of the Compendium* as follows:

- *Volume I* is devoted to multilateral instruments, that is to say, multilateral conventions as well as resolutions and other documents issued by multilateral organizations.

- *Volume II* covers interregional and regional instruments, including agreements, resolutions and other texts from regional organizations with an inclusive geographical context.

- *Volume III* is divided into three annexes covering three types of instruments that differ in their context or their origin from those included in the first two volumes:

    - Annex A reproduces investment-related provisions in free trade and regional integration agreements. The specific function and, therefore, the effect of such provisions is largely determined by the economic integration process which they are intended to promote and in the context of which they operate.

    - Annex B (the only section that departs from the chronological pattern) offers the texts of prototype bilateral treaties for the promotion and protection of foreign investments (BITs) of several developed and developing countries, as well as a list of these treaties concluded up to July 1995. The bilateral character of these treaties differentiates them from the bulk of the instruments included in this *Compendium*. Over 900 such treaties had been adopted by July 1995.

    - Annex C supplies the texts of documents prepared by non-governmental organizations; these give an indication of the broader environment in which the instruments collected here are prepared.

- *Volume IV*, divided into two parts, covers additional multilateral (Part One) and regional instruments (Part Two) not covered in *Volumes I* and *II*, including, but not limited to, those adopted between 1996 and the end of 1999.

- *Volume V* is divided into four parts, as follows:

    - Part One reproduces investment-related provisions in a number of additional free trade and economic integration agreements not covered in *Volume III*.

    - Part Two includes for the first time investment-related provisions in association agreements as well as bilateral and interregional cooperation agreements. These are divided into three annexes. Annex A is devoted to agreements signed between the countries members of the European Free Trade Association (EFTA) and third countries. Annex B covers investment-related provisions in agreements signed between the countries members of the European Community (EC) and third countries as well as other regional groups. Annex C includes types of bilateral agreements related to investment that differ from those covered in other parts.

    - Part Three contains the texts of a number of additional prototype BITs of several developed and developing countries, as well as a list of these treaties concluded between July 1995 and the end of 1998, when the total number of BITs concluded since 1959 reached over 1,730.

- Part Four reproduces additional texts of recent documents prepared by non-governmental organizations.

- *Volume VI* is divided into the following six parts:

  - Part One contains an additional multilateral instrument.

  - Part Two covers additional interregional and regional instruments, including agreements, resolutions and other texts from regional organizations with an inclusive geographical context.

  - Part Three reproduces investment-related provisions in a number of additional free trade and economic integration agreements not covered in previous volumes.

  - Part Four includes investment-related provisions in association agreements as well as bilateral and interregional cooperation agreements not covered in previous volumes.

  - Part Five contains the texts of a number of additional prototype BITs of several developed and developing countries not covered in previous volumes.

  - Part Six includes for the first time prototype double taxation treaties (DTTs).

- *Volume VII* is divided into the following three parts:

  - Part One contains an additional multilateral instrument.

  - Part Two reproduces investment-related provisions in a number of additional free trade and cooperation agreements signed between countries members of the European Free Trade Association (EFTA) and countries members of the European Community (EC) with third countries not covered in previous volumes.

  - Part Three contains the texts of a number of additional prototype BITs not covered in previous volumes.

- *Volume VIII* is divided into the following three parts:

  - Part One covers additional interregional and regional instruments, including agreements and other texts from regional organizations with an inclusive geographical context.

- Part Two reproduces investment-related provisions in a number of additional free trade, economic integration and cooperation agreements not covered in previous volumes.

- Part Three contains the texts of a number of additional prototype BITs not covered in previous volumes.

- *Volume IX* is divided into the following three parts:

  - Part One covers additional interregional and regional instruments, including agreements and other texts from regional organizations with an inclusive geographical context.

  - Part Two reproduces investment-related provisions in a number of additional free trade, economic integration and cooperation agreements not covered in previous volumes.

  - Part Three contains the texts of a number of additional prototype BITs not covered in previous volumes.

Within each of these subdivisions, instruments are reproduced in chronological order, except for the sections dedicated to prototype instruments.

The multilateral and regional instruments covered are widely differing in scope and coverage. Some are designed to provide an overall, general framework for FDI and cover many, although rarely all, aspects of investment operations. Most instruments deal with particular aspects and issues concerning FDI. A significant number address core FDI issues, such as the promotion and protection of investment, investment liberalization, dispute settlement and insurance and guarantees. Others cover specific issues, of direct but not exclusive relevance to FDI and TNCs, such as transfer of technology, intellectual property, avoidance of double taxation, competition and the protection of consumers and the environment. A relatively small number of instruments of this last category has been reproduced, since each of these specific issues often constitutes an entire system of legal regulation of its own, whose proper coverage would require an extended exposition of many kinds of instruments and arrangements.[a]

The *Compendium* is meant to be a collection of instruments, not an anthology of relevant provisions. Indeed, to understand a particular instrument, it is normally necessary to take its entire text into consideration. An effort has been made, therefore, to reproduce complete instruments, even though, in a number of cases, reasons of space and relevance have dictated the inclusion of excerpts.

The UNCTAD secretariat has deliberately refrained from adding its own commentary to the texts reproduced in the *Compendium*. The only exception to this rule is the boxes added to

---

[a] For a collection of instruments (or excerpts therefrom) dealing with transfer of technology, see UNCTAD, *Compendium of International Arrangements on Transfer of Technology: Selected Instruments* (Geneva: United Nations), United Nations publication, Sales No. E.01.II.D.28.

each instrument. They provide some basic facts, such as its date of adoption and date of entry

into force and, where appropriate, signatory countries. Also, a list of agreements containing investment-related provisions signed by the EFTA countries and by the EC countries with third countries or regional groups are reproduced in the *Compendium*. Moreover, to facilitate the identification of each instrument in the table of contents, additional information has been added, in brackets, next to each title, on the year of its signature and the name of the relevant institution involved.

Rubens Ricupero
Secretary-General of UNCTAD

Geneva, June 2002

ACKNOWLEDGEMENTS

Volume VIII of the *Compendium* was prepared by Abraham Negash under the overall direction of Karl P. Sauvant. Comments were received from Victoria Aranda, Americo Beviglia Zampetti and Joerg Weber. The volume was proof-read by Stijn Mentrop. The cooperation of the relevant countries and organizations from which the relevant instruments originate is acknowledged with gratitude.

CONTENTS

VOLUME VIII

PART ONE

INTERREGIONAL AND REGIONAL INSTRUMENTS

PART TWO

BILATERAL INSTRUMENTS

PART THREE

PROTOTYPE INSTRUMENTS

CONTENTS OF OTHER VOLUMES

VOLUME I
MULTILATERAL INSTRUMENTS

VOLUME II
REGIONAL INSTRUMENTS

REGIONAL INSTRUMENTS

VOLUME III

REGIONAL INTEGRATION, BILATERAL AND NON-GOVERNMENTAL INSTRUMENTS

ANNEX C. NON-GOVERNMENTAL INSTRUMENTS

VOLUME IV

MULTILATERAL AND REGIONAL INSTRUMENTS

PART ONE

MULTILATERAL INSTRUMENTS

PART TWO

REGIONAL INSTRUMENTS

VOLUME V

REGIONAL INTEGRATION, BILATERAL AND NON-GOVERNMENTAL INSTRUMENTS

PART ONE

INVESTMENT-RELATED PROVISIONS IN FREE TRADE AND ECONOMIC INTEGRATION AGREEMENTS

PART TWO

INVESTMENT-RELATED PROVISIONS IN ASSOCIATION AGREEMENTS, BILATERAL AND INTERREGIONAL COOPERATION AGREEMENTS

ANNEX A. INVESTMENT-RELATED PROVISIONS IN FREE TRADE AGREEMENTS SIGNED BETWEEN THE COUNTRIES MEMBERS OF THE EUROPEAN FREE TRADE ASSOCIATION AND THIRD COUNTRIES AND LIST OF AGREEMENTS SIGNED (END-1999)

ANNEX B. INVESTMENT-RELATED PROVISIONS IN ASSOCIATION, PARTNERSHIP AND COOPERATION AGREEMENTS SIGNED BETWEEN THE COUNTRIES MEMBERS OF THE EUROPEAN COMMUNITY AND THIRD COUNTRIESAND LIST OF AGREEMENTS SIGNED (END-1999)

ANNEX C.   OTHER BILATERAL INVESTMENT-RELATED AGREEMENTS

PART THREE

PROTOTYPE BILATERAL INVESTMENT TREATIES AND LIST OF BILATERAL INVESTMENT TREATIES (MID-1995 — END-1998)

PART FOUR

NON-GOVERNMENTAL INSTRUMENTS

VOLUME VI

PART ONE

MULTILATERAL INSTRUMENTS

PART TWO

INTERREGIONAL AND REGIONAL INSTRUMENTS

PART THREE

INVESTMENT-RELATED PROVISIONS IN FREE TRADE AND ECONOMIC INTEGRATION AGREEMENTS

PART FOUR

INVESTMENT-RELATED PROVISIONS IN ASSOCIATION AGREEMENTS, BILATERAL AND INTERREGIONAL COOPERATION AGREEMENTS

PART FIVE

PROTOTYPE BILATERAL INVESTMENT TREATIES

PART SIX

PROTOTYPE BILATERAL DOUBLE TAXATION TREATIES

VOLUME VII

PART ONE

MULTILATERAL INSTRUMENTS

PART TWO

BILATERAL INSTRUMENTS

PART THREE

PROTOTYPE INSTRUMENTS

CONTENTS

VOLUME IX

PART ONE

INTERREGIONAL AND REGIONAL INSTRUMENTS

PART TWO

BILATERAL INSTRUMENTS

PART THREE

PROTOTYPE INSTRUMENTS

PART ONE

INTERREGIONAL AND REGIONAL

INSTRUMENTS

PROTOCOL A/P1/11/84 RELATING TO COMMUNITY ENTERPRISES *

(ECONOMIC COMMUNITY OF WEST AFRICAN STATES)

The Protocol A/P1/11/84 Relating to Community Enterprises was signed by the Member States of Economic Community of West African States, namely Benin, Burkina Faso, Cape Verde, Côte d'Ivoire, Gambia, Ghana, Guinea, Guinea-Bissau, Liberia, Mali, Niger, Nigeria, Senegal, Sierra Leone and Togo on 23 November 1984.

THE HIGH CONTRACTING PARTIES

Recalling the provisions of Articles 2 and 32 of the Treaty of the Economic Community of West African States relating to the integration and development of the economies of Member States of the Community;

Recalling the provision of the Protocol relating to the definition of the concept of products originating from Member States of ECOWAS;

Recalling Resolution ECW/CM/VI/RES.26 of November 1979 of the Council of Ministers relating to the formulation of ECOWAS Regional Industrial Policy and Programme;

Recalling Decision A/DEC.1/5/85 dated 30th May, 1983 of the Authority relating to the adoption and the implementation of a single Trade Liberalisation Scheme for industrial Products originating from Member States and the classification of the Member States contained in Article 4 thereof;

Mindful of the fact that the responsibility for the economic development of the West African region rests with the Member States themselves;

Considering that in furtherance of the objectives of the Treaty, Community enterprises can be vital agents for the promotion of more rapid integration of the economies of the Member States through the provision of additional avenues for joint endeavours under a Community framework;

HAVE AGREED AS FOLLOWS;

---

* *Source*: Economic Community of West African States (1984). Protocol A/P1/11/84 Relating to Community Enterprises "; available on the Internet (http://www.ecowas.int/). [Note added by the editor.]

Article 1

DEFINITIONS

"Treaty" means the Treaty of the Economic Community of West African States signed in Lagos on the 28th May, 1975;

"Community" means the Economic Community of West African States established by Article 1 of the Treaty;

"Member State" means a Member State of the Community;

"Third Country" means a country other than a Member State of the Community;

"Authority" means the Authority of Heads of State and Government of the Community established by Article 5 of the Treaty;

"Council" means the Council of Ministers of the Community established by Article 6 of the Treaty;

"Executive Secretariat" and "Executive Secretary" means the Executive Secretariat and Executive Secretary of the Community as provided for under Article 8 of the Treaty;

"The Fund" means the Fund for Co-operation, Compensation and Development established by Article 50 of the Treaty;

"Selection Panel" means the Panel established by Article 11 of this Protocol;

"Community Enterprise" means an enterprise admitted to the status of a Community Enterprise under this Protocol and enjoying the benefits and guarantees granted thereunder;

"National Enterprises" means an enterprise that is registered in a Member State and operating under the national laws of the Member States;

"Inter-governmental enterprise" means an enterprise whose equity capital is owned entirely by two or more Member States;

"Citizen of the Community" means a citizen of the Community as defined in the Protocol relating to the definition of Community Citizen;

"National of a Member State" means a national of a Member State who is otherwise not qualified as a citizen of the Community;

"Unit of Account" means the unit of account specified in paragraph 3 of Article 6 of the Protocol relating to the Fund;

"Value Added" means value added as defined by Article 1 of the Protocol relating to the definition of the concept of products originating from Member States;

"Legal Persons of Member States" means institutions or companies in which Member States or their nationals own not less than 51% of the equity capital;

"Processing" shall have the same meaning ascribed to it in the Protocol relating to the definition of the concept of products originating from Member States.

Article 2

OWNERSHIP AND FORM OF COMMUNITY ENTERPRISES

1.   Subject to the provisions of this Protocol, an enterprise may be admitted to the status of Community Enterprise under this Protocol if its equity capital is owned by:

   a.   two or more Member States, or

   b.   two or more Member States and citizens or institutions of the Community or nationals or legal persons of a Member State or nationals or legal persons of third countries.

2.   Any enterprise in respect of which an application is made of admission to the status of a Community Enterprise, shall first have been incorporated as a public limited liability company or established as an inter-governmental enterprise in a Member State.

Article 3

CONDITIONS FOR THE APPROVAL OF A COMMUNITY ENTERPRISE

1.   No enterprise shall be admitted to the status of a Community Enterprise unless it complies with the provisions of Article 2 of this Protocol and in addition it satisfies the following conditions:

   a.   i.   In respect of an enterprise referred to in sub-paragraph (a) of paragraph 1 of Article 2 of this Protocol, its entire equity capital is vested in two or more Member States, or

   ii.   In respect of an enterprise referred to in sub-paragraph (b) of paragraph 1 of Article 2 of this Protocol, not less than 51% of its equity capital is vested in two or more Member States and citizens or institutions of the Community or nationals or legal persons of a Member State or nationals or legal persons of third countries; and

   b.   in accordance with Article 4 of Decision A/DEC.1/5/83 of the Authority.

   i.   in respect of Cape Verde, the Gambia, Guinea Bissau, Burkina Faso, Mali, Mauritania or Niger its equity capital is not less than 1.5 million units of accounts with an intended investment of not less than 6 million units of accounts, or

ii. in respect of Benin, Guinea, Liberia, Sierra Leone or Togo, its equity capital is not less than 2 million units of account with an intended investment of not less than 8 million units of account,

iii. in respect of Ivory Coast, Ghana, Nigeria or Senegal, its equity capital is not less than 2.5 million units of account with an intended investment of not less than 8 million units of account,

c. its Chairman and the majority of the members of its Board of Directors are citizens of the Community; and

d. its activities extend to two or more Member States with the objective of promoting through complementarity the economic integration of the Community; and

e. its Headquarters is in a Member State; and

f. its objectives are in accordance with the development policies and programmes of the Community as may be determined from time to time by the Council; and

g. it operations will not harm the interest of National Enterprises of Member States; and

h. all its shares are registered and confer the same rights; and

i. with respect to a manufacturing enterprise, its products originate within the Member States in accordance with the provisions of the Protocol relating to the definition of the concept of products origination from Member States of the Economic Community of West African States other than those relating to indigenous ownership and participation.

2. Notwithstanding the provisions of this Protocol, an enterprise may be admitted to the status of a Community Enterprise if it is or will be engaged solely in the purchase or sale of goods without undergoing any processing.

Article 4

ADDITIONAL CRITERIA FOR APPROVAL OF COMMUNITY ENTERPRISES

In addition to the conditions stipulated in Article 3 of this Protocol, the Selection Panel shall before recommending the admission of an enterprise to the status of a Community Enterprise and depending on the nature of the activities of the enterprise have regard to its ability to contribute to the following objectives:

a. the development of the Community in general and in particular, the industrially less-developed Member States;

b. the promotion of diversification in the economic activities of the Community;

c. the rational use of the resources of the Member States and their economic potential;

d.   the creation and the expansion of employment within the Community for nationals of the Member States;

e.   improved access of the Member States to international capital markets;

f.   the provision of satisfactory arrangements for the training of nationals of the Member States in administrative, technical, managerial and other skills with a view to securing the benefit of their knowledge and experience in the conduct of the enterprises;

g.   the promotion and development of indigenous technology and the transfer adaptation of imported one;

h.   the improvement of the balance of payments of Member States through significant savings on import from third countries and increase of trade within the Community and exports to third countries;

i.   the provision of sufficient and adequate environmental pollution controls and the restoration of the environment to its original state.

Article 5

APPLICATION FOR APPROVAL

1.   All applications for the admission of an enterprise to the status of a Community Enterprise shall be in writing and shall first be submitted to the Member State in which the enterprise is located or will be located for its sponsorship with a copy to the Executive Secretariat for information.

2.   On receipt of an application, the Member State shall acknowledge receipt and make its decision known to the applicant and the Executive Secretariat within three months of the receipt of such application.

3.   An Enterprise sponsored by a Member State shall submit through such Member State thirty copies in French and twenty in English of its application to the Executive Secretariat which shall acknowledge receipt both to the member States and the Enterprises concerned.

Article 6

INFORMATION REQUIRED FOR APPROVAL OF APPLICATION

1.   All applications for the admission of an enterprise to the status of a Community Enterprise shall be accompanied by a detailed description of the nature of the enterprise and a copy of its Memorandum and Articles of Association or equivalent documents.

2.   The particulars required under paragraph 1 of this Article shall where applicable include the following:

    a.   the name and address of the enterprise to be approved;

b.   a copy of its instrument of incorporation and a certificate showing the number of shares held by each shareholder;

c.   list and nationalities of shareholders;

d.   the names and nationalities of members of the Board of Directors;

e.   the goods produced or to be produced or services offered or to be offered;

f.   the actual or projected amount on investment and financing plan showing the amount to be invested in local and external currencies;

g.   date of commencement of construction;

h.   the day on which the enterprise is expected to commence operation or production in marketable quantities of the products specified;

i.   the locality or localities in which it is proposed to establish the enterprise;

j.   a detailed feasibility study on the enterprise which shall where applicable include a

      i.   detailed estimate and description and analysis of the projected markets, capital and production factors, required and size of the labour force, especially the size of personnel required from third countries;

      ii.   a production scheme indicating the annual volume and value of production and possibilities of expansions;

      iii.   a detailed inventory of the volume, value and origin of plant machinery, spare parts and all other equipment necessary for the establishment and operation of the enterprise after its admission and their expected sources of supply and the price structure for products to be manufactured and the estimated trading account figures for a ten-year period and cash flow;

      iv.   the projected scale of export to third countries;

      v.   the projected effect on trade within the Community;

      vi.   a detailed inventory in volume and value and origin of annual imports of raw materials and semi-processed goods essential to the operations of the enterprise after its admission.

      vii.   a programme of recruitment and training for workers who are citizens of the Community that would enable them to acquire the requisite skills. Such programme shall provide for a period at the end of which citizens of the Community shall replace personnel from third countries.

Article 7

1.   Upon the receipt of the application referred to in paragraph 3 of Article 5 of this Protocol, the Executive Secretariat shall:

    a.   acknowledge receipt and state the period required for an evaluation of the application which shall not exceed six months. The Executive Secretariat may during the evaluation of such application request the applicant for supplementary information and may determine a time limit in any case not exceeding six months, for the communication of such information;

    b.   forward a copy thereof to all Member States;

    c.   publish an extract of the application in the Official Journal of the Community and cause it to be published in the Official Gazettes of the Member States.

2.   The Member States shall acknowledge receipt and within four months from the date of the publication of an application in the Official Journal of the Community submit their observations thereon to the Executive Secretariat.

3.   Three months after the publication of an application in the Official Journal of the Community, the Executive Secretariat shall transmit the application together with all the relevant documents and observations received from the Member States to the Selection Panel for its consideration and recommendations.

4.   The Executive Secretariat shall forward the recommendations of the Selection Panel to the next meeting of the Council for its decision.

5.   The decision of the Council shall be published in the Official Journal of the Community and transmitted forthwith to the Member States which shall cause it to be published in their Official Gazettes.

Article 8

OBJECTION PROCEDURE

1.   Any Member State wishing to object to the admission of an enterprise to the status of a Community Enterprise shall within a period of three months from the date the application is published in the Official Journal of the Community forward to the Executive Secretariat in writing the reasons and justification for its objection.

2.   Any legal or natural person established or domiciled in a Member State wishing to object to the admission of an enterprise to the status of a Community Enterprise shall within the period specified in paragraph 1 of this Article submit in writing the reasons and justification for his objection to that Member State for transmission to the Executive Secretariat.

3.   Upon the receipt of an objection the Executive Secretariat shall investigate the matter and submit its findings to the Selection Panel for its recommendations and transmit them to the Council for its decision.

Article 9

APPROVAL AGREEMENT

1.   As soon as enterprise has been approved for admission to the status of a Community Enterprise by the Council the Executive Secretary shall on behalf of the Community enter into an agreement (hereinafter referred to as "the Approval Agreement") with the enterprise in the form annexed to this Protocol.

2.   The duration of the Approval Agreement shall be fixed by the Council on the recommendation of the Selection Panel bearing in mind the size and nature of the enterprise.

3.   The Approval Agreement shall be governed by the provisions of this Protocol.

Article 10

ROLE OF THE EXECUTIVE SECRETARIAT

The Executive Secretariat shall:

a.   receive and evaluate all applications for the admission of enterprises to the status of Community Enterprises, submit them to the Selection Panel for its recommendations and to the Council for its decision;

b.   keep a register of Community Enterprises and levy and collect from Community Enterprises such registration fees as may be determined by the Council;

c.   Monitor in co-operation with the Member States the implementation of training schemes instituted in pursuance with item (vii) of sub-paragraph (j) of paragraph 2 of Article 6 of this Protocol;

d.   monitor in co-operation with the Member States the results of benefits granted to Community Enterprise under this Protocol and advise the Council on the performance of such Community Enterprises;

e.   inform the Council of any change in the composition of the Board of Directors or in the control of a Community Enterprise;

f.   examine as early as possible any complaints or objections received affecting an Approval Agreement or the performance and conduct of a Community Enterprise after commencement of operations and submit them to the Selection Panel;

g.   supervise the execution of the Approval Agreement and the implementation of this Protocol generally;

h.   help Community Enterprise in their negotiations with Member States with a view to obtaining the most favourable fiscal regime, incentives and privileges in force in the Member States concerned.

Article 11

SELECTION PANEL

1.   There is hereby established a Selection Panel which shall consist of one representative from each Member State who may be assisted by advisers.

2.   It shall be the responsibility of the Selection Panel:

   a.   to examine al applications for the admission of enterprises to the status of Community Enterprises submitted to it by the Executive Secretariat and make recommendations thereon to the Council;

   b.   to deal with any complaints or objections affecting an Approval Agreement or the performance and conduct of a Community Enterprise.

Article 12

ROLE OF THE COUNCIL

The Council shall:

a.   admit enterprises to the status of Community Enterprises in accordance with the provisions of this Protocol;

b.   determine the basis and the rate for calculating the Community Levy as provided for in paragraph 1 of Article 14 of this Protocol;

c.   approve the use of the proceeds of the Community Levy as provided for in paragraph 3 of Article 14 of this Protocol;

d.   cause the suspension or cancellation of an Approval Agreement where a Community Enterprise has been fraudulent or acts contrary to the provisions of this Protocol;

e.   determine registration fees to be paid by Community Enterprises as provided for in paragraph (b) of Article 10 of this Protocol;

Article 13

DUTIES OF A COMMUNITY ENTERPRISE

1.   All enterprises which have been admitted to the status of Community Enterprises in accordance with the provisions of this Protocol shall:

   a.   submit progress reports, annual balance sheets and audited accounts to the relevant authorities of the Member States involved in the project with copies to the Executive Secretariat;

b.   furnish the Member States and the Executive Secretariat with information relating to the fulfilment of the conditions of any permit and the extent to which benefits and permits have been utilised;

c.   offer services or manufacture products within the Community of acceptable quality at competitive prices and in sufficient quantities;

d.   inform the Executive Secretariat of nay intended deviations form or difficulties in the implementation of the terms of an Approval Agreement, so as to enable any necessary re-assessment to be made between the parties to the Approval Agreement;

e.   comply with such audit as may be requested by the Executive Secretariat in collaboration with the relevant authorities of the Member State where they are located in order to ascertain compliance with the terms of the Approval Agreement;

f.   comply with such other conditions as may be imposed by the Council;

g.   for all other necessary purposes, co-operate fully with the representative of the Executive Secretariat and the Member States;

h.   not fix or alter the prices of its product or services without prior consultation with the Executive Secretariat and the competent authorities of the Member States where they are located.

2.   All shareholders of a Community Enterprise shall be entitled to a vote and to be informed about the activities of the enterprise.

3.   No dealings in the shares of a Community Enterprise shall take place without the approval of its Board of Directors and in no case shall such dealings head to a reduction of the equity capital of nationals, legal persons or governments of the Member States below the level prescribed in items (i) and (ii) of sub-paragraph (a) of paragraph 1 of Article 3 of this Protocol. All valid dealings in its shares shall be notified to the Executive Secretariat.

4.   Any decision relating to the alteration of the instrument of incorporation, increase and reduction in the capital and dissolution of a Community Enterprise, appointment and removal of members of the Board of Directors and change of location of the headquarters of a Community Enterprise shall previously be notified to the Executive Secretariat.

5.   All changes in the structure of a Community Enterprise that may reduce the effective control of citizens of the Community or nationals of the Member States in the day to day administration of that enterprise shall not be permitted.

Article 14

COMMUNITY LEVY

1.   In addition to such national taxes as a Community Enterprise may be subject to in a Member State where its headquarters is or where it has autonomous branches, subsidiaries or

affiliates a Community enterprise shall pay directly to the Community an annual Community Levy the basis and rate of which shall be determined by the Council, taking into consideration the level of development of the different Member States in accordance with the provisions of Article 4 of Decision A/DEC.1/5/83 of the Authority.

2. Notwithstanding the provisions of paragraph 1 of this Article, the Council may exempt a Community Enterprise from the payment of Community Levy for such period and in respect of such activities as it may determine.

3. The Community Levy paid in pursuance of the provisions of paragraph 1 of this Article shall be kept in a Special Facility of the Fund and the use of such Special Facility shall be determined by Council.

4. Regulations relating to the application of the provisions of this Article including the computation of Community Levy, exemption from or deferment of payment of Community Levy and other allowances shall be made by the Council.

Article 15

DUTIES OF THE MEMBER STATES

1. Each Member State shall:

   a. receive, study and evaluate all applications for the admission of an enterprise to the status of a Community Enterprise and forward such applications sponsored by them within three months to the Executive Secretariat for processing;

   b. take such steps as are necessary to give effect to the provisions of this Protocol and ensure that effect is given to the provisions of an Approval Agreement and any matters required to be done thereunder;

   c. not take such discriminatory or unreasonable measures as would adversely affect the management, maintenance, use, enjoyment, expansion, sale, liquidation or other disposition of the investment of Community Enterprises;

   d. assist Community Enterprise by taking all necessary steps to promote their objectives and operations and facilitate the realisation of those objectives including the granting of the necessary export and import licences;

   e. determine and approve the quota of employees who are nationals of third countries required from time to time by Community Enterprises and take measures to facilitate the granting of the necessary visas and entry, resident and work permits;

   f. transmit as soon as possible to the Executive Secretariat any complaint or objection by any interested party in respect of an application for approval, or the performance or conduct of a Community Enterprise after commencement of its activities;

g.   pay fair compensation to any Community Enterprise which sustains a loss as a result of the expropriation or nationalisation by it of the assets or shares of the Community Enterprises;

h.   refuse to grant import licence or import duties exemption for the import of products from third countries where in the opinion of the Council, the same or similar products produced by Community Enterprises or by other enterprises manufacturing the same or similar products in the Member States are available in sufficient quantity or quantities within the Community to meet the demand for such products or similar products at competitive prices.

2.   All shareholders shall be enabled by the Member States to exercise in a reasonable manner, all their rights, particularly with respect to their attendance at meetings of the organs of a Community Enterprise.

Article 16

GENERAL BENEFITS, GUARANTEES AND PRIVILEGES OF COMMUNITY ENTERPRISES

1.   No enterprise admitted to the status of a Community Enterprise shall be nationalised or expropriated by the government of any Member State except for valid reasons of public interest and whereupon fair and adequate compensation shall be promptly said.

2.   Subject to the provisions of this Article, no person who owns shares in a Community Enterprise shall be compelled by law while the Community Enterprise continues to enjoy the benefits, guarantees and privileges granted under this Protocol, to cede in whole or in part his interest in the Community Enterprise.

3.   Benefits granted to a Community Enterprise under this Protocol and particularly under the terms of an Approval Agreement shall not, except as provided under Article 21, be altered subsequently to its disadvantage.

4.   Community Enterprises shall have legal personality in all Member States and shall enjoy the rights and privileges and favourable treatment with regard to industrial, financial and other incentives or advantages granted as a result of their negotiations with relevant authorities and in accordance with the laws of the Member States concerned.

5.   Subject to legislation in force and economic conditions prevailing in the Member States the following privileges and benefits may be obtained for a Community Enterprise through negotiations with the Member State concerned.

i.   the remittance of funds for payment of normal commercial transactions;

ii.   the remittance of capital, including interests and dividends to the country of origin of shareholders and creditors in the event of sale or the liquidation of a Community Enterprise;

iii.   the transfer of profits at the rate fixed in accordance with the terms of the negotiations carried out with the Member State concerned out of the country in which the headquarters of a Community Enterprise is located after adequate provision has been made for re-investment, maintenance and replacement of assets and after payment of any tax due in respect of the Community Enterprise;

iv. the transfer of payment in respect of principal, interest and other financial charges where a loan has been granted to a Community Enterprise by a non-resident in accordance with the terms of the contract of the said loan;

v. the transfer of fees and other charges incurred by a Community Enterprise in the ordinary course of business outside the country of its principal place of business;

vi. the entry into the Member State of the requisite foreign managerial and technical personnel for employment or engagement in a Community Enterprise, if the requisite skills are not available within the Community.

6. Reasonable facilities shall be provided by the monetary authorities of the Member States concerned to personnel employed or engaged in a Community Enterprise for making remittances abroad in respect of maintenance of their families and other contractual obligations such as insurance premiums and all contributions to provident and pension funds.

7. Dividends paid to natural or legal persons who are shareholders of Community Enterprises may be exempted from withholding tax whether such shareholders are residents or non-residents of the Member States where such enterprises are established.

Article 17

SPECIAL ADDITIONAL PRIVILEGES

1. The provisions of this Article shall apply only to the Community Enterprises referred to in sub-paragraph (a) and (b) of paragraph 1 of Article 2 of this Protocol.

2. An Approval Agreement may, without prejudice to the right of products which otherwise enjoy Community tariff treatment, provide exceptionally that no other Approval Agreement under this Protocol may be entered into in respect of the same industrial or economic activity.

3. Where a Community Enterprise enjoys the benefits provided for in paragraph 2 of this Article:

a. the products of the enterprise shall not be subject to any form of tariff or non-tariff restrictions or barriers except as provided for under Article 26 of the Treaty;

b. products which are the same or similar to the products of that enterprise may be imported exceptionally into the Community or exempted from import duties where in the opinion of the Council the products of that enterprise are insufficient in quantity or quality to meet the demand for those products or similar products at a competitive price.

4. The provisions of paragraph 2 and sub-paragraph (b) of paragraph 3 of this Article are exceptional and can only be applied for a specified period and for a region defined by the Council and for a Community Enterprise operating in a priority sector or introducing a new

industrial or economic activity within the Community without undue distortion to the economic equilibrium of the Community.

Article 18

COMPENSATION

1.   For the purpose of paying compensation in pursuance of the provisions of sub-paragraph (g) of paragraph 1 of Article 15 of this Protocol, the assets and liabilities of Community Enterprise shall be valued in accordance with regulations that are in force in the Member States concerned.

2.   Compensation shall forthwith be paid to the Community Enterprise in the currency of the original investment or convertible currency as soon as the amount of compensation has been determined in accordance with the provisions of this Article.

3.   Any disagreement as to he amount of compensation payable or the method of valuation used or as to any aspect of compensation shall be settled in accordance with the provisions of Article 22 of this Protocol.

4.   No provision of this Article shall be construed as empowering a Community Enterprise to increase or minimize the loss or losses sustained.

Article 19

APPLICATION FOR COMPENSATION

1.   A Community Enterprise whose assets are nationalised or expropriated or shareholders whose shares have been expropriated shall apply to the Member State concerned for compensation and transmit a copy of such application to the Executive Secretariat. Such application shall be in thirty copies in French and twenty in English, and shall contain:

   a.   details of the circumstances of the expropriation or nationalisation;

   b.   a valuation certificate of the investment expropriated or nationalised;

   c.   relevant documents relating to the expropriation or nationalisation.

2.   The Executive Secretariat shall transmit without delay to all the Member States copies of an application for compensation.

3.   The Executive Secretariat shall within three months from the date on which the copies of an application for compensation are received by him, contact the relevant authorities of the Member State concerned with a view to reaching an amicable settlement on the matter.

4.   If after the expiration of six months the issue has not been amicably settled, the Executive Secretary shall refer the matter to the Council.

5.   An award for compensation shall be expressed and paid in the same currency in which the investment was made or in convertible currency.

Article 20

NON-ASSIGNMENT OF APPROVAL AGREEMENT

An Approval Agreement concluded under the provision of this Protocol shall not be assignable.,

Article 21

DEFAULT, REVOCATION, SUSPENSION, CANCELLATION AND TERMINATION OF THE APPROVAL AGREEMENT

1.   The Council may without prior notice revoke its decisions to admit an enterprise to the status of a Community enterprise or cause the immediate suspension or cancellation of an Approval Agreement if any of the provisions of this Protocol or an Approval Agreement if any of the provisions of this Protocol or an Approval Agreement are not complied with. The revocation or cancellation shall take effect from the date of the decision which admitted an enterprise to the status of a Community Enterprise.

2.   The Council shall take any of the actions specified in paragraph 1 of this Article for any of the following reasons:

   a.   that the Community Enterprise has committed fraud, misrepresentation or other illegal act or has failed either deliberately or through negligence to disclose some material fact or facts prior to the enterprise being admitted to the status of a Community Enterprise;

   b.   that the Community Enterprise has failed to carry out its activities on a scale to justify being admitted to the status of a Community Enterprise;

   c.   that the Community Enterprise has abused the exemptions from import duties granted to it;

   d.   that the Community Enterprise has committed such other act or omission as to constitute a breach of its Approval Agreement.

3.   For the purpose of this Article the term "material fact" in sub-paragraph (a) of paragraph 2 of this Article shall mean any fact the knowledge of which would have caused the Community not to have entered into an Approval Agreement, or to enter into an Approval Agreement substantially different from that which is in fact entered into.

4.   Either party to an Approval Agreement wishing to terminate it shall give to the other one year's notice in writing of its intention to do so.

5.   The termination of an Approval Agreement shall not affect on-going actions and projects and vested rights during its period of validity.

Article 22

SETTLEMENT OF DISPUTES

1.   Where a dispute arises between Member States as to the interpretation or application of the provisions of this Protocol or an Approval Agreement the dispute shall be settled in accordance with the rules and procedures laid down in Article 56 of the Treaty.

2.   Where a dispute arises as to the interpretation or application of the provisions of this Protocol or an Approval Agreement between the Community and a Community Enterprise or between a Member State and a Community Enterprise, the parties shall inform the Executive Secretariat and endeavour to settle the dispute amicably within six months from the date when the dispute arose.

3.   Where a dispute referred to in paragraph 2 of this Article cannot be settled amicably, either party to the dispute shall notify the Executive Secretariat of the existence of such a dispute and each party shall within a period of 90 days nominate an arbitrator from the panel of Arbitrators of the International Centre for the Settlement of Investment Disputes or the Panel of Arbitrators of the Community as may from time to time be constituted by the Executive Secretariat. The two arbitrators so nominated shall within thirty days elect a third arbitrator from either of the said two panels who shall preside over the proceedings of the arbitration. In the event of the failure of the two arbitrators to agree on the election of the third arbitrator, either party may request the President of the International Court of Justice to elect the third arbitrator from either of the said two panels.

4.   The arbitrators so nominated shall conduct the arbitration at the headquarters of the Community or at any other place within the Community as may be agreed by the parties.

5.   The procedure of the arbitration shall be determined by the arbitrators, but the presiding arbitrator shall have full power to settle all questions of procedure in any case of disagreement in respect thereto.

6.   All decisions of the arbitrators shall be by majority vote which decisions shall be final and biding on the parties to the arbitration.

7.   The Council may make regulations concerning the application of the provisions of this Article.

Article 23

AMENDMENT

1.   Any Member State may submit proposals for the amendment or revision of this Protocol to the Executive Secretariat.

2.   The Executive Secretariat shall communicate such proposals to the Member States not later than thirty days after their receipt. Amendments or revisions shall be considered by the Authority after the Member States have been given thirty days notice thereof.

3.   No amendment to this Protocol shall prejudice any rights acquired by a Community Enterprise in pursuance of the provisions of this Protocol prior to the coming into force of the amendment.

Article 24

APPLICATION

The provisions of this Protocol:

a.   shall apply to enterprises defined in paragraph 1 of Article 2 of this Protocol; and

b.   may apply to wholly privately-owned enterprises in which nationals or legal persons of Member States own not less than 70% of equity capital and for this purposes the Council shall prescribe the rules and regulations for the application of the provisions of this Protocol to enterprises specified in this sub-paragraph.

Article 25

ENTRY INTO FORCE

1.   This Protocol shall enter into force provisionally upon signature by the Authority of Heads of State and Government of Member States and definitively upon ratification by at least seven (7) signatory States in accordance with the constitutional procedures applicable for each signatory State.

2.   This Protocol and all instruments of ratification shall be deposited with the Executive Secretariat of the Community which shall transmit certified true copies of this Protocol to all Member States and notify them of the dates of deposit of instruments of ratification and shall register this Protocol with the Organisation of African Unity, the United Nations and such other organisations as the Council shall determine.

3.   This Protocol shall be annexed to and shall form an integral part of the Treaty.

In Faith Whereof, We, The Authority of Heads of State and Government of The Economic Community of West African States, Have Signed This Protocol.

Done at Lome, this 23rd Day of November, 1984 in Single Original in the English French Languages, both texts being equally Authentic.

ANNEX

SPECIMEN OF APPROVAL AGREEMENT

THIS APPROVAL AGREEMENT IS MADE THIS.......DAY OF 19.....IN........ BETWEEN The Economic Community of West African States (hereinafter referred to as "The Community") whose headquarters is at 6, King George V Road, Lagos, in the Federal Republic of Nigeria, represented by the Executive Secretary of the Community OF THE ONE PART and the Company (Name of the Company) (hereinafter referred to as "The Promoter") whose

Headquarters is at ...... incorporated under No ....and ad-mitted to the Status of Community Enterprise by Decision No........of the .....day of ...19......of the Council of Ministers of the Community and represented by ....(name and status) OF THE OTHER PART

In accordance with the provisions of the protocol of the community relating to community enterprises (hereinafter refered to as "the protocol")

The contracting parties have agreed as follows:

Article 1

COMMUNITY GUARANTEES, BENEFITS AND PRIVILEGES

As a Community Enterprise, the Promoter may enjoy the guaranteed benefits and privileges set out in Article 16, and contingently those set out in Article 17 of the Protocol as may be conferred.

Article 2

OBLIGATIONS OF PROMOTER

The Promoter hereby accepts and undertakes to comply with all the obligations provided for in the Protocol and in this Agreement. He shall begin his operations not later than the 31st of December, ...

Article 3

NOTICE

All orders, approvals, declarations, notices, communications or undertakings of any kind between the Community and the Promoter shall be in writing and the parties hereto shall not under any circumstances be permitted to allege or rely upon any oral order, approval, declaration, notice, communication or undertaking.

Article 4

LAW OF THE AGREEMENT

The law which shall govern this Agreement and in accordance with which it is to be construed shall be the Protocol and any Regulations or Decisions made or taken thereunder. In the case of issues not expressly covered by the Protocol and this Agreement the governing law shall be the Memorandum and Articles of Association of the Promoter and the law of the Country where the principal office, incorporated branches and subsidiaries of the Promoter are located.

Article 5

DECISIONS RELATING TO THE ARTICLE OF THE PROMOTER

The Promoter shall previously inform the Executive Secretariat of any decision taken by its Board of Directors or shareholders affecting the provisions of its Articles.

Article 6

LOCATION OF PROMOTER

The Promoter will be principally located in ....with branches and subsidiaries in ....

Article 7

PRODUCTS AND SERVICES

The products and/or services which shall be produced and/or provided by the Promoter under the terms of this Agreement are...

Article 8
FORCE MAJEURE

1.   Under this Agreement, force majeure means any unforeseeable, irresistible and insurmountable event independent of both parties occurring after the entry into force of this Agreement such as to impede the performance of either party obligations.

2.   Either party to the Agreement shall inform the other party of the occurrence of a force majeure within forty-eight (48) hours following the occurrence of such force majeure.

3.   Failure on the part of the parties to comply with any of the terms and conditions hereof shall not constitute grounds for termination or breach or give the parties any claims for damages insofar as the failure arises from force majeure as defined in paragraph (1) of this Article provided that the parties shall take all reasonable steps to minimise the effects of such failure and to fulfil the terms and conditions of this Agreement with the minimum of delay.

Article 9

ENTRY INTO FORCE AND DURATION OF AGREEMENT

This Agreement shall enter into force upon signature for a period of ....years and subject to revision after the first..........years.

Article 10

COMPLIANCE WITH NATIONAL LAWS

1.   The Promoter shall comply with the general laws and regulations in force in the Member States.

2.   With respect to fiscal laws and regulations in fore in the Member States the grant of investment incentives under this Agreement shall not release the Promoter of liabilities for any act, omission or things required to be done under the fiscal bases of the Member States to the extent of which such compliance is not inconsistent with any provision of the Protocol and of this Agreement.

Article 11

AMENDMENT AND REVISION

This Agreement may be amended and revised by the parties after the expiration of the period provided in Article 9. Any party wishing to amend or to revise this Agreement shall notify the other through written proposals which shall be discussed by common consent within six (6) months after the date of notification.

Article 12

TERMINATIONS, SUSPENSION AND INVALIDATION OF AGREEMENT

1.   This Agreement may be terminated at any time by either party provided that notice of one (1) year is given to other party.

2.   The termination of this Agreement shall not affect on-going actions or projects, vested rights of parties during its period of validity.

3.   This Agreement may be suspended or invalidated immediately without notice by the Council of Ministers of the Community, subject to conditions stipulated in Article 21 of the Protocol.

Article 13

RESIDUAL PROVISIONS

The provisions of the Protocol shall govern obligations, breach of contract, settlement of disputes and all such all other matters not provided for in this Agreement.

Article 14

ANNEXES

The following documents are annexed to this Agreement:

a.   The Protocol

b.   The Articles of the Promoter and any other document relating to him.

III.   SUPPORT MEASURES

*

SUPPLEMENTARY PROTOCOL A/SP.2/5/90 ON THE IMPLEMENTATION OF THE THIRD PHASE (RIGHT OF ESTABLISHMENT) OF THE PROTOCOL ON FREE MOVEMENT OF PERSONS, RIGHT OF RESIDENCE AND ESTABLISHMENT[*]

(ECONOMIC COMMUNITY OF WEST AFRICAN STATES)

The Supplementary Protocol A/Sp.2/5/90 on the Implementation of the Third Phase (Right of Establishment) of the Protocol on Free Movement of Persons, Right of Residence and Establishment was signed by the Member States of Economic Community of West African States, namely Benin, Burkina Faso, Cape Verde, Côte d'Ivoire, Gambia, Ghana, Guinea, Guinea-Bissau, Liberia, Mali, Niger, Nigeria, Senegal, Sierra Leone and Togo on 30 May 1990.

THE HIGH CONTRACTING PARTIES,

MINDFUL of Article 5 of the ECOWAS Treaty establishing the Authority of Heads of State and Government and defining its composition and functions;

MINDFUL of Article 27 of the ECOWAS Treaty relating to freedom of movement and residence within the Community;

MINDFUL of Protocol A/P.1/5/79 dated 29 May, 1979, on Free Movement of Persons, Right of Residence and Establishment;

MINDFUL or Protocol A/P.3/5/82 dated 29 May, 1979, establishing the Code of Citizenship of the Community;

MINDFUL of Protocol A/P.1/11/84 dated 23 November, 1984 on Community Enterprises;

MINDFUL of Supplementary Protocol A/SP.1/7/85 dated 6 July, 1985, establishing the Code of Conduct for the implementation of the Protocol on Free Movement of Persons, Right of Residence and Establishment;

CONSIDERING the deadline for the implementation of Phase II (Right of Residences) of the Protocol on Free Movement of Persons, Right of Residence and Establishment, which deadline will expire on 4 June, 1990;

CONVINCED of the imperative need to proceed to the third phase (Right of Establishment) of the Protocol on Free Movement of Persons, Right of Residence and Establishment, in-as-much-as the uniform implementation of the provisions of ECOWAS texts on free movement of persons, goods, services and capital by all Member States is a fundamental basis of Community

---

[*] *Source*: Economic Community of West African States (1990). "Supplementary Protocol A/Sp.2/5/90 on the Implementation of the Third Phase (Right of Establishment) of the Protocol on Free Movement of Persons, Right of Residence and Establishment "; available on the Internet (http://www.ecowas.int/). [Note added by the editor.]

building and a pre-requisite for the harmonious development of the economic, social and cultural activities of the States of the region which will ensure the welfare of their peoples;

HEREBY AGREE AS FOLLOWS:

CHAPTER 1

DEFINITIONS

Article 1

1.   In this Protocol, the following terms shall have the meanings assigned to them hereunder:

"Treaty" means the Treaty of the Economic Community of West African States;

"Community" means the Economic Community of West African States;

"Member State" or "Member States" means a Member State or Member States of the Economic Community of West African States;

"Host Member State" means the Member State or country of residence of the migrant worker;

"Member State of Origin" means the Member State or country of residence of the migrant worker or the country of which he is a national;

"Authority" means the Authority of Heads of State and Government established by Article 5 of the Treaty;

"Council" means the Council of Ministers established by Article 6 of the Treaty;

"Executive Secretary" and "Executive Secretariat" mean the Executive Secretary and the Executive Secretariat of the Community as defined in Article 8 of the Treaty.

"Commission" means the Trade, Customs, Immigration, Money and Payments Commission of the Community, as defined in Article 9 paragraph 1 (a) of the Treaty.

"Community Citizen" or "Community Citizens" means any national or nationals of a Member State fulfilling the conditions stipulated in the Protocol A/P.3/5/82 relating to the definition of Community Citizen;

"Right of Residence" means the right of a citizen who is a national of one Member State to reside in a Member State other than his State of origin which issues him with a residence card or permit that may or may not allow him to hold employment;

"Right of Establishment" means the right granted to a citizen who is a national of the Member State to settle or establish in another Member State other than his State of origin, and to have access to economic activities, to carry out these activities as well as to set up and manage enterprises, and in particular companies, under the same conditions as defined by the legislation of the host Member State for its own nationals;

"Residence Card" or "Residence Permit" means the document issued by the competent authorities of a Member State granting right of residence in the territory of the Member State;

"Resident" means any citizen, who is a national of one Member State, and who is accorded the right of residence.

"Migrant Worker" or "Migrant" means any citizen who is a national of one Member State, who has travelled from his country of origin to the territory of another Member State of which he is not a national and who seeks to hold employment there;

"Competent Administrations" or "Relevant Departments" means national Administrations of Member States responsible for immigration and emigration matters;

"Competent Authority of place of residence" means the competent local authority responsible for problems concerning the residence of foreigners in the territory of the host Member State;

"Fundamental Rights" means the right granted to any migrant worker by this Protocol and the Conventions of the International Labour Organisation (ILO) on the protection of the rights of migrant workers.

"Border area workers" means migrant workers who, while in employment in one Member State, maintain their normal residence in a neighbouring Member State, which is their country of origin and to which they return each day or at least once a week.

"Seasonal Workers" means migrant workers in employment or practising a business on their own account in one Member State of which they are not nationals, the activity being by its nature dependent on seasonal conditions and capable of being practised only during a part of the year.

"Itinerant Workers" means migrant workers who normally residing in one Member State, may have to travel to another Member State for a short period for the requirements of their activities.

"Company" means a company constituted under civil or commercial law or any other legal entity constituted under public or private law with the exception of non-profit-making companies.

2.   In this Protocol, the term "migrant workers" excludes:

   i.   Persons on official posting who are employed by international organisations and persons employed by a State outside the territory of that State, whose entry into the country and conditions of service are governed by general international law or by specific International Agreements or Conventions;

   ii.   Persons on official posting who are employed by a State outside the territory of that State for the implementation of co-operation programmes for development agreed on with the host country, the entry into the country and conditions of service of such persons being established by specific International Agreements or Conventions;

   iii.   Persons whose working relations with an employer have not been established in the host Member State;

iv.   Persons who become residents in their capacity as investors in a country other than their State of origin or who, since their arrival in that country, have been carrying out an economic activity as an employer.

CHAPTER II

ESTABLISHMENT OF OR ACCESS TO ENTERPRISES

Article 2

The right of establishment as defined in Article 1 above shall include access to non-salaried activities and the exercise of such activities as well as the creation and management of enterprises and companies which comply with the definition contained in Article 3 below are subject to the same conditions stipulated by the laws and regulations of the country of establishment for its own nationals.

Article 3

For the purpose of implementation of this Protocol, companies which are formed in accordance with the laws and regulations of a Member State with their headquarters, central seat of administration or principal establishment within the Community shall be considered in the same category as individual nationals of Member States. Where, however, only the statutory headquarters of the company are established in a Member State, activities of such a company should have effective and sustained links with the economy of the Member State.

CHAPTER III

PROVISIONS FOR SECTORS OF ECONOMIC ACITIVITY GOVERNED BY SPECIAL MEASURES WHERE SUCH ACTIVITY INVOLVES NON-NATIONALS

Article 4

1.   In matters of establishment and services, each Member State shall undertake to accord non-discriminatory treatment to nationals and companies of other Member States.

2.   If, however, for a specific activity, a Member State is unable to accord such treatment, the Member State must indicate as much, in writing, to the Executive Secretariat. Other Member States shall then not be bound to accord non-discriminatory treatment to nationals and companies of the State concerned.

3.   The provisions of this Protocol and measures taken as a result thereof shall be without prejudice to the application of legislative and administrative provisions, which provide a special treatment for non-nationals and are justified by exigencies of public order, security or public health.

4.   On the recommendation of the Commission, and on the proposal of the Council, the Authority shall take the relevant decision for the co-operation and harmonisation of legislative,

statutory and administrative provisions which, in at least one Member State, make access to certain non-salaried activities (liberal or non-liberal professionals) and the exercise of such activities subject to protective or restrictive measures.

5.   To facilitate access to non-salaried activities and the exercise of such activities, the Commission shall recommend to the Council, which shall propose to the Authority that decisions be taken for the mutual recognition at Community level of diplomas, certificates and other qualifications.

6.   Activities which, in a Member State, form part, even occasionally, of the exercise of public authority, shall be exempted from the provisions of this Protocol.

CHAPTER IV

PROVISIONS FOR THE PROMOTION AND PROTECTION OF CAPITAL FOR INVESTMENT OR ALREADY INVESTED IN THE ESTABLISHMENT OF AN ENTERPRISE OR FOR THE PURPOSE OF OBTAINING ACCESS TO ECONOMIC ACTIVITY

Article 5

Member States recognise the importance of capital (whether private or public) in the promotion of development co-operation and the need to take measures conducive to the promotion of such capital. Member States shall therefore undertake, jointly and severally to:

i.   implement measures to encourage participation in development efforts by economic operators who share the objectives and priorities of development co-operation and respect the law and regulations of their respective States ;

ii.   accord fair and equitable treatment to such capital to encourage and create conditions which favour investment of such capital;

iii.   promote effective co-operation between economic operators in their respective States.

Article 6

In order to further accelerate co-operation in their development efforts and increase directly productive investments, Member States shall undertake to adopt provisions which will facilitate and increase the flow of more stable private capital and enhance:

1.   co-financing of productive investment with the private sector;

2.   the activities and efficacy of domestic financial markets;

3.   access to international financial markets.

Article 7

1.   Assets and capital invested by ECOWAS citizens who are not nationals of the Member State of establishment, having been duly authorised, shall not be subject to any act of confiscation or expropriation on a discriminatory basis.

2.   Any act of confiscation, expropriation or nationalisation must be followed by fair and equitable compensation.

Article 8

In recognition of the intermediary role of national development finance institutions in attracting the flow of capital for development co-operation, Member States shall undertake to encourage, as part of their monetary and financial co-operation, the establishment or enhancement of:

1.   national or regional export financing and export credit guarantee institutions ; and

2.   regional payment mechanism likely to facilitate and promote intra-community trade.

Article 9

In recognition of the need to promote and protect the investments of each Member State in their respective territories, Member States shall undertake, in their mutual interest, to harmonise their national legislations, administrative rules and regulations governing the promotion and protection of investments in order to establish the foundations for the Community guarantee and insurance systems.

CHAPTER V

PROVISIONS GOVERNING THE MOVEMENT OF CAPITAL FOR INVESTMENT AND CURRENT PAYMENTS

Article 10

1.   In transactions involving movement of capital for investment and current payments, Member States shall refrain from taking exchange control measures which are incompatible with their obligations under the terms of this Protocol and earlier Community provisions, particularly Protocol A/P.1/11/84 of the Authority dated 23 November, 1984 and relating to Community Enterprises.

2.   However, such obligations shall not prevent Member States from taking the necessary protective measures for reasons of grave economic difficulty or serious balance of payment problems, provided that the decision-making bodies of the Community are given notification thereof.

Article 11

In the case of foreign exchange transactions related to investment and current payments, Member States shall, as far as possible, refrain from taking discriminatory measures and from according preferential treatment to nationals of third countries.

CHAPTER VI

CO-OPERATION BETWEEN RELEVANT ADMNINSTRATIONS IN MEMBER STATES

Article 12

The relevant authorities of Member States shall co-operate closely with one another and with the Executive Secretariat in accordance with the general conditions for the realisation of the right of establishment in order to:

1.   identify activities in which freedom of establishment has a particularly useful contribution to make to the development of production and trade and to deal with such activities in order of priority;

2.   eliminate administrative practices and procedures emanating either from internal legislation or from agreements earlier concluded between Member States which, if maintained, would be an impediment to the freedom of establishment;

3.   ensure that salaried workers of one Member State employed in the territory of another Member State shall remain in the said territory to carry out non-salaried activity on condition that they fulfill the requirements binding upon any ECOWAS citizen arriving from his State of origin for the purpose of carrying out a non-salaried activity;

4.   make possible the acquisition and exploitation of landed property situated in the territory of one Member State by a national of another Member State, in-so-far as this is permitted by the laws and regulations or the host Member State;

5.   eliminate restrictions to freedom of establishment in any sector of activity both in terms of conditions for the establishment of agencies, branches or subsidiaries and in terms of conditions of entry for staff of the parent establishment into the management or supervisory organs of the subsidiaries;

6.   co-ordinate as far as necessary with a view to making them equivalent, the guarantees required from companies by Member States to protect the interests of both partners and third parties.

CHAPTER VII

GENERAL AND MISCELLANEOUS PROVISIONS

Article 13

Member States shall undertake to institute all legislative and other measures which are in conformity with their constitutional procedures and necessary for the implementation of the provisions of this Protocol.

Article 14

Any dispute arising between Member States on the interpretation or implementation of this Protocol shall be resolved in accordance with the procedure for settlement of disputes as laid down in Article 56 of the Treaty.

Article 15

1.   Any Member State may submit proposals for amendment or revision of this Protocol.

2.   All proposals shall be forwarded to the Executive Secretary who shall communicate them to Member States within thirty (30) days of receiving them. Amendments or revisions shall be considered by the Authority at the expiration of the thirty- (30) days-period of notice granted to Member States.

CHAPTER VIII

DEPOSIT AND ENTRY INTO FORCE

Article 16

1.   This Supplementary Protocol shall enter into force, provisionally, upon signature by the Heads of State and Government and definitively, upon ratification by at least seven signatory States in accordance with the constitutional procedures of each signatory State.

2.   This Supplementary Protocol and all instruments of ratification shall be deposited with the Executive Secretariat, which shall forward certified copies of the instruments of ratification to all Member States and shall notify them of the dates of deposit of the instruments of ratification. This Protocol shall be registered with the Organisation of African Unity, the United Nations Organisation and such Organisations as may be determined by the Authority of Heads of State and Government.

3.   This Supplementary Protocol shall be annexed to the Treaty of which it shall form an integral part.

In Faith Whereof, We, Heads of State and Government of the Economic Community of West African States, Have Signed This Protocol.

*

REVISED TREATY OF CHAGUARAMAS ESTABLISHING THE CARIBBEAN COMMUNITY INCLUDING THE CARICOM SINGLE MARKET AND ECONOMY *

(THE CARIBBEAN COMMUNITY)

The Revised Treaty of Chaguaramas Establishing the Caribbean Community Including the Caricom Single Market and Economy is intended to update the 1973 Treaty. The Treaty Establishing the Caribbean Community reproduced in volume III of this *Compendium* was signed in Chaguaramas on 4 July 1973. The Revised Treaty has been open for signature to the States Members of the Community, namely Antigua and Barbuda, Bahamas, Barbados, Belize, Dominica, Grenada, Guyana, Jamaica, Montserrat, St. Kitts and Nevis, Saint Lucia, St. Vincent and the Grenadines, Suriname and Trinidad and Tobago since 2001.

CHAPTER TWO
INSTITUTIONAL ARRANGEMENTS

ARTICLE 10
Organs of the Community

1.   The principal Organs of the Community are:

   (a)   the Conference of Heads of Government; and

   (b)   the Community Council of Ministers which shall be the second highest organ.

2.   In the performance of their functions, the principal Organs shall be assisted by the following Organs:

   (a)   the Council for Finance and Planning;

   (b)   the Council for Trade and Economic Development; the Council for Foreign and Community Relations, and

   (c)   the Council for Human and Social Development.

---

* *Source*: The Caribbean Community Secretariat (2001). "Revised Treaty of Chaguaramas Establishing the Caribbean Community Including the Caricom Single Market and Economy"; available on the Internet (http://www. caricom.org/revisedtreaty.pdf) and (http://www.sice.oas.org/trade/caricom/caricind.asp). [Note added by the editor.]

ARTICLE 11
Composition of the Conference

1.   The Conference of Heads of Government shall consist of the Heads of Government of the Member States.

2.   Any Head of Government may designate a Minister or other person to represent him or her at any Meeting of the Conference.

ARTICLE 12
Functions and Powers of the Conference

1.   The Conference shall be the supreme Organ of the Community.

2.   Community. The Conference shall determine and provide policy direction for the

3.   Save as otherwise provided in this Treaty, the Conference shall be the final authority for the conclusion of treaties on behalf of the Community and for entering into relationships between the Community and international organizations and States.

4.   The Conference may take decisions for the purpose of establishing the financial arrangements necessary to defray the expenses of the Community and shall be the final authority on questions arising in relation to the financial affairs of the Community.

5.   Subject to the relevant provisions of this Treaty, the Conference shall exercise such powers as may be conferred on it by or under any Instrument elaborated by or under the auspices of the Community.

6.   The Conference may establish such Organs or Bodies as it considers necessary for the achievement of the objectives of the Community.

7.   The Conference may issue policy directives of a general or special character to other Organs and Bodies of the Community concerning the policies to be pursued for the achievement of the objectives of the Community and effect shall be given to such directives.

8.   Notwithstanding any other provision of this Treaty, the Conference may consider and resolve disputes between Member States.

9.   The Conference may consult with entities within the Caribbean Region or with other organizations and for this purpose may establish such machinery as it considers necessary.

10.   Subject to the provisions of this Chapter, the Conference shall regulate its own procedure and may decide to admit at its deliberations as observers representatives of non-Member States of the Community and other entities.

11.   The Bureau, consisting of the current Chairman and the immediately outgoing and incoming Chairmen of the Conference, shall perform the following functions:

>   (a)   initiating proposals for development and approval by the Ministerial Councils as it considers necessary;

(b)   updating the consensus of the Member States on issues falling to be determined by the Conference;

(c)   facilitating implementation of Community decisions, both at the regional and local levels, in an expeditious and informed manner;

(d)   providing guidance to the Secretariat on policy issues.

ARTICLE 13
The Community Council of Ministers

1.   The Community Council shall consist of Ministers responsible for Community Affairs and any other Minister designated by the Member States in their absolute discretion.

2.   The Community Council shall, in accordance with the policy directions established by the Conference, have primary responsibility for the development of Community strategic planning and co-ordination in the areas of economic integration, functional co-operation and external relations.

3.   In pursuance of paragraph 2, the Community Council shall:

(a)   approve the programmes of the Community on the basis, inter alia, of proposals emanating from other Community Organs;

(b)   subject to paragraph 5 of Article 20, amend proposals developed by the Ministerial Councils or request them to develop proposals for the achievement of Community objectives, and have responsibility for promoting and monitoring the implementation of Community decisions in the Member States.

4.   Without prejudice to the generality of the foregoing provisions, the Community Council shall;

(a)   subject to paragraph 4 of Article 12, examine and approve the Community budget;

(b)   mobilise and allocate resources for the implementation of Community plans and programmes;

(c)   establish, subject to the provisions of Article 26, a system of regional and national consultations in order to enhance the decision-making and implementation processes of the Community;

(d)   promote, enhance, monitor and evaluate regional and national implementation processes and, to this end, establish a regional technical assistance service;

(e)   function as a preparatory body for meetings of the Conference;

(f)   ensure the efficient operation and orderly development of the CSME, particularly by seeking to resolve problems arising out of its functioning, taking into account the work and decisions of COTED;

    (g)   receive and consider allegations of breaches of obligations arisIng under this Treaty, including disputes between Organs of the Community;

    (h)   on the instructions of the Conference, issue directives to Organs and to the Secretariat aimed at ensuring the timely implementation of Community decisions;

    (i)   undertake any additional functions remitted to it by the Conference, arising under this Treaty.

ARTICLE 14
The Council for Finance and Planning

1.   The Council for Finance and Planning shall consist of Ministers designated by the Member States. Each Member State shall be entitled to designate alternates to represent it on COFAP.

2.   Subject to the relevant provisions of Article 12, COFAP shall have primary responsibility for economic policy co-ordination and financial and monetary integration of Member States and, without prejudice to the generality of the foregoing, shall:

    (a)   establish and promote measures for the co-ordination and convergence of national macro-economic policies of the Member States and for the execution of a harmonised policy on foreign investment;

    (b)   promote and facilitate the adoption of measures for fiscal and monetary co-operation among the Member States, including the establishment of mechanisms for payment arrangements;

    (c)   recommend measures to achieve and maintain fiscal discipline by the Governments of the Member States;

    (d)   pending the establishment of a monetary union in the Community, recommend arrangements for the free convertibility of the currencies of the Member States on a reciprocal basis;

    (e)   promote the establishment and integration of capital markets in the Community, and

    (f)   undertake any additional functions remitted to it by the Conference arising under this Treaty.

3.   Under the direction of COFAP, the Committee of Central Bank Governors shall assist in the performance of the functions mentioned in paragraph 2 of this Article.

ARTICLE 15
The Council for Trade and Economic Development

1.   The Council for Trade and Economic Development shall consist of Ministers designated by the Member States. Each Member State shall be entitled to designate alternates to represent it on COTED.

2.   Subject to the provisions of Article 12, COTED shall be responsible for the promotion of trade and economic development of the Community. In particular, COTED shall:

(a)   promote the development and oversee the operation of the CSME;

(b)   evaluate, promote and establish measures to enhance production, quality control and marketing of industrial and agricultural commodities so as to ensure their international competitiveness;

(c)   establish and promote measures to accelerate structural diversification of industrial and agricultural production on a sustainable and regionally-integrated basis;

(d)   determine and promote measures for the accelerated development and marketing of services;

(e)   promote and develop policies and programmes to facilitate the transportation of people and goods;

(f)   promote measures for the development of energy and natural resources on a sustainable basis;

(g)   establish and promote measures for the accelerated development of science and technology;

(h)   promote and develop policies for the protection of and preservation of the environment and for sustainable development;

(i)   promote and develop, in collaboration with the Council for Foreign and Community Relations, co-ordinated policies for the enhancement of external economic and trade relations of the Community, and

j)   undertake any additional functions remitted to it by the Conference, arising under this Treaty.

ARTICLE 16
The Council for Foreign and Community Relations

1.   The Council for Foreign and Community Relations shall consist of Ministers Responsible for the Foreign Affairs of Member States. Each Member State shall be entitled to designate an alternate to represent it on COFCOR.

2.   Subject to the provisions of Article 12, COFCOR shall be responsible for determining relations between the Community and international organisations and Third States.

3.   Without prejudice to the generality of paragraph 2, COFCOR shall:

(a)   promote the development of friendly and mutually beneficial relations among the Member States;

(b) establish measures to co-ordinate the foreign policies of the Member States of the Community, including proposals for joint representation, and seek to ensure, as far as practicable, the adoption of Community positions on major hemispheric and international issues;

(c) co-ordinate the positions of the Member States in inter- governmental organisations in whose activities such States participate;

(d) collaborate with COTED in promoting and developing co-ordinated policies for the enhancement of external economic and trade relations of the Community;

(e) co-ordinate, in close consultation with the Member States, Community policy on International issues with the policies of States in the wider Caribbean Region in order to arrive at common positions in relation to Third States, groups of States and relevant inter-governmental organisations, and

(f) undertake any additional functions remitted to it by the Conference, arising under this Treaty.

4. Only Member States possessing the necessary competence with respect to the matters under consideration from time to time may take part in the deliberations of COFCOR.

ARTICLE 17
The Council for Human and Social Development

1. The Council for Human and Social Development shall consist of Ministers designated by the Member States. Each Member State shall be entitled to designate alternates to represent it on COHSOD.

2. Subject to the provisions of Article 12, COHSOD shall be responsible for the promotion of human and social development in the Community. In particular, COHSOD shall:

(a) promote the improvement of health, including the development and organisation of efficient and affordable health services in the Community;

(b) promote the development of education through the efficient organisation of educational and trainIng facilities In the Community, including elementary and advanced vocational training and technical facilities;

(c) promote and develop co-ordinated policies and programmes to improve the living and working conditions of workers and take appropriate measures to facilitate the organisation and development of harmonious labour and industrial relations in the Community;

(d) establish policies and programmes to promote the development of youth and women in the Community with a view to encouraging and enhancing their participation in social, cultural, political and economic activities;

(e) promote and establish programmes for the development of culture and sports in the Community;

(f)   promote the development of special focus programmes supportive of the establishment and maintenance of a healthy human environment in the Community, and

(g)   undertake any additional functions remitted to it by the Conference, arising under this Treaty.

3.   Without prejudice to the requirements of any otherprovision of this Treaty, COHSOD shall promote co-operation among the Member States in the areas set out in the schedule hereto in furtherance of the objectives set out in Article 5.

ARTICLE 18
Bodies of the Community

1.   There are hereby established as Bodies of the Community:

(a)   the Legal Affairs Committee; and

(b)   the Budget Committee.

2.   The Council of Central Bank Governors shall be redesignated the "Committee of Central Bank Governors" and recognised as a Body of the Community.

3.   The Organs of the Community may establish, as they deem necessary, other Bodies of the Community.

ARTICLE 19
Composition and Functions of Bodies of the Community

1.   The Legal Affairs Committee shall consist of the MInisters responsible for Legal Affairs or Attorneys-General of the Member States, or both, and shall be responsible for providing the Organs and Bodies, either on request or on its own initiative, with advice on treaties, international legal issues, the harmonisation of laws of the Community and other legal matters.

2.   The Budget Committee shall consist of senior officials of the Member States who shall perform their functions in a professional capacity. It shall examine the draft budget and work programme of the Community prepared by the Secretariat and submit recommendations to the Community Council.

3.   The Committee of Central Bank Governors shall consist of the Governors or Heads of the Central Banks of the Member States or their nominees. The Committee shall make recommendations to COFAP on matters relating to monetary co-operation, payments arrangements, free movement of capital, integration of capital markets, monetary union and any other related matters referred to it by the Organs of the Community.

4.   The procedures of Bodies shall be regulated, mutatis mutandis, by the relevant provisions of Articles 27 and 29.

ARTICLE 20
Co-operation by Community Organs

1.   Community Organs shall co-operate with each other for the achievement of Community objectives.

2.   The Bureau and the Community Council may initiate proposals for development by the Ministerial Councils within their respective areas of competence.

3.   Where a Community Organ proposes to develop a proposal which is likely to impact importantly on activities within the sphere of competence of another Community Organ, the first-mentioned Community Organ shall transmit such proposal to other interested Community Organs for their consideration and reaction before reaching a final decision on the proposal.

4.   Proposals approved by the Ministerial Councils shall be transmitted to the Community Council for prioritisation and resource allocation for their implementation.

5.   Proposals approved by the Ministerial Councils and transmitted to the Community Council for prioritisation and resource allocation for implementation may be returned by the Community Council to the originating Organ for modification. The Community Council may modify the proposal to the extent and in the manner agreed with the originating Organ.

6.   The Secretariat shall monitor the development and implementation of proposals for the achievement of Community objectives and keep the Community Council informed accordingly.

4.   Proposals approved by the Ministerial Councils shall be transmitted to the Community Council for prioritisation and resource allocation for their implementation.

5.   Proposals approved by the Ministerial Councils and transmitted to the Community Council for prioritisation and resource allocation for implementation may be returned by the Community Council to the originating Organ for modification. The Community Council may modify the proposal to the extent and in the manner agreed with the originating Organ.

6.   The Secretariat shall monitor the development and implementation of proposals for the achievement of Community objectives and keep the Community Council informed accordingly.

ARTICLE 21
Institutions of the Community

The following entities established by or under the auspices of the Community shall be recognised as Institutions of the Community:

- Caribbean Disaster Emergency Response Agency (CDERA);
- Caribbean Meteorological Institute (CMI);
- Caribbean Meteorological Organisation (CMO);
- Caribbean Environmental Health Institute (CEHI);
- Caribbean Agricultural Research and Development Institute (CARDI);
- Caribbean Regional Centre for the Education and Training of Animal Health and Veterinary Public Health Assistants (REPAHA);

- Association of Caribbean Community Parliamentarians (ACCP);
- Caribbean Centre For Developmental Administration (CARICAD);
- Caribbean Food and Nutrition Institute (CFNI),

and such other entities as may be designated by the Conference.

ARTICLE 22
Associate Institutions of the Community

The following entities with which the Community enjoys important functional relationships which contribute to the achievement of the objectives of the Community shall be recognised as Associate Institutions of the Community:

- Caribbean Development Bank (COB);
- University of Guyana (UG);
- University of the West Indies (UWI);
- Caribbean Law Institute / Caribbean Law Institute Centre (CLI/CLIC);
- the Secretariat of the Organisation of Eastern Caribbean States; .

and such other entities as may be designated by the Conference.

ARTICLE 23
The Secretariat

1.   The Secretariat shall be the principal administrative organ of the Community. The headquarters of the Community shall be located in Georgetown, Guyana.

2.   The Secretariat shall comprise a Secretary-General and such other staff as the Community may require. In the recruitment of such staff, consideration shall be given to securing the highest standards of efficiency, competence and integrity, bearing in mind the principle of equitable geographical distribution.

3.   The Secretary-General shall, in addition to the powers conferred by or under the Treaty, be the Chief Executive Officer of the Community and shall act in that capacity at all meetings of Community Organs and Bodies. He shall make an annual report to the Conference on the work of the Community.

4.   In the performance of their duties the Secretary-General and staff shall neither seek nor receive instructions from any Government of the Member States or from any other authority external to the Community. They shall refrain from any action which might reflect adversely on their position as officials of the Community and shall be responsible only to the Community.

5.   Member States undertake to respect the exclusively international character of the responsibilities of the Secretary-General and staff and shall not seek to influence them in the discharge of their responsibilities.

6.   The Conference shall approve the Staff Regulations governing the operations of the Secretariat.

7.   The Community Council shall approve the financial regulations governing the operations of the Secretariat.

8   The Secretary-General shall establish Staff Rules for the operation of the Secretariat.

ARTICLE 24
The Secretary-General

1.   The Secretary-General shall be appointed by the Conference, on the recommendation of the Community Council, for a term not exceeding five years and may be reappointed by the Conference.

2.   The Secretary-General shall be the Chief Executive Officer of the Community and shall, subject to the determinations of competent Organs of the Community and in accordance with the financial and other regulations, perform the following functions:

(a)   represent the Community;

(b)   develop, as mandated, decisions of competent Organs of the Community into implementable proposals;

(c)   identify and mobilise, as required, external resources to implement decisions at the regional level and undertake studies and develop decisions on relevant issues into implementable proposals;

(d)   implement, as mandated, decisions at the regional level for the achievement of Community objectives;

(e)   implement, with the consent of the Member State concerned, Community decisions which do not require legislative or administrative action by national authorities;

(f)   monitor and report on, as mandated, implementation of Community decisions; (g) initiate or develop proposals for consideration and decision by competent Organs in order to achieve Community objectives, and (h) such other functions assigned by the Conference or other competent Organs.

ARTICLE 25
Functions of the Secretariat

In addition to any functions which may be assigned to it by Organs of the Community, the Secretariat shall:

(a)   service meetings of the Organs and Bodies of the Community and take appropriate follow up action on determinations issuing from such meetings;

(b)   initiate, organise and conduct studies on issues for the achievement of the objectives of the Community;

(c)   provide, on request, services to the Member States of the Community on matters relating to the achievement of its objectives;

(d)   collect, store and disseminate to the Member States of the Community information relevant for the achievement of its objectives;

(e)   assist Community Organs in the development and implementation of proposals and programmes for the achievement of objectives of the Community;

(f)   co-ordinate in relation to the Community the activities of donor agencies, international, regional and national institutions for the achievement of objectives of the Community;

(g)   prepare the draft budget of the Community for examination by the Budget Committee;

(h)   provide, on request, technical assistance to national authorities to facilitate implementation of Community decisions;

(i)   conduct, as mandated, fact-finding assignments in the Member States, and

(j)   initiate or develop proposals for consideration and decision by competent Organs in order to achieve Community objectives.

ARTICLE 26
The Consultative Process

1.   In order to enhance the decision-making process in the Community, the Community Council, assisted by the Secretary-General, shall, in collaboration with competent authorities of the Member States, establish and maintain an efficient system of consultations at the national and regional levels.

2.   The system of consultations shall be structured to ensure that determinations of Community Organs and the Legal Affairs Committee are adequately informed by relevant information inputs and are reinforced by consultations undertaken at successively lower levels of the decision-making process.

ARTICLE 27
Common Voting Procedures
in Community Organs and Bodies

1.   Subject to paragraph 2 of this Article, each Member State represented on Community Organs and Bodies shall have one vote. A simple majority of Member States shall constitute a quorum.

2.   Member States, whose contributions to the regular budget of the Community are in arrears for more than two years, shall not have the right to vote except on matters relating to the CSME, but may otherwise participate in the deliberations of Community Organs and Bodies. The Conference may, nevertheless, permit such Member States to vote if it is satisfied that the failure to contribute is due to conditions beyond their control.

3.   Decisions on procedural issues in Community Organs shall be reached by a simple majority of Member States.

4.   Subject to the agreement of the Conference, a Member State may opt out of obligations arising from the decisions of competent Organs provided that the fundamental objectives of the Community, as laid down in the Treaty, are not prejudiced thereby.

5.   Prior to taking decisions on any issue falling to be determined by Community Organs, the Secretariat shall bring to the attention of the meeting the financial implications of such decisions and any other matters which may be relevant.

6.   Recommendations of Community Organs shall be made by a two-thirds majority of Member States and shall not be legally binding. Member States omitting to comply with recommendations shall inform the Secretariat in writing within six months stating the reasons for their non-compliance.

7.   Subject to the relevant provisions of this Treaty, Community Organs and Bodies shall establish their rules of procedure.

ARTICLE 28
Voting in the Conference

1.   Save as otherwise provided in this Treaty and subject to paragraph 2 of this Article and the relevant provisions of Article 27, the Conference shall take decisions by an affirmative vote of all its members and such decisions shall be binding.

2.   For the purpose of this Article abstentions shall not be construed as impairing the validity of decisions of the Conference provided that the Member States constituting three-quarters of the membership of the Community, vote in favour of such decisions.

3.   Omission by a Member State to participate in the vote shall be deemed an abstention within the meaning of paragraph 2 of this Article.

4.   Parties to a dispute or against which sanctions are being considered shall not have the right to vote on the issue falling to be determined.

ARTICLE 29
Voting in the Community Council and Ministerial Councils

1.   Save as otherwise provided in this Treaty and subject to the provisions of this Article and Article 27, the Ministerial Councils shall take decisions by a qualified majority vote and such decisions shall be binding.

2.   For the purposes of paragraph 1 of this Article a qualified majority vote means an affirmative vote of the Member States comprising no less than three-quarters of the membership of the Community.

3.   Where issues have been determined to be of critical importance to the national well-being of a Member State, in accordance with paragraph 4 of this Article, such decisions shall be reached by an affirmative vote of all Member States.

4.   Decisions that an issue is of critical importance to the national well-being of a Member State shall be reached by a two-thirds majority of the Member States.

5.   For the purposes of paragraph 3 of this Article abstentions shall not be construed as impairing the validity of decisions required to be reached by unanimity provided that Member States constituting not less than three-quarters of the membership of the Community vote in favour of such decisions.

CHAPTER THREE
ESTABLISHMENT, SERVICES, CAPITAL AND MOVEMENT OF COMMUNITY NATIONALS

ARTICLE 30
Scope of Application

1.   Save as otherwise provided in this Article and Article 31, the provisions of this Chapter shall apply to the right of establishment, the right to provide services and the right to move capital in the Community.

2.   Activities in a Member State involving the exercise of governmental authority shall, in so far as that Member State is concerned, be excluded from the operation of this Chapter.

3.   For the purposes of this Chapter, "activities involving the exercise of governmental uthority" means activities conducted neither on a commercial basis nor in competition with one or more economic enterprises, and includes:

(a)   activities conducted by a central bank or monetary authority or any other public entity, in pursuit of monetary or exchange rate policies;

(b)   activities forming part of a statutory system of social security or public retirement plans;

(c)   activities forming part of a system of national security or for the establishment or maintenance of public order; and

(d)   other activities conducted by a public entity for the account of or with the guarantee or using financial resources of the government.

ARTICLE 31
Treatment of Monopolies

1.   The Member States may determine that the public interest requires the exclusion or restriction of the right of establishment in any industry or in a particular sector of an industry.

2.   Where such a determination has been made:

(a)   if the determination results in the continuation or establishment of a government monopoly, the Member State shall adopt appropriate measures to ensure that the monopoly does not discriminate between nationals of Member States, save as otherwise provided In this Treaty, and is subject to the agreed rules of competition established for Community economic enterprises;

(b) if the determination results in the continuation or establishment of a private sector monopoly, the Member State shall, subject to the provisions of this Treaty, adopt appropriate measures to ensure that national treatment is accorded to nationals of other Member States in terms of participating in its operations.

ARTICLE 32
Prohibition of New Restrictions on the Right of Establishment

1.   The Member States shall not introduce in their territories any new restrictions relating to the right of establishment of nationals of other Member States save as otherwise provided in this Treaty.

2.   The Member States shall notify CO TED of existing restrictions on the right of establishment in respect of nationals of other Member States.

3.   (1)   The right of establishment within the meaning of this Chapter shall include the right to:

   (a)   engage in any non-wage-earning activities of a commercial, industrial, agricultural, professional or artisanal nature;

   (b)   create and manage economic enterprises referred to in paragraph 5(b) of this Article.

   (2)   For the purposes of this Chapter "non-wage earning activities" means activities undertaken by self-employed persons.

4.   The Community Council may, with the approval of the Conference and upon the recommendation of COTED or COFAP, as the case may be, enlarge the body of rights provided in paragraph 3 of this Article. The competent Organ shall establish basic criteria for Member States in order to safeguard against manipulation or abuse of such rights so as to gain an unfair advantage against other Member States, for example, in the areas of nationality criteria and in the operation of companies.

5.   For the purposes of this Chapter:

   (a)   a person shall be regarded as a national of a Member State if such person -

      (i)   is a citizen of that State;

      (ii)   has a connection with that State of a kind which entitles him to be regarded as belonging to or, if it be so expressed, as being a native or resident of the State for the purposes of the laws thereof relating to immigration; or

      (iii)   is a company or other legal entity constituted in the Member State in conformity with the laws thereof and which that State regards as belonging to it, provided that such company or other legal entity has been formed for gainful purposes and has its registered office and central administration, and carries on substantial activity, within the Community and which is substantially owned and effectively controlled by persons mentioned in sub- paragraphs (i) and (ii) of this paragraph;

(b)   "economic enterprises" includes any type of organisation for the production of or trade in goods or the provision of services (other than a non-profit organisation) owned or controlled by any person or entity mentioned in sub-paragraph (a) of this paragraph;

(c)   a company or other legal entity is:

   (i)   substantially owned if more than 50 per cent of the equity Interest therein is beneficially owned by nationals mentioned in sub-paragraph (a) (i) or (ii) of this paragraph;

   (ii)   effectively controlled if nationals mentioned in sub- paragraph (a) of this paragraph have the power to name a majority of its directors or otherwise legally to direct its actions.

ARTICLE 33
Removal of Restrictions on the Right of Establishment

1.   Subject to the provisions of Article 221 and Article 222, the Member States shall remove restrictions on the right of establishment of nationals of a Member State in the territory of another Member State.

2.   The removal of restrictions on the right of establishment mentioned in paragraph 1 of this Article shall also apply to restrictions on the setting up of agencies, branches or subsidiaries by nationals of a Member State in the territory of another Member State.

3.   Subject to the approval of the Conference, COTED, in consultation with COHSOD and COFAP, shall, within one year from the entry into force of this Treaty, establish a programme providing for the removal of restrictions on the right of establishment of nationals of a Member State in the territory of another Member State. The programme shall, *inter alia*:

(a)   identify the activities in respect of which the right of establishment shall not apply;

(b)   establish the conditions under which the right of establishment is to be achieved; and

(c)   set out the conditions, stages and time-frames for the removal of restrictions on the right of establishment.

4.   The Community Council may authorise a Member State whose nationals have been aggrieved by the violation of obligations set out in this Article, Article 32, Article 36 and Article 37 to take such measures as may be provided for in this Treaty.

ARTICLE 34
Management of Removal of Restrictions on the Right of Establishment

In performing its tasks set out in Article 33, COTED shall, inter alia:

(a)   accord priority to the removal of restrictions on activities in respect of which the right of establishment encourages the development of:

(i)   the production of trade in goods;

(ii)   the provision of services, which generate foreign exchange earnings;

(b)   require the Member States to remove administrative practices and procedures, the maintenance of which impede the exercise of the right of establishment;

(c)   require the Member States to remove all restrictions on the movement of managerial, technical and supervisory staff of economic enterprises and on establishing agencies, branches and subsidiaries of companies and other entities established in the Community;

(d)   establish measures to ensure the removal of restrictions on the right of establishment in respect of activities accorded priority treatment pursuant to paragraph (a) of this Article as they relate to:

(i)   the establishment, in the territories of the Member States, of agencies, branches or subsidiaries belonging to an economic enterprise;and

(ii)   the conditions governing the entry of managerial, technical or supervisory personnel employed in such agencies, branches and subsidiaries, including the spouses and immediate dependent family members of such personnel;

(e)   take appropriate measures to ensure close collaboration among competent national authorities in order to improve their knowledge of the particular situation regarding the relevant activities within the Community;

(f)   require the Member States to ensure that nationals of one Member State may have access to land, buildings and other property situated in the territory of another Member State, other than for speculative purposes or for a purpose potentially destabilising to the economy, on a non-discriminatory basis, bearing in mind the importance of agriculture for many national economies;

(g)   ensure concordance in the Member States regarding the protection afforded the interests of partners, members and other persons with financial interests in companies and other entities.

ARTICLE 35
Acceptance of Diplomas, Certificates, and other Evidence of Qualifications

1.   COHSOD, in consultation with the competent Organ, shall establish common standards and measures for accreditation or when necessary for the mutual recognition of diplomas, certificates and other evidence of qualifications of the nationals of the Member States in order to facilitate access to, and engagement in, employment and non-wage-earning activities in the Community.

2.   The Member States shall establish or employ, as the case may be, appropriate mechanisms to establish common standards to determine equivalency or accord accreditation to diplomas, certificates and other evidence of qualifications secured by nationals of other Member States.

3.   COHSOD shall also establish measures for the co-ordination of legislative and administrative requirements of the Member States for the participation of Community nationals in employment and for the conduct of non-wage-earning activities in the Community.

ARTICLE 36
Prohibition of New Restrictions on the Provision of Services

1.   The Member States shall not introduce any new restrictions on the provision of services in the Community by nationals of other Member States except as otherwise provided in this Treaty.

2.   Without prejudice to the provisions relating to the right of establishment, persons providing services may, in order to provide such services, temporarily engage in approved activities in the Member State where the services are to be provided under the same conditions enjoyed by nationals of that Member State.

3.   The Member States shall notify COTED of existing restrictions on the provision of services in respect of nationals of other Member States.

4.   For the purposes of this Chapter, "services" means services provided against remuneration other than wages in any approved sector and "the provision of services" means the supply of services:

   (a)   from the territory of one Member State into the territory of another Member State;

   (b)   in the territory of one Member State to the service consumer of another Member State;

   (c)   by a service supplier of one Member State through commercial presence in the territory of another Member State; and

   (d)   by a service supplier of one Member State through the presence of natural persons of a Member State in the territory of another Member State.

ARTICLE 37
Removal of Restrictions on Provision of Services

1.   Subject to the provisions of this Treaty, Member States shall abolish discriminatory restrictions on the provision of services within the Community in respect of Community nationals.

2.   Subject to the approval of the Conference, COTED, in consultation with other competent Organs, shall, within one year from the entry into force of this Treaty, establish a programme for the removal of restrictions on the provision of such services in the Community by Community nationals.

3.   In establishing the programme mentioned in paragraph 2 of this Article, COTED shall:

   (a)   accord priority to services which directly affect production costs or facilitate the trade in goods and services which generate foreign exchange earnings;

   (b)   require the Member States to remove administrative practices and procedures, the maintenance of which impede the exercise of the right to provide services;

   (c)   establish measures to ensure the abolition of restrictions on the right to provide services in respect of activities accorded priority treatment in accordance with sub-paragraph (a) of this paragraph, both in terms of conditions for the provision of services in the territories of Member States as well as the conditions governing the entry of personnel, including their spouses and immediate dependent family members, for the provision of services;

   (d)   take appropriate measures to ensure close collaboration among competent national authorities in order to improve their knowledge of the conditions regarding relevant activities within the Community, and

   (e)   require the Member States to ensure that nationals of one Member State have on a non-discriminatory basis, access to land, buildings and other property situated in the territory of another Member State for purposes directly related to the provision of services, bearing in mind the importance of agriculture for many national economies.

ARTICLE 38
Removal of Restrictions on Banking, Insurance and Other Financial Services

1.   Subject to the provisions of this Chapter, the Member States shall remove discriminatory restrictions on banking, insurance and other financial services.

2.   Subject to the approval of the Conference, COFAP, in consultation with other competent Organs of the Community, may exclude certain financial services from the operation of the provisions of this Article.

ARTICLE 39
Prohibition of New Restrictions on Movement of Capital and Current Transactions

The Member States shall not introduce any new restrictions on the movement of capital and payments connected with such movement and on current payments and transfers, nor render more restrictive existing regulations except as provided in Article 43 and Article 46.

ARTICLE 40
Removal of Restrictions on Movement of Capital and Current Transactions

1.   The Member States shall, in order to ensure the proper functioning of the CSME, remove among themselves:

(a)   restrictions on the movement of capital payments;

(b)   restrictions on all current payments including payments for goods and services and other current transfers.

2.   COFAP, subject to the approval of the Conference, shall establish in collaboration with the Committee of Central Bank Governors a programme for the removal of the restrictions mentioned in paragraph 1 of this Article.

3.   For the purpose of this Article, capital and related payments and transfers include:

(a)   equity and portfolio investments;
(b)   short-term bank and credit transactions;
(c)   payment of interest on loans and amortization;
(d)   dividends and other income on investments after taxes;
(e)   repatriation of proceeds from the sale of assets; and
(f)   other transfers and payments relating to investment flows.

ARTICLE 41
Authorisation to Facilitate Movement of Capital

1.   The Member States shall, where necessary and subject to paragraph 2 of this Article, grant the authorisations required for the movement of capital mentioned in Article 40 on a non-discriminatory basis.

2.   A loan intended for State purposes may require prior notification to the State in which it is being issued or placed.

ARTICLE 42
Co-ordination of Foreign Exchange Policies and Exchange of Information

1.   The Member States shall take such measures as are necessary to coordinate their foreign exchange policies in respect of the movement of capital between them and third States.

2.   The Member States shall keep the competent authorities in other Member States informed of significant unusual movements of capital within their knowledge to and from third States.

ARTICLE 43
Restrictions to Safeguard Balance-of-Payments

1.   In the event of serious balance-of-payments and external financial difficulties or threat thereof a Member State may, consistently with its international obligations and subject to paragraph 5 of this Article, adopt or maintain restrictions to address such difficulties.

2.   The restrictions which may be adopted or maintained pursuant to paragraph 1 of this Article may include quantitative restrictions on imports, restrictions on the right of establishment, restrictions on the right to provide services, restrictions on the right to move capital or on payments and transfers for transactions connected therewith. However, such restrictions:

   (a)   shall, subject to the provisions of this Treaty, not discriminate among Member States or against Member States in favour of third States;

   (b)   shall at all times seek to minimise damage to the commercial, economic or financial interests of any other Member State;

   (c)   shall not exceed those necessary to deal with the circumstances described in paragraph 1 of this Article; and

   (d)   shall be temporary but in any event not longer than a period of eighteen (18) months and be phased out progressively as the situation described in paragraph 1 improves.

3.   In determining the incidence of such restrictions, the Member State concerned may accord priority to activities which are essential to its economic stability. Such restrictions shall not be adopted or maintained for the purpose of protecting a particular sector in contravention of the relevant provisions of this Treaty, due regard being paid in either case to any special factors which may be affecting the reserves of such Member State or its need for reserves.

4.   Restrictions adopted or maintained pursuant to paragraph 1 of this Article, or any changes therein, shall be promptly notified within three (3) working days to COFAP and to COTED, and, in any event, the Member State concerned shall immediately consult with the competent Organ if and when requested.

5.   COFAP shall establish procedures for periodic consultations including, where possible and desirable, prior consultations with the objective of making recommendations to the Member State concerned for the removal of the restrictions.

6.   The consultations referred to in paragraph 5 of this Article shall:

   (a)   be designed to assist the Member State concerned to overcome its balance-of-payments and external financial difficulties;

   (b)   assess the balance-of-payments situation of the Member State concerned and the restrictions adopted or maintained under this Article, taking into account, inter alia:

(i)   the nature and extent of the balance-of-payments and the external financial difficulties;

(ii)   the external economic and trading environment of the Member State applying the restrictions; and

(iii)   alternative corrective measures which may be available.

7.   The consultations shall address the compliance of any restrictions with paragraph 2 of this Article and, in particular, the progressive phase-out of restrictions in accordance with paragraph 2(d).

8.   In such consultations, all findings of statistical and other facts presented by the Committee of Central Bank Governors relating to foreign exchange, monetary reserves and balance-of-payments, shall be accepted and conclusions shall be based on the assessment by the Committee of the balance-of-payments and the external financial situation of the Member State concerned.

ARTICLE 44
Measures to Facilitate Establishment, Provision
of Services and Movement of Capital

1.   In order to facilitate the exercise of the rights provided for in this Chapter, COTED and COFAP shall, subject to the approval of the Conference, adopt appropriate measures for:

(a)   the establishment of market intelligence and information systems in the Community;

(b)   harmonised legal and administrative requirements for the operation of partnerships, companies, or other entities;

(c)   abolition of exchange controls in the Community, and free convertibility of the currencies of the Member States;

(d)   the establishment of an integrated capital market in the Community;

(e)   convergence of macro-economic performance and policies through the co-ordination or harmonisation of monetary and fiscal policies, including, in particular, policies relating to interest rates, exchange rates, tax structures and national budgetary deficits;

(f)   the establishment of economical and efficient land, sea and air transport services throughout the Community, and

(g)   the establishment of efficient communication services.

2.   COFAP and COTED shall establish a comprehensive set of rules in respect of the areas listed in paragraph 1 of this Article for approval by the Conference.

ARTICLE 45
Movement of Community Nationals

Member States commit themselves to the goal of free movement of their nationals within the Community.

ARTICLE 46
Movement of Skilled Community Nationals

1.   Without prejudice to the rights recognised and agreed to be accorded by Member States in Articles 32, 33, 37, 38 and 40 among themselves and to Community nationals, Member States have agreed, and undertake as a first step towards achieving the goal set out in Article 45, to accord to the following categories of Community nationals the right to seek employment in their jurisdictions:

> (a)   University graduates;
> (b)   media workers;
> (c)   sportspersons;
> (d)   artistes; and
> (e)   musicians,

recognised as such by the competent authorities of the receiving Member States.

2.   Member States shall establish appropriate legislative, administrative and procedural arrangements to:

> (a)   facilitate the movement of skills within the contemplation of this Article;
>
> (b)   provide for movement of Community nationals into and within their jurisdictions without harassment or the imposition of impediments, including:
>
>> (i)   the elimination of the requirement for passports for Community nationals travelling to their jurisdictions;
>>
>> (ii)   the elimination of the requirement for work permits for Community nationals seeking approved employment in their jurisdictions;
>>
>> (iii)   establishment of mechanisms for certifying and establishing equivalency of degrees and for accrediting institutions;
>>
>> (iv)   harmonisation and transferability of social security benefits.

3.   Nothing in this Treaty shall be construed as inhibiting Member States from according Community nationals unrestricted access to, and movement within, their jurisdictions subject to such conditions as the public interest may require.

4.   The Conference shall keep the provisions of this Article under review in order to:

> (c)   enlarge, as appropriate, the classes of persons entitled to move and work freely in the Community; and

(d)   monitor and secure compliance therewith.

ARTICLE 47
Restrictions to Resolve Difficulties or Hardships
Arising from the Exercise of Rights

1.   Where the exercise of rights granted under this Chapter creates serious difficulties in any sector of the economy of a Member State or occasions economic hardships in a region of the Community, a Member State adversely affected thereby may, subject to the provisions of this Article, apply such restrictions on the exercise of the rights as it considers appropriate in order to resolve the difficulties or alleviate the hardships.

2.   Where a Member State:

   (a)   intends to apply restrictions in accordance with paragraph 1 of this Article, it shall, prior to applying those restrictions, notify the competent Organ of that intention and the nature of the restrictions;

   (b)   is unable to comply with sub-paragraph (a) of this paragraph, it shall, upon applying the restrictions in accordance with paragraph 1, immediately notify the competent Organ of the application and nature of the restrictions.

3.   The Member State shall, at the time of application of the restrictions mentioned in paragraph 1, submit to COTED or COFAP, as the case may require, a programme setting out the measures to be taken by that Member State to resolve the difficulties or to alleviate the hardships.

4.   The competent Organ shall give its earliest consideration to the programme, and:

   (a)   make a determination in respect of the appropriateness of the restrictions and whether they shall be continued; and

   (b)   where it decides that the restrictions shall be continued, determine:

      (i)   the adequacy of the programme; and
      (ii)   the period for which the restrictions should continue.

The competent Organ, in making a determination under sub-paragraph (b) of this paragraph, may impose such conditions as it considers necessary.

5.   Restrictions applied by a Member State pursuant to paragraph 1 of this Article shall be confined to those necessary:

   (a)   to resolve the difficulties in the affected sectors;

   (b)   to alleviate economic hardships in a particular region.

6.   In applying restrictions mentioned in paragraph 5, Member States shall:

   (a)   minimise damage to the commercial or economic interests of any other Member

State; or

(b)   prevent the unreasonable exercise of rights granted under this Chapter, the exclusion of which could impair the development of the CSME.

7.   The Member States, in applying restrictions pursuant to paragraph 1 of this Article, shall not discriminate and:

(a)   shall progressively relax them as relevant conditions improve;

(b)   may maintain them only to the extent that conditions mentioned in paragraph 1 of this Article continue to justify their application.

8.   If COTED or COFAP, as the case may require, is not satisfied that Member States applying restrictions are acting in accordance with the provisions of paragraph 6 of this Article, it may recommend to the Member States adversely affected thereby alternative arrangements to the same end.

ARTICLE 48
Waiver of Obligations to Grant Rights

1.   Notwithstanding any provision in this Chapter, a Member State may apply to the Community Council for a waiver of the requirement to grant any of the rights mentioned in paragraph 1 of Article 30 in respect of any industry, sector or enterprise.

2.   An application for a waiver within the meaning of paragraph 1 of this Article shall:

(a)   be made prior to the establishment of the relevant programme for the removal of restrictions on the rights mentioned in paragraph 1;

(b)   identify the rights in respect of which the waiver is required;

(c)   set out the circumstances justifying the grant of the waiver; and

(d)   indicate the period for which the waiver is required.

3.   The Community Council may require the applicant to furnish such additional information as the Council may specify.

4.   Where the Community Council is satisfied that the waiver should be granted, it shall grant a waiver for a period not exceeding five years, subject to such terms and conditions as the Community Council may determine.

5.   A Member State which has been granted a waiver within the meaning of paragraph 1 of this Article:

(a)   shall not, while the waiver is in force, be entitled to espouse a claim on behalf of its nationals against another Member State in respect of the rights for which the waiver was granted;

(b)   shall:

(i)   at the termination of the period of the waiver, remove the restrictions and notify the Community Council; or

(ii)   where the Member State removes the restrictions before the end of the period of the waiver; notify the Community Council accordingly.

ARTICLE 49
Special Provisions for Less Developed Countries

Where in this Chapter; the Member States or competent Organs are required to remove restrictions on the exercise of the rights mentioned in paragraph 1 of Article 30 the special needs and circumstances of the Less Developed Countries shall be taken into account.

ARTICLE 50
Accelerated Implementation

Nothing in this Chapter shall be construed as precluding the Member States from adopting measures to remove restrictions on the right of establishment, the right to provide services or the right to move capital within the Community earlier than is required by these provisions

CHAPTER FOUR
POLICIES FOR SECTORAL DEVELOPMENT

PART ONE
INDUSTRIAL POLICY

ARTICLE 51

Objectives of the Community Industrial Policy

1.   The goal of the Community Industrial Policy shall be market-Ied, internationally competitive and sustainable production of goods and services for the promotion of the Region's economic and social development.

2.   In fulfilment of the goal set out in paragraph 1 of this Article, the Community shall pursue the following objectives:

(a)   cross-border employment of natural resources, human resources, capital, technology and management capabilities for the production of goods and services on a sustainable basis;

(b)   linkages among economic sectors and enterprises within and among the Member States of the CSME;

(c)   promotion of regional economic enterprises capable of achieving scales of production to facilitate successful competition in domestic and extra-regional markets;

(d)   establishment of a viable micro and small economic enterprise sector;

(e)   enhanced and diversified production of goods and services for both export and domestic markets;

(f)   sustained public and private sector collaboration in order to secure market-led production of goods and services;

(g)   ˙ enhanced industrial production on an environmentally sustainable basis;

(h)   balanced economic and social development in the CSME bearing in mind the special needs of disadvantaged countries, regions and sectors within the meaning of Article I; and

(i)   stable industrial relations.

ARTICLE 52
Implementation of Community Industrial Policy

1.   In order to achieve the objectives of its industrial policy, the Community shall promote, *inter alia*:

(a)   the co-ordination of national industrial policies of the Member States;

(b)   the establishment and maintenance of an investment-friendly environment, including a facilitative administrative process;

(c)   the diversification of the products and markets for goods and services with a view to increasing the range and value of exports;

(d)   the organisation and development of product and factor markets;

(e)   the development of required institutional, legal, technical, financial, administrative and other support for the establishment or development of micro and small economic enterprises throughout the Community; and

(f)   in collaboration with the social partners, the advancement of production integration.

2.   The Community shall establish a special regime for disadvantaged countries, regions and sectors.

3.   COTED shall, in collaboration with competent organs and bodies of the Community and the private sector; establish criteria for according special consideration to particular industries and sectors. Such criteria shall include, in particular; arrangements relating to the prospects of the industry for successful production integration.

4.   COTED shall collaborate with competent agencies to assist the Member States in designing appropriate policy instruments to support industries, which may include effective export promotion policies, financing policies, incentives and technology policies.

5.   In implementing the Community Industrial Policy, COTED shall have regard to the provisions of this Treaty relating to environmental protection.

6.   The Member States undertake to establish and maintain appropriate macro-economic policies supportive of efficient production in the Community. In addition, they shall undertake to put in place arrangements for; inter alia:

(a)   effective payment mechanisms;

(b)   the avoidance of double taxation;

(c)   harmonised legislation in relevant areas;

(d)   the elimination of bureaucratic impediments to deployment of investments in industrial enterprises;

(e)   the improvement of infrastructure and co-operation in the areas of air and maritime transport;

(f)   communications systems.

7.   In order to facilitate the implementation of the Community Industrial Policy, COTED shall, in collaboration with competent organs and agencies:

(a)   develop strategies for the development and dissemination of market information and appropriate mechanisms to facilitate acquisition, storage and retrieval of such information;

(b)   promote the establishment and development of capital markets in the Member States; and

(c)   encourage the Member States to establish and develop export markets, especially in non-traditional sectors, through the development of sector-specific incentives and appropriate policy instruments.

8.   For the purpose of this Article, "production integration" includes:

(a)   the direct organisation of production in more than one Member State bya single economic enterprise;

(b)   complementary production involving collaboration among several economic enterprises operating in one or more Member States to produce and use required inputs in the production chain; and

(c)   co-operation among economic enterprises in areas such as purchasing, marketing, and research and development.

ARTICLE 53
Micro and Small Economic Enterprise Development

1. The Community shall adopt appropriate policy measures to encourage the development of competitive micro and small economic enterprises in the Member States.

2. Without prejudice to the generality of the foregoing, the competent Organ shall encourage policy initiatives and the establishment of effective programmes to foster a facilitative legal, economic, and administrative framework in the Member States to enhance micro and small economic enterprise development, and shall promote:

    (a)   the development of the capacities of national and regional support agencies for micro and small economic enterprises, including the creation of entrepreneurial centres, byorganising technical assistance inclusive of planning, delivery and evaluation of support services to the sector;

    (b)   access to, improvement in the quality o~ and opportunities for training and education in areas such as technical skills, entrepreneurial competence and business management for micro and small entrepreneurs;

    (c)   access by micro and small economic enterprises to the technical assistance provided by the support agencies;

    (d)   the establishment, development or modernising, as the case may require, of financial institutions to provide, to micro and small economic enterprises, services by way of appropriate and innovative instruments;

    (e)   innovation within the micro and small enterprise sector; and

    (f)   the creation of, and access to, trade and technology information networks.

3. For the purposes of this Article, micro and small economic enterprises shall be economic enterprises within the meaning of Article 32 that satisfy such other criteria as may be determined by the competent authorities.

ARTICLE 54
Development of the Services Sector

1. COTED shall, in collaboration with the appropriate Councils, promote the development of the services sector in the Community in order to stimulate economic complementarities among, and accelerate economic development in, the Member States. In particular; COTED shall promote measures to achieve:

    (a)   increased investment in services;

    (b)   increased volume, value and range of trade in services within the Community and with third States;

    (c)   competitiveness in the modes of delivering services; and

(d)   enhanced enterprise and infrastructural development, including that of micro and small service enterprises.

2.   In order to achieve the objectives set out in paragraph 1, the Member States shall, through the appropriate Councils, collaborate in:

(a)   designing programmes for the development of human resources to achieve competitiveness in the provision of services;

(b)   establishing a regime of incentives for the development of and trade in services; and

(c)   adopting measures to promote the establishment of an appropriate institutional and administrative framework and, in collaboration with the Legal Affairs Committee, promote the establishment of the appropriate legal framework to support the services sector in the Community.

3.   In the establishment of programmes and policies of the Community for the development of the services sector; the relevant Councils shall give priority to:

(a)   the efficient provision of infrastructural services including telecommunications, road, air; maritime and riverain transportation, statistical data generation and financial services;

(b)   the development of capacity-enhancing services including education services, research and development services;

(c)   the development of services which enhance cross-sector competitiveness;

(d)   the facilitation of cross-border provision of services which enhance the competitiveness of the services sector; and

(e)   the development of informatics and other knowledge-based services.

ARTICLE 55
Sustainable Tourism Development

1.   The Community shall, in collaboration with competent international organisations, formulate proposals for sustainable tourism development. These proposals shall recognise the importance of the tourism sub-sector to the economic development of the Region, and the need to conserve its cultural and natural resources and to maintain a balance between a healthy ecology and economic development.

2.   The programme for sustainable tourism development shall have the following objectives:

(a)   an enhanced image for the Region as a tourist destination;

(b)   a diversified tourism product of a consistently high quality;

(c)   an expanded market-base;

(d)   education programmes designed to ensure that appropriate practices are pursued by service.providers;

(e)   linkages with other sectors in the economy;

(f)   conservation of the natural and cultural resources of the Region through proper management; and

(g)   appropriate infrastructure and other services in support of tourism, considering the natural and social carrying-capacity of the Member States.

PART THREE
COMMON SUPPORTIVE MEASURES

ARTICLE 66
Protection of Intellectual Property Rights

COTED shall promote the protection of intellectual property rights within the Community by, inter alia:

(a)   the strengthening of regimes for the protection of intellectual property rights and the simplification of registration procedures in the Member States;

(b)   the establishment of a regional administration for intellectual property rights except copyright;

(c)   the identification and establishment, by the Member States of mechanisms to ensure:

(i)   the use of protected works for the enhanced benefit of the Member States;

(ii)   the preservation of indigenous Caribbean culture; and

(iii)   the legal protection of the expressions of folklore, other traditional knowledge and national heritage, particularly of indigenous populations in the Community;

(d)   increased dissemination and use of patent documentation as a source of technological information;

(e)   public education;

(f)   measures to prevent the abuse of intellectual property rights by rights-holders or the resort to practices which unreasonably restrain trade or adversely affect the international transfer of technology; and

(g)   participation by the Member States in international regimes for the protection of intellectual property rights.

ARTICLE 69
Harmonisation of Investment Incentives

1.   The Member States shall harmonise national incentives to investments in the industrial, agricultural and services sectors.

2.   COFAP shall, consistently with relevant international agreements, formulate proposals for the establishment of regimes for the granting of incentives to enterprises in the sectors mentioned in paragraph 1. In particular, such proposals shall accord support for industries considered to be of strategic interest to the Community.

3.   In formulating the proposals mentioned in paragraph 2, COFAP shall give due consideration to the peculiarities of the industries concerned and, without prejudice to the generality of the foregoing, may provide for the following:

(a)   national incentives to investment designed to promote sustainable, export-led industrial and service-oriented development;

(b)   investment facilitation through the removal of bureaucratic impediments; and

(c)   non-discrimination in the granting of incentives among Community nationals.

ARTICLE 72
Double Taxation Agreements

1.   The Member States shall conclude among themselves an agreement for the avoidance of double taxation in order to facilitate the free movement of capital in the Community.

2.   The Member States shall conclude their double taxation agreements with third States on the basis of mutually agreed principles which shall be determined by COFAP.

ARTICLE 73
Industrial Relations

COHSOD shall, in consultation with COTED, formulate proposals and adopt appropriate measures for the promotion of harmonious, stable and enlightened industrial relations in the Community. In formulating such measures and proposals, COHSOD shall, inter alia. promote:

(a)   the objectives of full employment, improved living and working conditions; adequate social security policies and programmes; tripartite consultations among governments, workers' and employers' organisations; and cross-border mobility of labour;

(b)   recognition of the principle of non-discriminatory treatment among Community workers in the pursuit of employment within the Community;

(c)   the establishment and maintenance of effective mechanisms for the enhancement of industrial relations, particularly that of collective bargaining; and

(d)   awareness among Community workers and employers that international competitiveness is essential for social and economic development of Member States and requires collaboration of employers and workers for increased production and productivity in Community enterprises.

ARTICLE 77
Special Provisions for Less Developed Countries

Where in this Chapter Member States or competent Organs are required to adopt measures for the achievement of the Community Industrial Policy, the special needs and circumstances of the Less Developed Countries shall be taken into account.

CHAPTER FIVE
TRADE POLICY

PART THREE
SUBSIDIES

ARTICLE 96
Determination of a Subsidy

For the purpose of this Part, a subsidy shall be deemed to exist if there is a financial contribution by a Government or any public body within the territory of a Member State (hereinafter referred to as "government} where:

(a)   a government practice involves direct transfer of funds (e.g., grants, loans and equity infusion) or potential direct transfer of funds or liabilities (e.g., loan guarantees);

(b)   government revenue that is otherwise due is foregone or not collected (e.g., fiscal incentives, such as tax credits);

(c)   a government purchases goods or provides goods or services other than general infrastructure;

(d)   a government makes payments to a funding mechanism, or directs or entrusts to a private body the conduct of activities mentioned in sub-paragraphs (a), (b) and (c) which are normally conducted by governments; and a benefit is thereby conferred. (e) there is any form of income or price support,

ARTICLE 97
Types of Subsidies

1.   A subsidy within the meaning of Article 96 shall be categorised as follows:

    (a)   a prohibited subsidy;

    (b)   a subsidy which:

        (i)   causes injury to a domestic industry; or

(ii)   results in nullification or impairment of benefits accruing directly or indirectly to any Member State; or

(iii)   seriously prejudices the interests of any Member State; or

(c)   a subsidy which causes serious adverse effects to a domestic industry of any Member State such as to cause damage which would be difficult to repair:

Provided that the subsidy is specific to an enterprise or industry or group of enterprises or industries within the jurisdiction of the granting Member State.

2.   For the purpose of this Chapter a determination of whether a subsidy as defined in Article 92 is specific shall be governed by the following:

(a)   in order to determine whether a subsidy referred to in paragraph 1 of this Article is specific to an enterprise or industry or group of enterprises or industries (referred to in this Part as "certain enterprises, / within the jurisdiction of the granting authority, the following criteria shall apply:

(i)   where the granting authority, or the legislation pursuant to which the granting authority operates, explicitly limits access to a subsidy to certain enterprises, such a subsidy shall be specific;

(ii)   where the granting authority, or the legislation pursuant to which the granting authority operates, establishes objective criteria or conditions governing the eligibility for, and the amount o~ a subsidy, specificity shall not exist, provided that the eligibility is automatic and that such criteria and conditions are strictly adhered to. The criteria or conditions must be clearly spelled out in law, regulation, or other official document, so as to be capable of verification;

(iii)   if notwithstanding any appearance of non-specificity resulting from the application of the principles laid down in sub-sub-paragraphs (i) and (ii), there are reasons to believe that the subsidy may in fact be specific, other factors may be considered. Such factors are: use of a subsidy programme by a limited number of certain enterprises, predominant use of certain enterprises, the granting of disproportionately large amounts of subsidy to certain enterprises, and the manner in which discretion has been exercised by the granting authority in the decision to grant a subsidy. In applying this sub- paragraph, account shall be taken of the extent of diversification of economic activities within the jurisdiction of the granting authority, as well as of the length of time during which the subsidy programme has been in operation;

(b)   a subsidy which is limited to certain enterprises located within a designated geographical region within the jurisdiction of the granting authority shall be specific. It is understood that the setting or change of generally applicable tax rates by all levels of government entitled to do so shall not be deemed to be a specific subsidy for the purposes of this Part;

(c)   any subsidy falling under the provisions of Article 99 shall be deemed to be specific;

(d)   any determination of specificity under the provisions of this Article shall be clearly substantiated on the basis of positive evidence.

ARTICLE 98
Entitlement to Take Action
Against Subsidised Products

1.   A Member State may take action against subsidised products where:

(a)   the products have benefited from a prohibited subsidy;

(b)   the subsidy is specific and has caused any of the effects referred to in Article 112; and

(c)   the subsidy is specific and does not conform to the provisions of Article 108.

2.   Notwithstanding the provisions of paragraph 1, a Member State shall not take definitive action against products which are believed to be benefitting from subsidies referred to in Article 97 if the Member State aggrieved thereby has not:

(a)   promulgated legislation to permit the introduction of counter measures or countervailing duties against subsidised imports;

(b)   consulted with the Member State which is alleged to have introduced or to be maintaining subsidies identified in Article 97;

(c)   notified COTED of the alleged subsidisation based on preliminary investigations and failure of consultations; and

(d)   received authorisation from COTED to introduce countervailing duties or countermeasures as a result of a definitive determination of the existence of prohibited subsidies which cause nullification, impairment, serious prejudice or adverse effects caused by subsidisation.

3.   Consultations for the purposes of this Part shall follow the procedures set out in *Annex II*.

ARTICLE 99
Prohibited Subsidies

1.   Subject to this Treaty, a Member State shall neither grant nor maintain subsidies referred to in paragraph 2.

2.   The following subsidies within the meaning of Article 96 shall be prohibited:

(a)   subsidies contingent, in law or in fact, whether solely or as one of several other conditions, upon export performance, including those listed in Schedule V; and

(b)   subsidies contingent, whether solely or as one of several other conditions, upon the use of domestic over imported goods. 3. Nothing in this Article shall be construed as applying to agricultural commodities produced in the Community.

ARTICLE 100
Preliminary Investigation of Prohibited Subsidies

1.   An application for an investigation may be made in writing by or on behalf of a domestic industry to the competent authority where the industry has reason to believe that a prohibited subsidy referred to in Article 99 has been granted or maintained by another Member State. The authority shall examine the application and determine, on the basis of the facts available, whether to initiate an investigation.

2.   An investigation initiated pursuant to paragraph 1 of this Article shall be deemed to be a preliminary investigation. The authority shall give public notice of the preliminary investigation to inform the concerned Member State, other Member States and the interested parties all of whom shall be afforded adequate time to submit information required and to make comments.

3.   The authority shall make a preliminary determination whether a prohibited subsidy has been granted or maintained and, where the determination is affirmative, invite the concerned Member States and interested parties to defend their interests.

4.   A request for investigation by the domestic industry under this Article or under Article 106 or 112 shall be accompanied by information set out in the *Illustrative List at Annex 111 (a).*

5.   Wherever the term "domestic industry" is used in this Chapter, it shall mean domestic industry as defined in *Annex I.*

ARTICLE 101
Request for Consultations Relating
to Prohibited Subsidies

1.   Whenever a Member State has reason to believe, pursuant to Article 99 that a prohibited subsidy has been granted or is maintained by a Member State, the aggrieved or any other Member State may request consultations with the Member State believed to be granting or maintaining the subsidy. The aggrieved Member State shall notify COTED of the request for consultations. A request for consultations shall include a statement of the available evidence with regard to the existence and nature of the alleged prohibited subsidy.

2.   Upon receipt of a request for consultations under paragraph 1, the Member State believed to be granting or maintaining the subsidy shall reply within 10 days and shall furnish the relevant information requested and shall promptly enter into consultations which shall be concluded within 30 days of the date of request for such consultations unless the parties agree to extend the consultations to a mutually agreed date. The purpose of the consultations shall be to clarify the facts relating to the existence and type of the alleged subsidy and to arrive at a mutually agreed solution.

ARTICLE 102
Reference to COTED to Investigate
Prohibited Subsidies

1.   If no mutually agreed solution is reached at the completion of 30 days from the date of the request for the consultations referred to in Article 101, or at such time as the parties agree, or if the Member State believed to be granting or maintaining the subsidy refuses to co-operate, the Member State requesting consultations or any other Member State interested in such consultations may refer the matter to COTED which shall carry out an investigation to establish whether the subsidy in question is a prohibited subsidy.

2.   The referral of the matter to COTED for an investigation shall not prevent the aggrieved Member State from taking, on a provisional basis, which shall not be sooner than 60 days from the date of initiation of investigations under paragraph 1 of Article 103 counter-measures to forestall injury or to prevent further injury to its domestic industry.

ARTICLE 103
Investigation by COTED of
Prohibited Subsidies

1.   Whenever COTED decides to carry out an investigation pursuant to Article 102, such an investigation by COTED shall proceed as expeditiously as possible. COTED may appoint competent experts to advise whether the subsidy falls to be classified as a prohibited subsidy, in which case COTED shall set a time limit for the examination of the evidence by the competent experts. COTED shall make its determination and issue its report which shall, unless extenuating circumstances arise, not exceed 90 days from the date of receipt of request for the investigation.

2.   The results of an investigation carried out pursuant to Article 102 shall be made available to all Member States for information and to afford the concerned Member States an opportunity to arrive at a mutually agreed solution within 30 days from the date of issue of the report failing which COTED shall adopt the recommendations of the report.

3.   If COTED is satisfied, based on the results of the investigation, that the subsidy in question is a prohibited subsidy and that the concerned Member States cannot reach a mutually agreed solution, it shall, subject to Article 104, require the offending Member State to withdraw the subsidy within a specified time-frame. Where the offending Member State fails to comply, COTED shall authorise the aggrieved Member State to take counter-measures on the products which benefit from such a subsidy.

ARTICLE 104
Withdrawal of Prohibited Subsidies

1.   Notwithstanding the investigation confirming the existence of a prohibited subsidy in paragraph 3 of Article 103, COTED shall not impose a requirement for the Member States to withdraw such a subsidy sooner than specified in this paragraph as follows:

    (a)   with respect to subsidies contingent upon export performance:

        (i)   the Member States with per capita GNP of less than one thousand United States dollars shall be allowed to maintain such subsidies; and

(ii)   other Member States shall be allowed to maintain such subsidies until 1 January 2003;

(b)   with respect to subsidies contingent upon the use of domestic over imported inputs, the Member States with per capita GNP of less than one thousand United States dollars shall be allowed to maintain such subsidies until 2003.

2.   Whenever the results of an investigation by COTED prove that the alleged subsidy is not a prohibited subsidy, any provisional countervailing measures which might have been imposed shall be promptly withdrawn and any bond or deposit which might have been effected, released or refunded, as the case may be. If the provisional measures referred to in this paragraph have materially retarded the exports of the Member State which was wrongfully alleged to have introduced or maintained prohibited subsidies, COTED shall, upon application from such a Member State, assess the effects of the provisionally applied measures and determine the nature and extent of compensation which is warranted and recommend compensation in accordance with its assessment.

3.   From the date of entry into force of this Treaty until the expiration of the dates mentioned in paragraph 1, no provisional measures shall be imposed where it has been determined by preliminary investigations that prohibited subsidies are maintained.

ARTICLE 105
Subsidies Causing Injury, Nullification, Impairment or Serious Prejudice

A Member State may take action against subsidised imports from any other Member State where it can be established, based on an investigation, that the effect of the subsidy has been:

(a)   injury to its domestic industry;

(b)   nullification or impairment of benefits which it expects under this Treaty; or

(c)   serious prejudice to its interests.

2.   Serious prejudice shall be deemed to exist in the case where:

(a)   the total ad valorem subsidisation of a product exceeds 5 per cent;

(b)   subsidies cover operating losses sustained by an industry;

(c)   subsidies cover operating losses sustained by an enterprise, other than one-time measures which are non-recurrent and cannot be repeated for that enterprise and which are given merely to provide time for the development of long-term solutions and to avoid acute social problems; or

(d)   subsidies are granted in the form of forgiveness of government- held debt and government grants to cover debt repayment.

3.   Notwithstanding the provisions of this Article, serious prejudice shall not be found if the Member State granting the subsidy in question demonstrates that the effect of the subsidy has not been:

(a)   to displace or impede the imports of like products from the Member State exporting to the Member State which has introduced or maintains the subsidy;

(b)   to displace or impede the exports of a like product from the affected exporting Member State into the market of a third Member State;

(c)   a significant price undercutting by the subsidised product as compared with the price of a like product of another Member State in the same market or a significant price suppression or price depression;

(d)   lost sales of another Member State in the same market; or

(e)   an increase in its market share within the CSME.

4.   The provisions of this Article shall not apply to Part Three.

ARTICLE 106
Preliminary Investigation of Subsidies Causing Injury,
Nullification, Impairment or Serious Prejudice

1.   An application for an investigation may be made in writing by or on behalf of a domestic industry to the national authority where the industry has reason to believe that a subsidy referred to in Article 105 has been granted or is maintained by another Member State and has caused injury, or resulted in nullification, impairment or serious prejudice to its interests.

2.   An application under paragraph 1 shall include sufficient information about the existence of a subsidy and, if possible, its amount, injury and a causal link between the subsidised products and the alleged injury.

3.   An application to initiate an investigation shall be considered to have been made by or on behalf of a domestic industry if it is supported by those domestic producers whose collective output constitutes more than 50 per cent of the total production of the like product by that proportion of the domestic industry expressing support for or opposition to the application. The investigation shall not be initiated where the domestic producers expressly supporting the application account for less than 25 per cent of the total production of the like product produced by the domestic industry.

4.   Upon receipt of a request for such an investigation, the authority shall examine the application and determine, on the basis of the facts available, whether to initiate an investigation. If the authority decides to initiate an investigation, it shall issue a public notice to that effect, invite the concerned Member State, other interested Member States and interested parties to submit required information and comments.

5.   An investigation initiated pursuant to paragraph 1 shall be deemed to be a preliminary investigation. The authority shall inform the concerned Member State and all interested parties of the results of the investigation.

6.   For the purpose of this Part, "like product" shall be interpreted to mean a product which is identical, i. e. , alike in all respects to the product under consideration, or in the absence of such a product, another product, which, although not alike in all respects, has characteristics closely resembling those of the product under consideration.

ARTICLE 107
Request for Consultations Relating to Subsidies Causing
Injury, Nullification, Impairment or Serious Prejudice

1.   Whenever a Member State has reason to believe that a subsidy within the meaning of Article 96 has been granted or is maintained by another Member State, and that imports from such a Member State have resulted in any of the effects mentioned in paragraph 1(b) of Article 97, the first-mentioned Member State may approach the Member State believed to be granting a subsidy with a request for consultations.

2.   A request for consultations shall include a statement of available evidence with regard to
-

(a)   the existence and nature of the subsidy; and

(b)   the injury caused to the domestic industry; or

(c)   the impairment or nullification of benefits of exporting to other Member States in the Community; or

(d)   serious prejudice to its interests.

3.   Upon receipt of a request for consultations under paragraph 1, the Member State believed to be granting or maintaining the subsidy shall reply within 10 days, and shall furnish relevant information and enter into consultations within 30 days of the date of the request. The purpose of the consultations shall be to clarify the facts relating to the existence, type and effect of the alleged subsidy and to arrive at a mutually agreed solution.

ARTICLE 108
Reference to COTED to Investigate Subsidies Causing
Injury, Nullification, Impairment or Serious Prejudice

1.   If no mutually agreed solution is reached at the completion of 60 days from the date of request for consultations, or on a date mutuallyagreed, the Member State requesting consultations may refer the matter to COTED which shall initiate an investigation, make a determination to resolve the dispute and issue a report within 120 days of the date of the request for an investigation by the aggrieved Member State.

2.   A decision by COTED to initiate an investigation shall not prevent the aggrieved Member State from taking, on a provisional basis, countermeasures which shall not be sooner than 60 days from the date of initiation of a preliminary investigation by the national authority to forestall or prevent further adverse effects.

ARTICLE 109
Investigation by COTED of Subsidies Causing Injury, Nullification, Impairment or Serious Prejudice

1.   In order to arrive at a determination of the existence, degree and effect of subsidisation, and remedial action which may be taken pursuant to the referral of a complaint of alleged subsidisation mentioned in Article 108, CO TED shall -

(a)   carry out an investigation into the circumstances relating to the alleged grant or maintenance of the subsidy by the offending Member State; the investigation is to be completed within 120 days of the date of receipt of a complaint regarding alleged subsidisation by an offending Member State; and

(b)   upon receipt of the report arising from the investigation, promptly make available the report to the concerned Member States to facilitate consultation and to permit the Member states concerned to arrive at a mutually acceptable solution.

ARTICLE 110
Consequences of Failure to Remove Subsidies Causing Injury, Nullification, Impairment or Serious Prejudice

1.   If no mutually acceptable solution is reached within 30 days of the date of issue of the report by COTED, and COTED is satisfied:

(a)   of the existence of a subsidy within the meaning of Article 105; and

(b)   that the subsidy has caused injury to the enterprise in the aggrieved Member State; or

(c)   that the subsidy has impaired or nullified benefits expected of the aggrieved Member State with respect to its exports to the Community; or

(d)   that the effect of the subsidy was to seriously prejudice the interests of the Member State, then in such a case, COTED shall request the Member State which has granted or maintained the subsidy to take appropriate steps to remedy the effects of the subsidy within six months of the date of the issue of the report by COTED.

2.   If, at the end of the period of six months allowed by COTED to the Member State granting or maintaining the subsidy to remedy the effects of the subsidy, the Member State fails to comply and in the absence of agreement on compensation COTED shall authorise the aggrieved Member State to impose countervailing duties at a rate equivalent to the amount of subsidisation for such time and under such conditions as COTED may prescribe.

ARTICLE 111
Types of Subsidies Causing Serious Adverse Effects

1.   The Member States shall not ordinarily impose or introduce countervailing duties or take countermeasures on products which benefit from:

(a)   subsidies which are not specific within the meaning of Article 97; or

(b)   subsidies which are specific within the meaning of Article 97 but which satisfy all of the conditions set out in this sub-paragraph hereunder:

    (i)   subsidies granted for research activities conducted by enterprises or by higher education or research establishments on a contract basis with firms if the assistance covers not more than 75 per cent of the costs of industrial research or 50 per cent of the costs of pre- competitive development activity and provided that such assistance is limited exclusively to:

        (aa)   costs of personnel (researchers, technicians and other supporting staff employed exclusively in the research activity);

        (bb)   costs of instruments, equipment, land and buildings used exclusively and permanently (except when disposed of on a commercial basis) for the research activity;

        (cc)   costs of consultancy and equivalent services used exclusively for the research activity, including bought-in research, technical knowledge, patents, etc.;

        (dd)   additional overhead costs incurred directly as a result of the research activity;

        (ee)   other running costs (such as those of materials, supplies and the like), incurred directly as a result of the research activity.

(c)   subsidies granted to assist disadvantaged regions within the territory of a Member State given pursuant to a general framework of regional development and that are non-specific within eligible regions provided that:

    (i)   each disadvantaged region must be a clearly designated contiguous geographical area with a definable economic and administrative identify;

    (ii)   the Region is considered as disadvantaged on the basis of neutral and objective criteria, indicating that the region's difficulties arise out of more than temporary circumstances; such criteria must be clearly spelled out in law, regulation, or other official document, so as to be capable of verification;

    (iii)   the criteria shall include a measurement of economic development which shall be based on at least one of the following factors:

        (aa)   one of either income per capita or household income per capita, or GDP per capita, which must not be above 85 per cent of the average for the territory concerned;

        (bb)   unemployment rate, which must be at least 110 per cent of the average for the territory concerned;

(d)   subsidies granted to assist entities in the adaptation of existing facilities to new environmental requirements imposed by law and/or regulations which result in greater constraints and financial burden on enterprises provided that the subsidies

         (i)   are a one-time non-recurring measure; and

         (ii)   are limited to 20 per cent of the cost of adaptation; and

         (iii)   do not cover the cost of replacing and operating the assisted investment, which must be fully borne by firms; and

         (iv)   are directly linked to and proportionate to a firm's planned reduction of nuisances and pollution, and do not cover any manufacturing cost savings which may be achieved; and

         (v)   are available to all firms which can adopt the new equipment and/or production processes.

(e)   subsidies granted to assist enterprises to undertake training or retraining of employees, whether or not the enterprise is new, and the upgrading of existing facilities to facilitate transition to competitive status within the Community, provided that such subsidies are not specific.

2.   The Member States shall notify COTED of any subsidy mentioned in paragraph 1. Any Member State may request further information regarding a notified subsidy programme and COTED shall review annually all notified subsidies referred to in paragraph 1.

ARTICLE 112
Preliminary Investigation of Subsidies
Causing Serious Adverse Effects

1.   A domestic industry may submit to the competent authority an application for an investigation to verify that serious adverse effects have been caused by imports which benefit from subsidies referred to in Article 111.

2.   Upon receipt of an application for an investigation to verify adverse effects, the authority shall examine the application, and, on the basis of the available facts, determine whether to initiate an investigation.

3.   The investigation referred to in paragraph 2 shall be deemed a preliminary investigation. The authority shall give public notice of its decision to initiate a preliminary investigation and the concerned Member State, other interested Member States, and the interested persons shall all be invited to provide relevant information and make comments.

4.   The results of the preliminary investigation shall be made available to the concerned Member State, other interested Member States and the interested persons to enable them to defend their interests.

ARTICLE 113
Request for Consultations Relating to Subsidies
Causing Serious Adverse Effects

1.   Whenever a Member State has reason to believe that imports from another Member State benefited from subsidies within the meaning of Article 111 and such imports have resulted in serious adverse effects to a domestic industry so as to cause damage which would be difficult to repair, the Member State aggrieved may request consultations with the Member State granting or maintaining the subsidy.

2.   The Member State alleged to be granting the subsidy which caused adverse effects shall reply within 10 days of the date of the request for consultations and shall enter into the consultations requested by the aggrieved Member State. If there is no mutual agreement within 60 days of the date of the request for such consultations or on a later date which was mutually agreed or if the Member State refuses to co-operate, the aggrieved Member State may refer the matter to COTED and request COTED to carry out an investigation.

ARTICLE 114
Investigation by COTED of Subsidies
Causing Serious Adverse Effects

1.   The referral of the matter to COTED for an investigation shall not prevent the aggrieved Member State from imposing on a provisional basis not sooner than 60 days from the date of initiation of the preliminary investigation referred to in Article 106, countermeasures to forestall or prevent further adverse effects.

2.   If COTED is satisfied that the investigation requested isjustified, COTED shall carry out the investigation, make a determination and issue a report within 120 days from the date when the request was referred.

3.   Where the results of the investigation carried out by COTED demonstrate that the subsloised imports caused serious adverse effects to the domestic industry of the aggrieved Member State requesting the investigation, COTED shall recommend that the offending Member State modify the programme of subsidies in such a way as to remove the adverse effects complained of.

ARTICLE 115
Consequences of Failure to Eliminate or
Establish Adverse Effects of Subsidies

1.   If the offending Member State fails to implement the recommendations of CO TED within 6 months of the date of issue of the report referred to in paragraph 2 of Article 114, COTED shall authorise the aggrieved Member State to impose appropriate countervailing duties commensurate with the nature and degree of serious adverse effects determined to exist.

2.   Whenever the results of an investigation by COTED prove that serious adverse effects have not been caused by subsidised imports referred to in paragraph 1 of Article 111, the Member State alleging that its domestic industry has suffered serious adverse effects shall promptly refund any duties which might have been provisionally imposed and where such provisional duties had materially retarded the exports of the Member State complained against,

CO TED shall, upon application from such State, assess the effects of the provisionally applied duties and determine the nature and extent of compensation which is warranted and require compensation in accordance with its assessment.

ARTICLE 116
Imposition of Provisional Measures and Countervailing Duties

1.   Notwithstanding anything to the contrary in this Chapter; a Member State aggrieved by the application or maintenance of prohibited subsidies or by subsidies which cause injury, or result in nullification, impairment, or serious prejudice, or cause serious adverse effects, as the case may be, shall introduce provisional measures only on the basis of the following rules:

(a)   Provisional measures may be applied only if -

(i)   a preliminary investigation has been initiated in accordance with the provisions of this Chapter; a public notice has been given to that effect and interested persons have been given adequate opportunities to submit information and make comments;

(ii)   an affirmative preliminary determination has been made of the existence of a prohibited subsidy, or a subsidy causing injury, nullification, impairment, serious prejudice, or a subsidy causing serious adverse effects, as the case may be;

(iii)   consultations were requested and undertaken, COTED was notified and requested to investigate and the authorities concerned judge such measures necessary to prevent injury being caused during the investigation;

(b)   Provisional measures may take the form of provisional countervailing duties guaranteed by cash deposits or bonds equal to the amount of the subsidisation calculated on a provisional basis;

(c)   Provisional measures shall not be applied sooner than 60 days from the date of initiation of the preliminary investigation;

(d)   The application of provisional measures shall be limited to as short a period as possible, not exceeding 120 days.

2.   Where investigations by COTED continue beyond the period allowed for the maintenance of provisional measures under sub-paragraph 1 (d), the Member State imposing the measures may continue with such measures until a definitive determination is made by COTED.

3.   The Member States which are parties to an investigation to verify the existence and the effect of alleged subsidisation, may seek or accept, as the case may be, undertakings from the Member State alleged to have granted or to be maintaining a subsidy. Undertakings may take the form of.

(a)   withdrawal, or limiting the amount of the subsidy to such an extent that injury, nullification, impairment, serious prejudice or serious adverse effects, as the case may be, are eliminated; or

(b)   a guarantee from the exporter benefiting from the subsidy to raise his price to such an extent that the injurious effect is eliminated.

4.   If a Member State accepts a voluntary guarantee pursuant to sub- paragraph 3(b), then the accepting Member State shall notify COTED and promptly suspend proceedings, and any provisional measures which may have been imposed shall be withdrawn with immediate effect.

5.   In the event that investigations to determine subsidisation have been concluded and the evidence proves injury, nullification, impairment or serious prejudice, or serious adverse effects, as the case may be, a Member State may impose countervailing duties retroactively to account for the entire period during which provisional measures have been in force. Such retroactively applied duties shall take into account the definitively assessed countervailing duties and the amount guaranteed by cash deposit or bond and:

(a)   where the definitive countervailing duties are higher than the provisional duties, the difference shall not be collected;

(b)   where the definitive countervailing duties are lower than the provisional duties, the excess of the deposit shall be refunded or the bond released promptly.

6.   No Member State shall impose countervailing duties other than provisional countervailing duties without prior authorisation from COTED and the determination and imposition of definitive countervailing duties shall be governed by the relevant provisions of the WTO Agreement on Subsidies and Countervailing Measures.

7.   COTED shall keep under review all counter-measures imposed by the Member States and shall ensure that the Member States observe the conditions and timetable for review and withdrawal of counter-measures that it may have authorised.

8.   The Member States undertake to co-operate in establishing harmonised legislation and procedures in accordance with the provisions of this Chapter.

CHAPTER SEVEN
DISADVANTAGED COUNTRIES, REGIONS
AND SECTORS

PART THREE
SPECIAL REGIME FOR LESS DEVELOPED COUNTRIES

ARTICLE 160
Import Duties

Where a less developed country has suffered or is likely to suffer loss of revenue as a result of the importation of goods eligible for Community treatment, COTED may, on application made in that behalf by the less developed country, authorise the imposition of import duties on such goods for such time and on such terms and conditions as COTED may decide.

ARTICLE 161
Community Origin

The Member States agree that in the determination and operation of the criterion of substantial transformation pursuant to Article 84, the special needs of the less developed countries shall be taken into account.

ARTICLE 162
Incentive Regimes

The Member States agree that in the establishment of any programme for incentives in the Community provided for in Article 52 and Article 69, the special needs of the less developed countries shall be taken into account.

ARTICLE 163
The Common External Tariff

The Member States agree that in the implementation of the Common External Tariff provided for in Article 82, the special needs of the less developed countries shall be taken into account.

ARTICLE 164
Promotion of Industrial Development

1.   Upon application made in that behalf by the less developed countries, GOTED may, if necessary, as a temporary measure in order to promote the development of an industry in any of these States, authorise such States to suspend Community origin treatment to any description of imports eligible therefor on grounds of production in one or more less developed countries.

2.   COTED may, in taking decisions pursuant to paragraph 1 of this Article, establish terms and conditions including a phasing-out period during which Member States and the Community shall provide support measures and the industry implement the necessary programmes for achieving competitiveness.

3.   The grant of authorisation pursuant to paragraph 1 of this Article shall be by means of a decision supported by the affirmative votes of all the less developed countries and at least two of the more developed countries.

ARTICLE 165
Public Undertakings

Paragraph 1 of Article 94 hall not apply to the less developed countries.

ARTICLE 166
Use of Technological and Research Facilities

The more developed countries undertake to provide opportunities for the use of their technological and research facilities by the less developed countries.

ARTICLE 167
Special Provisions for Belize

Belize shall be allowed to impose import duties or quantitative restrictions on beer and cigarettes produced in the Community for a period ending 31 December 2000

CHAPTER EIGHT
COMPETITION POLICY AND CONSUMER PROTECTION

PART ONE

ARTICLE 168
Scope of Chapter

The rules of competition shall not apply to -

(a)   combinations or activities of employees for their own reasonable protection as employees;

(b)   arrangements for collective bargaining on behalf of employers or employees for the purpose of fixing terms and conditions of employment;

(c)   business conduct within the meaning of Article 177duly notified to COTED in accordance with Article 170;

(d)   negative clearance rulings within the meaning of Article 180 or exemptions within the meaning of Articles 181 and 183;

(e)   activities of professional associations designed to develop or enforce professional standards of competence reasonably necessary for the protection of the public and approved by the Commission.

ARTICLE 169
Objectives of Community Competition Policy

1.   The goal of the Community Competition Policy shall be to ensure that the benefits expected from the establishment of the CSME are not frustrated by anti- competitive business conduct.

2.   In fulfilment of the goal set out in paragraph 1 of this Article, the Community shall pursue the following objectives:

(a)   the promotion and maintenance of competition and enhancement of economic efficiency in production, trade and commerce;

(b)   subject to this Treaty, the prohibition of anti-competitive business conduct which prevents, restricts or distorts competition or which constitutes the abuse of a dominant position in the market; and

(c)   the promotion of consumer welfare and protection of consumer interests.

ARTICLE 170
Implementation of Community Competition Policy

1.   In order to achieve the objectives of the Community Competition Policy,

(a)   the Community shall:

(i)   subject to Articles 164, 177, 178 and 179 of this Treaty, establish appropriate norms and institutional arrangements to prohibit and penalise anti-competitive business conduct; and

(ii)   establish and maintain information systems to enable enterprises and consumers to be kept informed about the operation of markets within the GSME;

(b)   the Member States shall:

(i)   take the necessary legislative measures to ensure consistency and compliance with the rules of competition and provide penalties for anti-competitive business conduct;

(ii)   provide for the dissemination of relevant information to facilitate consumer choice;

(iii)   establish and maintain institutional arrangements and administrative procedures to enforce competition laws; and

(iv)   take effective measures to ensure access by nationals of other Member States to competent enforcement authorities including the courts on an equitable, transparent and non-discriminatory basis.

2.   Every Member State shall establish and maintain a national competition authority for the purpose of facilitating the implementation of the rules of competition.

3.   Every Member State shall require its national competition authority to:

(a)   co-operate with the Commission in achieving compliance with the rules of competition;

(b)   investigate any allegations of anti-competitive business conduct referred to the authority by the Commission or another Member State;

(c)   co-operate with other national competition authorities in the detection and prevention of anti-competitive business conduct, and the exchange of information relating to such conduct.

4.   Nothing in this Article shall be construed as requiring a Member State to disclose confidential information, the disclosure of which would be prejudicial to the public interest or to

the legitimate commercial interests of enterprises, public or private. Confidential or proprietary information disclosed in the course of an investigation shall be treated on the same basis as that on which it was provided.

5.   Within 24 months of the entry into force of this Treaty, the Member States shall notify COTED of existing legislation, agreements and administrative practices inconsistent with the provisions of this Chapter. Within 36 months of entry into force of this Treaty, COTED shall establish a programme providing for the repeal of such legislation, and termination of agreements and administrative practices.

ARTICLE 171
Establishment of the Competition Commission

For the purposes of implementation of the Community Competition Policy, there is hereby established a Competition Commission (hereinafter called "the Commission) having the composition, functions and powers hereinafter set forth.

ARTICLE 172
Composition of the Commission

1.   The Commission shall comprise seven members appointed by the Regional Judicial and Legal Services Commission to serve on the Commission. The Regional Judicial and Legal Services Commission shall appoint a Chairman from among the members so appointed.

2.   The Commission shall comprise persons, collectively having expertise or experience in commerce, finance, economics, law, competition policy and practice, international trade and such other areas of expertise or experience as may be necessary.

3.   A Commissioner shall be appointed for a term of five years and such appointment may be renewed for a further period of not more than five years as determined by the Regional Judicial and Legal Services Commission.

4.   A Commissioner may be removed from office only for inability to perform the functions of his office or for misbehaviour and shall otherwise be subject to the disciplinary procedures of the Regional Judicial and Legal Services Commission.

5.   A Commissioner shall be removed only on the vote of the Judicial and Legal Services Commission that represents not less than three-quarters of all the Members of the Commission.

6.   A Commissioner may at any time resign the office of Commissioner by writing under his hand addressed to the Chairman of the Judicial and Legal Services Commission.

7.   A Commissioner shall not enter upon the duties of the office unless he has taken and subscribed before the Chairman of the Judicial and Legal Services Commission, the Oath of Office set out in the Annex to this Treaty.

8.   Notwithstanding the foregoing provisions of this Article, the Conference shallon the recommendation of COTED execute the functions required to be carried out by the Regional Judicial and Legal Services Commission where the Parties to the Agreement Establishing the Caribbean Court of Justice are less than seven.

ARTICLE 173
Functions of the Commission

1.   The Commission shall:

  (a)   apply the rules of competition in respect of anti-competitive cross-border business conduct;

  (b)   promote and protect competition in the Community and co- ordinate the implementation of the Community Competition Policy; and

  (c)   perform any other function conferred on it by any competent body of the Community.

2.   In discharging the functions setout in paragraph 1, the Commission shall:

  (a)   monitor anti-competitive practices of enterprises operating in the CSME, and investigate and arbitrate cross-border disputes;

  (b)   keep the Community Competition Policy under review and advise and make recommendations to COTED to enhance its effectiveness;

  (c)   promote the establishment of institutions and the development and implementation of harmonised competition laws and practices by the Member States to achieve uniformity in the administration of applicable rules;

  (d)   review the progress made by the Member States in the implementation of the legal and institutional framework for enforcement;

  (e)   co-operate with competent authorities in the Member States;

  (f)   provide support to the Member States in promoting and protecting consumer welfare;

  (g)   facilitate the exchange of relevant information and expertise; and

  (h)   develop and disseminate information about competition policy, and consumer protection policy.

3.   The Commission may, by directions in writing and subject to such conditions as it thinks fit, delegate any of its functions to one or more of its members.

ARTICLE 174
Powers of the Commission

1.   Subject to Articles 175 and 176, the Commission may, in respect of cross-border transactions or transactions with cross-border effects, monitor, investigate, detect, make determinations or take action to inhibit and penalise enterprises whose business conduct prejudices trade or prevents, restricts or distorts competition within the CSME.

2.   The Commission may, in accordance with applicable nationallaws, in the conduct of its investigations:

(a)   secure the attendance of any person before it to give evidence;

(b)   require the discovery or production of any document or part thereof; and

(c)   take such other action as may be necessary in furtherance of the investigation.

3.   The Commission may, on the basis of its investigations, make determinations regarding the compatibility of business conduct with the rules of competition and other related provisions of the Treaty.

4.   The Commission shall, to the extent required to remedy or penalise anti- competitive business conduct referred to in Article 177:

(a)   order the termination or nullification as the case may require, of agreements, conduct, activities or decisions prohibited by Article 170;

(b)   direct the enterprise to cease and desist from anti-competitive business conduct and to take such steps as are necessary to overcome the effects of abuse of its dominant position in the market, or any other business conduct inconsistent with the principles of fair competition set out in this Chapter;

(c)   order payment of compensation to persons affected; and

(d)   impose fines for breaches of the rules of competition.

5.   The Commission may enter into such arrangements for the provision of services as may be necessary for the efficient performance of its functions.

6.   The Member States shall enact legislation to ensure that determinations of the Commission are enforceable in their jurisdictions.

7.   The Commission may establish its own rules of procedure.

ARTICLE 175
Determination of Anti-Competitive Business Conduct:
Procedure of Commission on Request

1.   A Member State may request an investigation referred to in paragraph 1 of Article 174 where it has reason to believe that business conduct by an enterprise located in another Member State prejudices trade and prevents, restricts or distorts competition in the territory of the requesting Member State.

2.   Where COTED has reason to believe that business conduct by an enterprise in the CSME prejudices trade and prevents, restricts or distorts competition within the CSME and has or is likely to have cross-border effects, COTED may request an investigation referred to in paragraph 1 of Article 174.

3.   Requests under paragraphs 1 and 2 shall be in writing and shall disclose sufficient information for the Commission to make a preliminary assessment whether it should proceed with the investigation.

4.   Upon receipt of a request mentioned in paragraph 3, the Commission shall consult with the interested parties and shall determine on the basis of such consultations whether:

> (a)   the investigation is within the jurisdiction of the Commission; and

> (b)   the investigation is justified in all the circumstances of the case.

5.   The consultations shall be concluded within 30 days of the date of receipt of the request for the investigation, unless the parties agree to continue the consultations for a longer period.

6.   Where the Commission decides to conduct the investigation, the Commission shall:

> (a)   notify the interested parties and COTED;

> (b)   complete the investigation within 120 days from the date of receipt of the request for the investigation; and

> (c)   where the circumstances so warrant, extend the time period for completion of the investigation and notify the interested parties.

7.   Where the Commission decides to conduct an enquiry following an investigation, the Commission shall afford any party complained of the opportunity to defend its interest.

8.   At the conclusion of an enquiry, the Commission shall notify the interested parties of its determination.

9.   Where the Commission determines that a party has engaged in anti- competitive business conduct, it shall also require the party to take the action necessary to remove the effects of the anti-competitive business conduct.

10.   Where a specific course of action is required under paragraph 9, the enterprise concerned shall take the appropriate course of action within 30 days of the date of notification. If the concerned enterprise cannot comply, it shall notify the Commission and request an extension.

11.   If the enterprise cannot comply within the time period specified and fails to inform the Commission, the Commission may apply to the Court for an order.

12.   A party which is aggrieved by a determination of the Commission under paragraph 4 of Article 174 in any matter may apply to the Court for a review of that determination.

ARTICLE 176
Determination of Anti-Competitive Business Conduct:
Procedure of Commission Proprio Motu

1.   Where the Commission has reason to believe that business conduct by an enterprise in the CSME prejudices trade and prevents, restricts, or distorts competition within the CSME and has

cross-border effects, the Commission shall request the national competition authority to undertake a preliminary examination of the business conduct of the enterprise.

2.   Where a request is made under paragraph 1, the national competition authority shall examine the matter and report its findings to the Commission within such time as may be determined by the Commission.

3.   Where the Commission is not satisfied with the outcome of its request, the Commission may initiate its own preliminary examination into the business conduct of the enterprise referred to in paragraph 1.

4.   Where the findings of the preliminary examination under paragraphs 2 and 3 require investigation, the Commission and the Member State concerned shall hold consultations to determine and agree on who should have jurisdiction to investigate.

5.   If there is a difference of opinion between the Commission and the Member State regarding the nature and effects of the business conduct or the jurisdiction of the investigating authority, the Commission shall:

    (a)   cease any further examination of the matter; and

    (b)   refer the matter to COTED for its decision.

6.   Nothing in this Article shall prejudice the right of the Member State to initiate proceedings before the Court at any time.

7.   Where there is a finding that the Commission has jurisdiction to investigate the matter, the Commission shall follow the procedures set out in paragraphs 5, 6, 7 and 8 of Article 175.

ARTICLE 177
Prohibition of Anti-Competitive Business Conduct

1.   A Member State shall, within its jurisdiction, prohibit as being anti-competitive business conduct, the following:

(a)   agreements between enterprises, decisions by associations of enterprises, and concerted practices by enterprises which have as their object or effect the prevention, restriction or distortion of competition within the Community;

    (b)   actions by which an enterprise abuses its dominant position within the Community; or

    (c)   any other like conduct by enterprises whose object or effect is to frustrate the benefits expected from the establishment of the CSME.

2.   Anti-competitive business conduct within the meaning of paragraph 1 includes the following:

    (a)   the direct or indirect fixing of purchase or selling prices,

(b)   the limitation or control of production, markets, investment or technical development;

(c)   the artificial dividing up of markets or restriction of supply sources;

(d)   the application of unequal conditions to parties undertaking equivalent engagements in commercial transactions thereby causing a competitive disadvantage;

(e)   making the conclusion of a contract subject to the acceptance by the other party to the contract of additional obligations which, by their nature or according to commercial practice, have no connection with the subject matter of the contract;

(f)   unauthorised denial of access to networks or essential infrastructure;

(g)   predatory pricing;

(h)   price discrimination;

(i)   loyalty discounts or concessions;

(j)   exclusionary vertical restrictions; and

(k)   bid-rigging.

3.   Subject to Article 168, a Member State shall ensure that all agreements and decisions within the meaning of paragraph 1 of this Article shall be null and void within its jurisdiction.

4.   An enterprise shall not be treated as engaging in anti-competitive business conduct if it establishes that the activity complained of:.

(a)   contributes to:

(i)   the improvement of production or distribution of goods and services; or
(ii)   the promotion of technical or economic progress, while allowing consumers a fair share of the resulting benefit;

(b)   imposes on the enterprises affected only such restrictions as are indispensable to the attainment of the objectives mentioned in sub-paragraph (a); or

(c)   does not afford the enterprise engaged in the activity the possibility of eliminating competition in respect of a substantial part of the market for goods or services concerned.

ARTICLE 178
Determination of Dominant Position

For the purposes of this Chapter:

(a)   an enterprise holds a dominant position in a market if by itself or together with an interconnected enterprise, it occupies such a position of economic strength as will enable it to operate in the market without effective constraints from its competitors or potential competitors;

(b)   any two enterprises shall be treated as interconnected enterprises if one of them is a subsidiary of the other or both of them are subsidiaries of the same parent enterprise.

ARTICLE 179
Abuse of a Dominant Position

1.   Subject to paragraph 2 of this Article, an enterprise abuses its dominant position in a market if it prevents, restricts or distorts competition in the market and, in particular but without prejudice to the generality of the foregoing, it:

(a)   restricts the entry of any enterprise into a market;

(b)   prevents or deters any enterprise from engaging in competition in a market;

(c)   eliminates or removes any enterprise from a market;

(d)   directly or indirectly imposes unfair purchase or selling prices or other restrictive practices;

(e)   limits the production of goods or services for a market to the prejudice of consumers;

(f)   as a party to an agreement, makes the conclusion of such agreement subject to acceptance by another party of supplementary obligations which, by their nature or according to commercial usage, have no connection with the subject of the agreement;

(g)   engages in any business conduct that results in the exploitation of its customers or suppliers, so as to frustrate the benefits expected from the establishment of the CSME.

2.   In determining whether an enterprise has abused its dominant position, consideration shall be given to:

(a)   the relevant market defined in terms of the product and the geographic context;

(b)   the concentration level before and after the relevant activity of the enterprise measured in terms of annual sales volume, the value of assets and the value of the transaction;

(c)   the level of competition among the participants in terms of number of competitors, production capacity and product demand;

(d)   the barriers to entry of competitors; and

    (e)   the history of competition and rivalry between participants in the sector of activity.

3.   An enterprise shall not be treated as abusing its dominant position if it establishes that:

    (a)   its behaviour was directed exclusively to increasing efficiency in the production, provision or distribution of goods or services or to promoting technical or economic progress and that consumers were allowed a fair share of the resulting benefit;

    (b)   it reasonably enforces or seeks to enforce a right under or existing by virtue of a copyright, patent, registered trade mark or design; or

    (c)   the effect or likely effect of its behaviour on the market is the result of superior competitive performance of the enterprise concerned.

ARTICLE 180
Negative Clearance Rulings

1.   In any case where a Member State is uncertain whether business conduct is prohibited by paragraph 1 of Article 177, such a Member State may apply to the Commission for a ruling on the matter. If the Commission determines that such conduct is not prohibited by paragraph 1 of Article 177, it shall issue a negative clearance ruling to this effect.

2.   Subject to paragraph 3, a negative clearance ruling shall be conclusive of the matters stated therein in any judicial proceedings in the Community.

3.   The Court may, on an application of the Commission, review a decision of the Commission where the decision was induced by deceit or improper means.

ARTICLE 181
De Minimis Rule

The Commission may exempt from the provisions of this Part any business conduct referred to it if it considers that the impact of such conduct on competition and trade in the CSME is minimal.

ARTICLE 182
Powers of the COTED Respecting Community
Competition Policy and Rules

Subject to this Treaty, COTED shall develop and establish appropriate policies and rules of competition within the Community including special rules for particular sectors.

ARTICLE 183
Exemptions

1.   Where COTED determines, pursuant to Article 182, that special rules shall apply to specific sectors of the Community, it may suspend or exclude the application of Article 177 to such sectors pending adoption of the relevant rules.

2.   COTEO may, on its own initiative or pursuant to an application by a Member State in that behalf exclude or suspend the application of Article 177 to any sector or any enterprise or group of enterprises in the public interest.

PART TWO
CONSUMER PROTECTION

ARTICLE 184
Promotion of Consumer Interests in the Community

1.   The Member States shall promote the interests of consumers in the Community by appropriate measures that:

(a)   provide for the production and supply of goods and the provision of services to ensure the protection of life, health and safety of consumers;

(b)   ensure that goods supplied and services provided in the CSME satisfy regulations, standards, codes and licensing requirements established or approved b y competent bodies in the Community;

(c)   provide, where the regulations, standards, codes and licensing requirements referred to in paragraph (b) do not exist, for their establishment and implementation;

(d)   encourage high levels of ethical conduct for those engaged in the production and distribution of goods and services to consumers;

(e)   encourage fair and effective competition in order to provide consumers with greater choice among goods and services at lowest cost;

(f)   promote the provision of adequate information to consumers to enable the making of informed choices;

(g)   ensure the availability of adequate information and education programmes for consumers and suppliers;

(h)   protect consumers by prohibiting discrimination against producers and suppliers of goods produced in the Community and against service providers who are nationals of other Member States of the Community;

(i)   encourage the development of independent consumer organisations;

(j)   provide adequate and effective redress for consumers.

2.   For the purpose of this Part, "consumer" means any person:

(a)   to whom goods or services are supplied or intended to be supplied in the course of business carried on by a supplier or potential supplier; and

(b)   who does not receive the goods or services in the course of a business carried on by him.

ARTICLE 185
Protection of Consumer Interests in the Community

The Member States shall enact harmonised legislation to provide, inter alia:

(a)   for the fundamental terms of a contract and the implied obligations of parties to a contract for the supply of goods or services;

(b)   for the prohibition of the inclusion of unconscionable terms in contracts for the sale and supply of goods or services to consumers;

(c)   for the prohibition of unfair trading practices, particularly such practices relating to misleading or deceptive or fraudulent conduct;

(d)   for the prohibition of production and supply of harmful and defective goods and for the adoption of measures to prevent the supply or sale of such goods including measures requiring the removal of defective goods from the market;

(e)   that the provision of services is in compliance with the applicable regulations, standards, codes and licensing requirements;

(f)   that goods supplied to consumers are labelled in accordance with standards and specifications prescribed by the competent authorities;

(g)   that hazardous or other goods whose distribution and consumption are regulated by law are sold or supplied in accordance with applicable regulations;

(h)   that goods or materials, the production or use of which is likely to result in potentially harmful environmental effects, are labelled and supplied in accordance with applicable standards and regulations;

(i)   that producers and suppliers are liable for defects in goods and for violation of product standards and consumer safety standards which occasion loss or damage to consumers;

(j)   that violations of consumer safety standards by producers or suppliers are appropriately sanctioned and relevant civil or criminal defences to such violations are available to defendants.

ARTICLE 186
Action by the Commission to Provide Support in the
Promotion of Consumer Welfare and Protection of Consumer Interests

1.   The Commission shall, for the purpose of providing support to the Member States in the enhancement of consumer education and consumer welfare:

(a)   promote in the Community the elaboration, publication and adoption of fair contract terms between suppliers and consumers of goods and services produced or traded in the CSME;

(b)   take such measures as it considers necessary to ensure that the Member States discourage and eliminate unfair trading practices, including misleading or deceptive conduct, false advertising, bait advertising, referral selling and pyramid selling;

(c)   promote in the Member States product safety standards as part of a programme of consumer education in order to assist the consumer to make informed choices concerning the purchase of consumer goods;

(d)   keep under review the carrying on of commercial activities in the Member States which relate to goods supplied to consumers in such States or produced with a view to their being so supplied, or which relate to services supplied for consumers with a view to identifying practices which may adversely affect the interests of consumers;

(e)   educate and guide consumers generally in the practical resolution of their problems and in the best use of their income and credit, using such techniques and means of communications as are available;

(f)   confer, on request, with consumer organisations of the Member States and offer such advice and information as may be appropriate for the resolution of their consumer problems; (g) establish the necessary co-ordination with government agencies and departments for the effective education and guidance of consumers having regard to the programmes, activities and resources of each agency or department;

(h)   conduct research and collect and collate information in respect of matters affecting the interests of consumers;

(i)   compile, evaluate and publicise enactments for the protection of consumers in such States and recommend to COTEO the enactment of legislation considered necessary or desirable for the protection of consumers;

(j)   promote, after consultation with the competent standardising agency and other public and private agencies or organisations, the establishment of quality standards for consumer products;

(k)   promote and monitor, after consultation with relevant agencies and departments of Government, the enforcement of legislation affecting the interests of consumers, including, but not limited to, legislation relating to weights and measures, food and drugs adulteration, the control of standards and price controls;

(l)   make recommendations to COTED for the enactment of legislation by the Member States for the effective enforcement of the rights of consumers.

2.   The Commission shall:

(a)   draw to the attention of COTED business conduct by enterprises which impacts adversely on consumer welfare;

(b)   collaborate with competent Organs of the Community to promote consumer education and consumer welfare.

*

ADDITIONAL PROTOCOL TO THE CONVENTION FOR THE PROTECTION OF INDIVIDUALS WITH REGARD TO AUTOMATIC PROCESSING OF PERSONAL DATA REGARDING SUPERVISORY AUTHORITIES AND TRANSBORDER DATA FLOWS *

(THE COUNCIL OF EUROPE)

The Additional Protocol to the Convention for the Protection of Individuals With Regard to Automatic Processing of Personal Data Regarding Supervisory Authorities and Transborder Data Flows (ETS N° 181) was opened for signature in Strasbourg on 8 November 2001, by the Signatories of the Treaty ETS N° 108 and by the European Communities, and for the accession by the States having acceded to the Council of Europe Convention for the Protection of Individuals with Regard to Automatic Processing of Personal (ETS N°108). Treaty ETS N°108 is reproduced in Volume II of this *Compendium*.

Preamble

The Parties to this additional Protocol to the Convention for the Protection of Individuals with regard to Automatic Processing of Personal Data, opened for signature in Strasbourg on 28 January 1981 (hereafter referred to as "the Convention");

Convinced that supervisory authorities, exercising their functions in complete independence, are an element of the effective protection of individuals with regard to the processing of personal data;

Considering the importance of the flow of information between peoples;

Considering that, with the increase in exchanges of personal data across national borders, it is necessary to ensure the effective protection of human rights and fundamental freedoms, and in particular the right to privacy, in relation to such exchanges of personal data,

Have agreed as follows:

Article 1 – Supervisory authorities

1.   Each Party shall provide for one or more authorities to be responsible for ensuring compliance with the measures in its domestic law giving effect to the principles stated in Chapters II and III of the Convention and in this Protocol.

---

* *Source*: The Council of Europe (2001). "Additional Protocol to the Convention for the Protection of Individuals With Regard to Automatic Processing of Personal Data Regarding Supervisory Authorities and Transborder Data Flows (ETS N° 181)"; available on the web site of the Council of Europe's Treaty Office, at (http://conventions.coe.int). [Note added by the editor.]

2.　　a.　　To this end, the said authorities shall have, in particular, powers of investigation and intervention, as well as the power to engage in legal proceedings or bring to the attention of the competent judicial authorities violations of provisions of domestic law giving effect to the principles mentioned in paragraph 1 of Article 1 of this Protocol.

　　　　b.　　Each supervisory authority shall hear claims lodged by any person concerning the protection of his/her rights and fundamental freedoms with regard to the processing of personal data within its competence.

3.　　The supervisory authorities shall exercise their functions in complete independence.

4.　　Decisions of the supervisory authorities, which give rise to complaints, may be appealed against through the courts.

5.　　In accordance with the provisions of Chapter IV, and without prejudice to the provisions of Article 13 of the Convention, the supervisory authorities shall co-operate with one another to the extent necessary for the performance of their duties, in particular by exchanging all useful information.

Article 2 – Transborder flows of personal data to a recipient which is not subject to the jurisdiction of a Party to the Convention

1.　　Each Party shall provide for the transfer of personal data to a recipient that is subject to the jurisdiction of a State or organisation that is not Party to the Convention only if that State or organisation ensures an adequate level of protection for the intended data transfer.

2.　　By way of derogation from paragraph 1 of Article 2 of this Protocol, each Party may allow for the transfer of personal data:

　　　　a.　　if domestic law provides for it because of :

　　　　　　– specific interests of the data subject, or

　　　　　　– legitimate prevailing interests, especially important public interests, or

　　　　b.　　if safeguards, which can in particular result from contractual clauses, are provided by the controller responsible for the transfer and are found adequate by the competent authorities according to domestic law.

Article 3 – Final provisions

1.　　The provisions of Articles 1 and 2 of this Protocol shall be regarded by the Parties as additional articles to the Convention and all the provisions of the Convention shall apply accordingly.

2.　　This Protocol shall be open for signature by States Signatories to the Convention. After acceding to the Convention under the conditions provided by it, the European Communities may sign this Protocol. This Protocol is subject to ratification, acceptance or approval. A Signatory to this Protocol may not ratify, accept or approve it unless it has previously or simultaneously ratified, accepted or approved the Convention or has acceded to it. Instruments of ratification, acceptance or approval of this Protocol shall be deposited with the Secretary General of the Council of Europe.

3.	a.	This Protocol shall enter into force on the first day of the month following the expiry of a period of three months after the date on which five of its Signatories have expressed their consent to be bound by the Protocol in accordance with the provisions of paragraph 2 of Article 3.

	b.	In respect of any Signatory to this Protocol which subsequently expresses its consent to be bound by it, the Protocol shall enter into force on the first day of the month following the expiry of a period of three months after the date of deposit of the instrument of ratification, acceptance or approval.

4.	a.	After the entry into force of this Protocol, any State which has acceded to the Convention may also accede to the Protocol.

	b.	Accession shall be effected by the deposit with the Secretary General of the Council of Europe of an instrument of accession, which shall take effect on the first day of the month following the expiry of a period of three months after the date of its deposit.

5.	a.	Any Party may at any time denounce this Protocol by means of a notification addressed to the Secretary General of the Council of Europe.

	b.	Such denunciation shall become effective on the first day of the month following the expiry of a period of three months after the date of receipt of such notification by the Secretary General.

6.	The Secretary General of the Council of Europe shall notify the member States of the Council of Europe, the European Communities and any other State which has acceded to this Protocol of:

	a.	any signature;

	b.	the deposit of any instrument of ratification, acceptance or approval;

	c.	any date of entry into force of this Protocol in accordance with Article 3;

	d.	any other act, notification or communication relating to this Protocol.

In witness whereof the undersigned, being duly authorised thereto, have signed this Protocol.

Done at Strasbourg, this 8th day of November 2001, in English and in French, both texts being equally authentic, in a single copy which shall be deposited in the archives of the Council of Europe. The Secretary General of the Council of Europe shall transmit certified copies to each member State of the Council of Europe, the European Communities and any State invited to accede to the Convention.

List of Declarations Made With Respect to Treaty No. 181

Additional Protocol to the Convention for the Protection of Individuals with regard to Automatic Processing of Personal Data, regarding supervisory authorities and transborder data flows

Complete chronology on: 20/02/02

Germany:

Declaration contained in a Note verbale from the Permanent Representation of Germany, dated 5 November 2001, handed to the Secretary General of the Council of Europe at the time of signature of the instrument, on 8 November 2001 - Or. Engl./Germ.

Article 1, paragraph 3, of the Additional Protocol (as well as paragraph 2 of its Preamble) provides that supervisory authorities shall exercise their functions in complete independence.

The Federal Republic of Germany recalls its statement made at the meeting of 6 to 8 June 2000 of the Consultative Committee, set up by virtue of Article 18 of the Convention for the Protection of Individuals with regard to Automatic Processing of Personal Data, that the existing practice for supervising data protection in Germany meets the requirements of Article 1, paragraph 3, of the Additional Protocol because the supervisory authorities responsible for data protection - even where they are incorporated in a hierarchical administrative structure - exercise their functions in complete independence.

The preceding statement concerns Article(s): 1

United Kingdom:

Declaration contained in a letter from the Permanent Representative of the United Kingdom, dated 8 November 2001, handed to the Secretary General of the Council of Europe at the time of signature of the instrument, on 8 November 2001 - Or. Engl.

The Government of the United Kingdom declares that the United Kingdom's signature of the Additional Protocol is extended to the Bailiwicks of Jersey and Guernsey and the Isle of Man, being territories for whose international relations the United Kingdom is responsible.

The preceding statement concerns Article(s):

*

CONVENTION ESTABLISHING THE EUROPEAN FREE TRADE ASSOCIATION *
CONSOLIDATED VERSION[1]
[excerpts]

(EUROPEAN FREE TRADE ASSOCIATION SCRETARIAT)

The Convention Establishing the European Free Trade Association was originally signed on 4 January 1960. It applies mainly to the relations between Switzerland on the one hand and the other EFTA States on the other. It served for over 30 years as an institutional framework for the co-operation among the EFTA States which, still today, applies mainly to free trade in goods. The EFTA member States, namely Iceland, Liechtenstein, Norway and Switzerland, amended the Convention on 21 June 2001 thereby introducing significant changes and modernizing and bringing it up to a similar level of co-operation as is the cases between the EFTA States and the European Community. The following exerpts are from the Convention as amended in 2001, including Annexes and reservations.

The Republic of Iceland, the Principality of Liechtenstein, the Kingdom of Norway and the Swiss Confederation (hereinafter referred to as the "Member States");

...

Resolved to deepen the co-operation instituted within the European Free Trade Association, further facilitating the free movement of goods, aiming at the progressive attainment of free movement of persons and the progressive liberalisation of trade in services and investment, further opening up the public procurement markets in the EFTA States, and providing for the appropriate protection of intellectual property rights, under fair conditions of competition;

Building on their respective rights and obligations under the Agreement establishing the World Trade Organization and other multilateral and bilateral instruments of co-operation;

...

Have agreed as follows:

---

*   *Source*: The European Free Trade Association Secretariat (2001). "Convention establishing the European Free Trade Association ", available on the Internet (http://secretariat.efta.int/library/legal/vaduz/). [Note added by the editor.]
[1] This consolidated version of the Convention forms an integral part of the Convention as Annex XX to the Agreement amending the Convention.

CHAPTER I: OBJECTIVES

ARTICLE 2
Objectives

The objectives of the Association shall be

(a)   to promote a continued and balanced strengthening of trade and economic relations between the Member States with fair conditions of competition, and the respect of equivalent rules, within the area of the Association;

(b)   the free trade in goods;

(c)   to progressively liberalise the free movement of persons;

(d)   the progressive liberalisation of trade in services and of investment;

(e)   to provide fair conditions of competition affecting trade between the Member States;

(f)   to open the public procurement markets of the Member States;

(g)   to provide appropriate protection of intellectual property rights, in accordance with the highest international standards.

CHAPTER VI: RULES OF COMPETITION

ARTICLE 18
Competition

1.   Member States recognise that the following practices are incompatible with this Convention in so far as they frustrate the benefits arising from this Convention:

(a)   agreements between enterprises, decisions by associations of enterprises and concerted practices between enterprises which have as their object or result the prevention, restriction or distortion of competition;

(b)   abuse by one or more undertakings of a dominant position in the territories of the Member States as a whole or in a substantial part thereof.

2.   Should a Member State consider that a given practice is incompatible with this Article, it may ask for consultations in accordance with the procedures set out in Article 47 and take appropriate measures under the conditions set out in paragraph 2 of Article 40 to deal with the difficulties resulting from the practice in question.

CHAPTER VII: PROTECTION OF INTELLECTUAL PROPERTY

ARTICLE 19

1.   Member States shall grant and ensure adequate and effective protection of intellectual property rights, and provide for measures for the enforcement of such rights against infringement thereof, counterfeiting and piracy, in accordance with the provisions of this Article, Annex J to this Agreement and the international agreements referred to therein.

2.   Member States shall accord to each other's nationals treatment no less favourable than that they accord to their own nationals. Exemptions from this obligation must be in accordance with the substantive provisions of Article 3 of the TRIPS Agreement.

3.   Member States shall grant to each other's nationals treatment no less favourable than that accorded to nationals of any other State. Exemptions from this obligation must be in accordance with the substantive provisions of the TRIPS Agreement, in particular Articles 4 and 5 thereof.

4.   Member States agree, upon request of any Member State, to review the provisions on the protection of intellectual property rights contained in the present Article, with a view to further improve levels of protection and to avoid or remedy trade distortions caused by actual levels of protection of intellectual property rights.

CHAPTER VIII: FREE MOVEMENT OF PERSONS

ARTICLE 20
Movement of persons

1.   Freedom of movement of persons shall be secured among Member States in accordance with the provisions set out in Annex K and in the Protocol to Annex K on the free movement of persons between Liechtenstein and Switzerland.

2.   The objective of this Article for the benefit of the nationals of the Member States shall be:

   (a)   to accord a right of entry, residence, access to work as employed persons, establishment on a self-employed basis and the right to stay in the territory of the Member States;

   (b)   to facilitate the provision of services in the territory of the Member States, and in particular to liberalise the provision of services of brief duration;

   (c)   to accord a right of entry into, and residence in, the territory of the Member States to persons without an economic activity in the host State;

   (d)   to accord the same living, employment and working conditions as those accorded to nationals.

ARTICLE 21
Coordination of social security systems

In order to provide freedom of movement of persons, the Member States shall make provision, in accordance with Appendix 2 of Annex K and with the Protocol to Annex K on the free movement of persons between Liechtenstein and Switzerland, for the coordination of social security systems with the aim in particular of:

(a)   securing equality of treatment;

(b)   determining the legislation applicable;

(c)   aggregating, for the purpose of acquiring and retaining the right to benefit and of calculating the amount of benefit, of all periods taken into consideration by the national legislation of the States concerned;

(d)   paying benefits to persons resident in the territories of the Member States;

(e)   fostering mutual administrative assistance and cooperation between authorities and institutions.

ARTICLE 22
Mutual recognition of professional qualifications

In order to make it easier for nationals of the Member States to take up and pursue activities as workers and self-employed persons, the Member States shall take the necessary measures, as contained in Appendix 3 to Annex K and in the Protocol to Annex K on the free movement of persons between Liechtenstein and Switzerland, concerning the mutual recognition of diplomas, certificates and other evidence of formal qualifications, and the coordination of the provisions laid down by law, regulation or administrative action in the Member States concerning the taking up and pursuit of activities by workers and self-employed persons.

CHAPTER IX: INVESTMENT

SECTION I: ESTABLISHMENT

ARTICLE 23
Principles and scope

1.   Within the framework of, and subject to, the provisions of this Convention, there shall be no restrictions on the right of establishment of companies or firms, formed in accordance with the law of a Member State and having their registered office, central administration or principal place of business in the territory of the Member States. This shall also apply to the setting up of agencies, branches or subsidiaries by companies or firms of any Member State established in the territory of any other Member State.

The right of establishment shall include the right to set up, acquire and manage undertakings, in particular companies or firms within the meaning of paragraph 2, under the conditions laid down for its own undertakings by the law of the Member State where such establishment is effected, subject to the provisions set out hereafter.

2.   For the purposes of this Chapter:

(a)   "subsidiary" of a company shall mean a company which is effectively controlled by the first company;

(b)   "companies or firms" shall mean companies or firms constituted under civil or commercial law, including cooperative societies, and other legal persons governed by public or private law, save for those which are non-profit-making; in order to be considered as a company or firm of a Member State, the company or firm shall have a real and continuous link with the economy in that Member State.

3.   Annexes L to O contain specific provisions and exemptions regarding the right of establishment. The Member States shall endeavour to eliminate gradually remaining discriminations, which they may maintain in accordance with Annexes L to O. The Member States agree to review the present provision, including its Annexes, within two years after the entry into force of the Agreement amending the Convention establishing the European Free Trade Association of 21 June 2001 with a view to reducing, and ultimately eliminating, the remaining restrictions.

4.   From the date of entry into force of the Agreement amending the Convention establishing the European Free Trade Association of 21 June 2001, neither Member State shall adopt new, or more, discriminatory measures as regards the establishment and operation of companies or firms of another Member State, in comparison with the treatment accorded to its own companies or firms.

5.   In sectors covered by an exemption as contained in Annexes L to O, each Member State shall accord to companies or firms of another Member State treatment no less favourable than that accorded to companies or firms of third parties other than the European Community. As regards any new agreements concluded between any Member State and the European Community, the Member States further undertake to extend to each other, on the basis of reciprocity, the benefits of such agreements, subject to a decision by the Council.

6.   The right of establishment in the field of road, rail and air transport shall be governed by the provisions of Article 35 and Annexes P and Q, subject to the specific provisions and exemptions set out in Annexes L and M.

7.   The right of establishment of natural persons shall be governed by the provisions of Article 20, Annexes K and the Protocol to Annex K on movement of persons between Liechtenstein and Switzerland.

ARTICLE 24
National treatment

1.   Within the scope of application of this Chapter, and without prejudice to any special provisions contained herein:

(a)   Member States shall grant treatment no less favourable than that accorded to their own companies or firms;

(b)   each Member State may regulate the establishment and operation of companies or firms on its territory, in so far as these regulations do not discriminate against companies or firms of the other Member States in comparison to its own companies or firms.

2.   The provisions of this Article do not preclude the application by a Member State of particular rules concerning the establishment and operation in its territory of branches and agencies of companies of another Member State not incorporated in the territory of the first Member State, which are justified by legal or technical differences between such branches and agencies as compared to branches and agencies of companies incorporated in its territory. The difference in treatment shall not go beyond what is strictly necessary as a result of such legal or technical differences.

ARTICLE 25
Financial market regulation

1.   In respect of financial services, this Chapter does not prejudice the right of the Member States to adopt measures necessary for prudential grounds in order to ensure the protection of investors, depositors, policy holders, or persons to whom a fiduciary duty is owed, or to ensure the integrity and stability of the financial system. These measures shall not discriminate against companies or firms of the other Member States in comparison to its own companies or firms.

2.   Nothing in this Chapter shall be construed to require a Member State to disclose information relating to the affairs and accounts of individual customers or any confidential or proprietary information in the possession of public entities.

ARTICLE 26
Recognition

1.   A Member State may enter into an agreement or arrangement with a particular State providing for the recognition of standards, criteria for authorization, licensing or certification of service suppliers, in which case it shall offer adequate opportunity for any other Member State to negotiate its accession to such an agreement or arrangement or to negotiate comparable ones with it.

2.   Where a Member State accords recognition as provided for in paragraph 1 autonomously, it shall afford adequate opportunity for any other Member State to demonstrate that experience, licences or certifications obtained or requirements met in that other Member State's territory should be recognised.

3.   A Member State shall not accord recognition in a manner which would constitute a means of discrimination between countries in the application of its standards or criteria for the authorisation, licensing or certification of service suppliers, or a disguised restriction to establishment in the services sector.

ARTICLE 27
Exceptions

1.   The provisions of this Chapter shall not apply, so far as any given Member State is concerned, to activities which in that Member State are connected, even occasionally, with the exercise of official authority.

2.   The provisions of this Chapter and measures taken in pursuance thereof shall not prejudice the applicability of provisions laid down by law, regulation or administrative action providing for special treatment for foreign companies or firms on grounds of public policy, public security, public health or the environment.

3.   Subject to the requirement that such measures are not applied in a manner which would constitute a means of arbitrary or unjustifiable discrimination between States where like conditions prevail, or a disguised restriction on trade in services, nothing in this Convention shall be construed to prevent the adoption or enforcement by any Member State of measures:

    (a)   inconsistent with Article 24, provided that the difference in treatment is aimed at ensuring the equitable or effective[4] imposition or collection of direct taxes in respect of services or service suppliers of other Member States;

    (b)   inconsistent with paragraph 5 of Article 23, provided that the difference in treatment is the result of an agreement on the avoidance of double taxation or provisions on the avoidance of double taxation in any other international agreement or arrangement by which the Member State is bound.

---

[4]   Measures that are aimed at ensuring the equitable or effective imposition or collection of direct taxes include measures taken by a Member under its taxation system which:

    (i)   apply to non-resident service suppliers in recognition of the fact that the tax obligation of non-residents is determined with repsect to taxable items sourced or located in the Member State's territory; or

    (ii)   apply to non-residents in order to ensure the imposition or collection of taxes in the Member State's territory; or

    (iii)   apply to non-residents or residents in order to prevent the avoidance or evasion of taxes, including compliance measures; or

    (iv)   apply to consumers of services supplied in or from the territory of another Member State in order to ensure the imposition or collection of taxes of such consumers derived from sources in the Member State's territory; or

    (v)   distinguish service suppliers subject to tax on worldwide taxable items from other service suppliers, in recognition of the difference in the nature of the tax base between them; or

    (vi)   determine, allocate or apportion income, profit, gain, loss, deduction or credit of resident persons or branches, or between related persons or branches of the same person, in order to safeguard the Member State's tax base.

Tax terms or concepts in paragraph 3(a) of Article 27 and in this footnote are determined according to tax definitions and concepts, or equivalent or similar definitions and concepts, under the domestic law of the Member State taking the measure.

SECTION II: CAPITAL MOVEMENTS

ARTICLE 28

1.   Within the framework of this Chapter, there shall be no restrictions between the Member States on the movement of capital relating to the establishment in another Member State's territory of a company or firm of that Member State.

2.   The movement of capital not relating to establishment between the Member States shall be ensured in accordance with the international agreements to which they are parties.

3.   The Member States agree to review the present provision within two years after the entry into force of the Agreement amending the Convention establishing the European Free Trade Association of 21 June 2001 in order to broaden the scope of, and ultimately eliminate the remaining restrictions to, the movement of capital.

CHAPTER X: TRADE IN SERVICES

ARTICLE 29
Principles and scope

1.   Within the framework of, and subject to, the provisions of this Convention, there shall be no restrictions on the right to supply services within the territory of the Member States in respect of natural persons, companies or firms of Member States who are established in a Member State other than that of the natural person, company or firm for whom the services are intended.

2.   For the purposes of this Chapter, services shall be considered to be "services" within the meaning of this Convention where they are normally supplied for remuneration

   (a)   from the territory of one Member State into the territory of another Member State;

   (b)   in the territory of a Member State to the service consumer of another Member State in accordance with paragraph 7 below;

   (c)   by service supplier of a Member State, through presence of natural persons of that Member State in the territory of another Member State in accordance with paragraph 7 below.

3.   Annexes L to O contain specific provisions and exemptions regarding the right to supply services. The Member States shall endeavour to eliminate gradually remaining discriminations, which they may maintain in accordance with Annexes L to O. The Member States agree to review the present provision, including its Annexes, within two years after the entry into force of the Agreement amending the Convention establishing the European Free Trade Association of 21 June 2001 with a view to reducing, and ultimately eliminating, the remaining restrictions.

4.   From the date of entry into force of the Agreement amending the Convention establishing the European Free Trade Association of 21 June 2001, neither Member State shall adopt new, or more, discriminatory measures as regards services or service suppliers of another Member State, in comparison with the treatment accorded to its own like services or service suppliers.

5.   In sectors covered by an exemption as contained in Annexes L to O, each Member State shall accord to services or service suppliers of another Member State treatment no less favourable than that accorded to like services or service suppliers of third parties other than the European Community. As regards any new agreements concluded between any Member State and the European Community, the Member States further undertake to extend to each other, on the basis of reciprocity, the benefits of such agreements, subject to a decision by the Council.

6.   The right to supply services in the field of road, rail and air transport shall be governed by the provisions of Article 35 and Annexes P and Q, subject to the specific provisions and exemptions set out in Annex M.

7.   The supply or consumption of services by natural persons as provided for in paragraphs 2(b) and (c) shall be governed by the relevant provisions of Article 20, Annex K and the Protocol to Annex K on movement of persons between Liechtenstein and Switzerland, in accordance with the principles set out hereinafter.

ARTICLE 30
National treatment

Within the scope of application of this Chapter, and without prejudice to any special provisions contained herein:

(a)   Member States shall grant treatment no less favourable than that accorded to their own natural persons, companies or firms providing services;

(b)   each Member State may regulate services activities within its territory in so far as these regulations do not discriminate against natural persons, companies or firms of the other Member States in comparison to its own natural persons, companies or firms.

ARTICLE 31
Financial market regulation

1.   In respect of financial services, this Chapter does not prejudice the right of the Member States to adopt measures necessary for prudential grounds in order to ensure the protection of investors, depositors, policy holders, or persons to whom a fiduciary duty is owed, or to ensure the integrity and stability of the financial system. These measures shall not discriminate against natural persons, companies or firms of the other Member States in comparison to its own natural persons, companies or firms.

2.   Nothing in this Chapter shall be construed to require a Member State to disclose information relating to the affairs and accounts of individual customers or any confidential or proprietary information in the possession of public entities.

ARTICLE 32
Recognition

1.   The mutual recognition between the Member States of diplomas, certificates and other evidence of formal qualifications, and the coordination of the provisions laid down by law, regulation or administrative action in the Member States concerning the taking up and pursuit of

activities by natural persons, shall be governed by the relevant provisions of Article 22, Annex K and Appendix 3 thereto and the Protocol to Annex K on movement of persons between Liechtenstein and Switzerland.

2.   A Member State may enter into an agreement or arrangement with a particular State providing for the recognition of standards, criteria for authorization, licensing or certification of service suppliers, in which case it shall offer adequate opportunity for any other Member State to negotiate its accession to such an agreement or arrangement or to negotiate comparable ones with it.

3.   Where a Member State accords recognition as provided for in paragraph 2 autonomously, it shall afford adequate opportunity for any other Member State to demonstrate that experience, licences or certifications obtained or requirements met in that other Member State's territory should be recognised.

4.   A Member State shall not accord recognition in a manner which would constitute a means of discrimination between countries in the application of its standards or criteria for the authorisation, licensing or certification of service suppliers, or a disguised restriction to trade in services.

ARTICLE 33
Exceptions

1.   The provisions of this Chapter shall not apply, so far as any given Member State is concerned, to activities which in that Member State are connected, even occasionally, with the exercise of official authority.

2.   The provisions of this Chapter and measures taken in pursuance thereof shall not prejudice the applicability of provisions laid down by law, regulation or administrative action providing for special treatment of foreign service suppliers on grounds of public policy, public security, public health or the environment.

3.   Subject to the requirement that such measures are not applied in a manner which would constitute a means of arbitrary or unjustifiable discrimination between States where like conditions prevail, or a disguised restriction on trade in services, nothing in this Convention shall be construed to prevent the adoption or enforcement by any Member State of measures:

    (a)   inconsistent with Article 30, provided that the difference in treatment is aimed at ensuring the equitable or effective[5] imposition or collection of direct taxes in respect of services or service suppliers of other Member States;

---

[5]   Measures that are aimed at ensuring the equitable or effective imposition or collection of direct taxes include measures taken by a Member under its taxation system which:

    (i)   apply to non-resident service suppliers in recognition of the fact that the tax obligation of non-residents is determined with repsect to taxable items sourced or located in the Member State's territory; or

    (ii)   apply to non-residents in order to ensure the imposition or collection of taxes in the Member State's territory; or

    (iii)   apply to non-residents or residents in order to prevent the avoidance or evasion of taxes, including compliance measures; or

(b)   inconsistent with paragraph 5 of Article 29, provided that the difference in treatment is the result of an agreement on the avoidance of double taxation or provisions on the avoidance of double taxation in any other international agreement or arrangement by which the Member State is bound.

ARTICLE 34
Public procurement

Nothing in this Chapter shall be construed to impose any obligations with respect to public procurement.

ARTICLE 35
Transport

The Member States shall liberalise the access to each other's transport markets for the carriage of passengers and goods by road, rail and air in accordance with the provisions set out in Annex P and Annex Q respectively.

CHAPTER XII: PUBLIC PROCUREMENT

ARTICLE 37

1.   The Member States reaffirm their rights and obligations under the WTO Agreement on Government Procurement (GPA). Under this Convention, the Member States broaden the scope of their commitments under the WTO Government Procurement Agreement with an aim to pursue liberalisation in public procurement markets in accordance with Annex R.

2.   To this effect, the Member States shall secure non-discriminative, transparent and reciprocal access to their respective public procurement markets and shall ensure open and effective competition based on equal treatment.

CHAPTER XIII: CURRENT PAYMENTS

ARTICLE 38

Current payments connected with the movement of goods, persons, services or capital as defined in Article 28 between Member States within the framework of the provisions of this Convention shall be free of all restrictions.

(iv)   apply to consumers of services supplied in or from the territory of another Member State in order to ensure the imposition or collection of taxes of such consumers derived from sources in the Member State's territory; or

(v)   distinguish service suppliers subject to tax on worldwide taxable items from other service suppliers, in recognition of the difference in the nature of the tax base between them; or

(vi)   determine, allocate or apportion income, profit, gain, loss, deduction or credit of resident persons or branches, or between related persons or branches of the same person, in order to safeguard the Member State's tax base.

Tax terms or concepts in paragraph 3(a) of Article 27 and in this footnote are determined according to tax definitions and concepts, or equivalent or similar definitions and concepts, under the domestic law of the Member State taking the measure.

CHAPTER XIV: EXCEPTIONS AND SAFEGUARDS

ARTICLE 39
Security exceptions

Nothing in this Convention shall prevent a Member State from taking any measures:

(a)   which it considers necessary to prevent the disclosure of information contrary to its essential security interests;

(b)   which relate to the production of, or trade in, arms, munitions and war materials or other products or services indispensable for defence purposes or to research, development or production indispensable for defence purposes, provided that such measures do not impair the conditions of competition in respect of products or services not intended for specifically military purposes;

(c)   which it considers essential to its own security in the event of serious internal disturbances affecting the maintenance of law and order, in time of war or serious international tension constituting threat of war or in order to carry out obligations it has accepted for the purpose of maintaining peace and international security.

ARTICLE 40
Safeguard measures

1.   If serious economic, societal or environmental difficulties of a sectorial or regional nature liable to persist are arising, a Member State may unilaterally take appropriate measures under the conditions and procedures set out in Article 41.

2.   Such safeguard measures shall be restricted with regard to their scope and duration to what is strictly necessary in order to remedy the situation. Priority shall be given to such measures as will least disturb the functioning of this Convention.

3.   The safeguard measures shall apply with regard to all Member States.

4.   This Article is without prejudice to the application of specific safeguard provisions set out in the Annexes to this Convention or of special safeguard measures in accordance with Article 5 of the WTO Agreement on Agriculture.

ARTICLE 41

1.   A Member State which is considering taking safeguard measures under Article 40, shall, without delay, notify the other Member States through the Council and shall provide all relevant information.

2.   The Member States shall immediately enter into consultations in the Council with a view to finding a commonly acceptable solution.

3.   The Member State concerned may not take safeguard measures until one month has elapsed after the date of notification under paragraph 1, unless the consultation procedure under paragraph 2 has been concluded before the expiration of the stated time limit. When exceptional

circumstances requiring immediate action exclude prior examination, the Member State concerned may apply forthwith the protective measures strictly necessary to remedy the situation.

4.   The Member State concerned shall, without delay, notify the measures taken to the Council and shall provide all relevant information.

5.   The safeguard measures taken shall be the subject of consultations in the Council every three months from the date of their adoption with a view to their abolition before the date of expiry envisaged, or to the limitation of their scope of application.

Each Member State may at any time request the Council to review such measures.

CHAPTER XVIII: GENERAL PROVISIONS

ARTICLE 49
Obligations under other international agreements

1.   Nothing in this Convention shall be regarded as exempting any Member State from obligations which it has undertaken by virtue of agreements with third States or multilateral agreements to which they are parties.

2.   This Convention shall be without prejudice to the rules applicable to Member States governed by the Agreement on the European Economic Area, the Nordic cooperation and the regional union between Switzerland and Liechtenstein

ARTICLE 50
Rights and obligations of the Member States

The Member States shall take all appropriate measures, whether general or particular, to ensure fulfilment of the obligations arising out of this Convention. They shall abstain from any measure which could jeopardize the attainment of the objectives of this Convention.

ARTICLE 51
Transparency

1.   The Member States shall publish their laws, or otherwise make publicly available their laws, regulations, procedures and administrative rulings and judicial decisions of general application as well as the international agreements which may affect the operation of this Convention.

2.   The Member States shall promptly respond to specific questions and provide, upon request, information to each other on matters referred to in paragraph 1.

ARTICLE 52
Confidentiality

The representatives, delegates and experts of the Member States, as well as officials and other servants acting under this Convention shall be required, even after their duties have ceased, not to disclose information of the kind covered by the obligation of professional secrecy, in particular information about undertakings, their business relations or their cost components.

ARTICLE 53
Annexes

1. The Annexes, Appendices and Protocols to this Convention shall form an integral part of it.

2. The Annexes to this Convention are the following:

Annex A	on Rules of Origin
Annex B	on mutual administrative assistance in customs matters
Annex C	List of agricultural goods and goods processed from agricultural raw materials referred to in paragraph 1 of Article 8
Annex D	List of tariff concessions to agricultural products
Annex E	Seeds
Annex F	Organic agriculture
Annex G	Sanitary and phytosanitary measures
Annex H	Procedure for the provision of information in the field of technical regulations and of rules on Information Society services
Annex I	Mutual recognition in relation to conformity assessment
Annex J	Intellectual property rights
Annex K	Movement of persons
Annex L	Reservations by Iceland on investment and services
Annex M	Reservations by Liechtenstein on investment and services
Annex N	Reservations by Norway on investment and services
Annex O	Reservations by Switzerland on investment and services
Annex P	Land transport
Annex Q	Air transport
Annex R	Public procurement
Annex S	Organs, committees and other bodies set up by the Council

Annex T   Arbitration.

Annex U   List of territories to which Article 58 applies.

The Council may decide to amend the provisions to this paragraph.

3.   The Council may decide to amend Annexes A, C, H, S and T, as well as the Appendices to Annexes E, F, K, P, Q and R, unless otherwise provided in the Annexes.

4.   The Committee established under Annex I may decide to amend Article 4 of that Annex as well as Appendices 1 and 2 thereto. It shall inform the Council of its decision-making.

ARTICLE 54
Ratification

1.   This Convention shall be ratified by the signatory States. The instruments of ratification shall be deposited with the Government of Sweden, which shall notify all other signatory States.

2.   The Government of Norway shall act as Depositary as of 17 November 1995.

3.   The Council may decide to amend the provisions of this Article.

ARTICLE 55
Entry into force

This Convention shall enter into force on the deposit of instruments of ratification by all signatory States.

ARTICLE 56
Accession and association

1.   Any State may accede to this Convention, provided that the Council decides to approve its accession, on such terms and conditions as may be set out in that decision. The instrument of accession shall be deposited with the Depositary, which shall notify all other Member States. This Convention shall enter into force in relation to an acceding State on the date indicated in that decision.

2.   The Council may negotiate an agreement between the Member States and any other State, union of States or international organisation, creating an association embodying such reciprocal rights and obligations, common actions and special procedures as may be appropriate. Such an agreement shall be submitted to the Member States for acceptance and shall enter into force provided that it is accepted by all Member States. Instruments of acceptance shall be deposited with the Depositary, which shall notify all other Member States.

3.   Any State acceding to this Convention shall apply to become a party to the free trade agreements between the Member States on the one hand and third states, unions of states or international organisations on the other.

ARTICLE 57
Withdrawal

1.   Any Member State may withdraw from this Convention provided that it gives twelve months' notice in writing to the Depositary, which shall notify all other Member States.

2.   Before the withdrawal takes effect, the Member States shall agree on appropriate arrangements and equitable cost-sharing relating to the withdrawal.

ARTICLE 58
Territorial application

This Convention shall apply to the territories of the Member States except as provided for in Annex U.

ARTICLE 59
Amendment

Except as otherwise provided for in this Convention, an amendment to the provisions of this Convention shall be subject to a decision of the Council which shall be submitted to the Member States for acceptance in accordance with their internal legal requirements. It shall enter into force, unless otherwise provided, on the first day of the second month following the deposit of the instruments of acceptance by all Member States with the Depositary, which shall notify all other Member States.

ANNEX J TO THE CONVENTION
INTELLECTUAL PROPERTY RIGHTS (ART. 19)

ARTICLE 1
Intellectual property

"Intellectual property" comprises in particular copyright, including computer programmes and databases, as well as neighbouring rights, trademarks for goods and services, geographical indications, including appellations of origin, for goods and services, industrial designs, patents, plant varieties, topographies of integrated circuits, as well as undisclosed information.

ARTICLE 2
International conventions

1.   The Member States reaffirm their obligations set out in the international agreements to which they are parties, in particular the following multilateral agreements:

-    WTO Agreement of 15 April 1994 on Trade-Related Aspects of Intellectual Property Rights (TRIPS Agreement);

-    Paris Convention of 20 March 1883 for the Protection of Industrial Property (Stockholm Act, 1967);

- Berne Convention of 9 September 1886 for the Protection of Literary and Artistic Works (Paris Act, 1971); and

- International Convention of 26 October 1961 for the Protection of Performers, Producers of Phonograms and Broadcasting Organisations (Rome Convention).

2. The Member States which are not parties to one or more of the agreements listed below shall undertake to obtain their adherence to the following multilateral agreements before 1 January 2005:

- the Geneva Act (1999) of the Hague Agreement Concerning the International Registration of Industrial Designs;

- the WIPO Copyright Treaty (Geneva 1996); and

- the WIPO Performances and Phonogram Treaty (Geneva 1996).

3. The Member States agree to promptly hold expert consultations, upon request of any Member State, on activities relating to the identified or to future international conventions on harmonization, administration and enforcement of intellectual property rights and on activities in international organizations, such as the WTO and the World Intellectual Property Organization (WIPO), as well as relations of the Member States with third States on matters concerning intellectual property.

ARTICLE 3
Patents

The Member States shall ensure in their national laws at least the following:

(a) adequate and effective patent protection for inventions in all fields of technology. For Liechtenstein and Switzerland this means protection on a level corresponding to the one in the European Patent Convention of 5 October 1973, as implemented in national law. For Iceland and Norway this means protection on a level corresponding to the one in the Agreement on the European Economic Area of 2 May 1992, as implemented in national law;

(b) an additional term of protection for pharmaceuticals and plant protection products which shall be calculated from the expiry of the maximum term of patent of 20 years for a period equal to the period which elapsed between the filing date of the patent application and the date of the first market authorization of the product, reduced by a period of five years. Such additional protection shall cover a period of five years at the most and shall be granted under the following conditions:

- the product is protected by a patent in force;

- there has been an official marketing authorization procedure for the medicinal or plant protection product;

- the marketing of the patented product has been postponed by administrative procedures regarding authorization of market access, so that the effective use of the patent amounts to less than 15 years;

- the effective protection conferred by the patent and the additional protection shall together not exceed 15 years.

ARTICLE 4
Designs

The Member States shall ensure in their national laws adequate and effective protection of industrial designs by providing in particular a period of protection of five years from the date of application with a possibility of renewal for at least four consecutive periods of five years each. The Member States may provide for a shorter period of protection for designs of component parts used for the purpose of the repair of a product.

ARTICLE 5
Geographical indications

The Member States shall ensure in their national laws adequate and effective means to protect geographical indications, including appellations of origin, with regard to all products and services.

ARTICLE 6
Acquisition and maintenance of intellectual property rights

Where the acquisition of an intellectual property right is subject to the right being granted or registered, the Member States shall ensure that the procedures for grant or registration are of the same level as that provided in the TRIPS Agreement, in particular Article 62.

ARTICLE 7
Enforcement of intellectual property rights

The Member States shall provide for enforcement provisions under their national laws of the same level as that provided in the TRIPS Agreement, in particular Articles 41 to 61.

ANNEX L

RESERVATIONS BY ICELAND
(CHAPTER IX – INVESTMENT AND CHAPTER X – TRADE IN SERVICES)

As of the entry into force of the Agreement amending the Convention establishing the European Free Trade Association of 21 June 2001, Iceland will grant Switzerland treatment identical to that granted to Norway and Liechtenstein pursuant to the Agreement on the European Economic Area.

As regards air transport, foreign investment will continue to be subject to the current Icelandic legislation.

The Member States agree to review the reservation on air transport within two years after the entry into force of the Agreement amending the Convention establishing the European Free Trade Association of 21 June 2001 with the aim of eliminating the remaining restrictions on air transport.

ANNEX M

RESERVATIONS BY LIECHTENSTEIN
(CHAPTER IX – INVESTMENT AND CHAPTER X – TRADE IN SERVICES)

The term "unbound" shall mean that Liechtenstein does not commit itself with respect to the specified item.

Sector or subsector	Reservations	Chapter to which reservations apply
I. HORIZONTAL RESERVATIONS		
ALL SECTORS		
The level of commitments in a particular services sector shall not be construed to supersede the level of commitments taken with respect to any other services sector to which such service is an input or to which it is otherwise related. CPC numbers indicated in brackets are references to the UN Provisional Central Product Classification (Statistical Papers Series M No. 77, Provisional Central Product Classification, Department of International Economics and Social Affairs, Statistical Office of the United Nations, New York, 1991). Notwithstanding paragraph 4 of Articles 23 and 29, Liechtenstein may incorporate new limitations in sectors that are subject to an "unbound"-reservation to the extent that such limitations do not affect the overall balance of rights and obligations under the present Convention. Liechtenstein shall inform the Council in advance of its intent to introduce such new limitations by written notification. On receiving such written notification, any other Member State may request consultations. Liechtenstein and that Member State shall enter into such consultations. This provision shall be reviewed within two years after the entry into force of the Agreement amending the Convention establishing the European Free Trade Association, with a view to its elimination.		
	Unbound for subsidies, tax incentives and tax credits.	Trade in services and Investment
	Treatment accorded to subsidiaries of third country companies formed in accordance with the law of an EEA Member State and having registered office, central administration or principal place of business within an EEA Member State is not extended to branches or agencies established in an EEA Member State by a third-country company.	Trade in services and Investment
	Treatment less favourable may be accorded to subsidiaries of third countries having only their registered office in the territory of an EEA Member State unless they show that they possess an effective and continuous link with the economy of one of the EEA Member States.	Trade in services and Investment
	The establishment of a commercial presence by a legal entity (including branches) is subject to the requirement that no objection for reasons of national economy	

Sector or subsector	Reservations	Chapter to which reservations apply
	(balanced proportion of national and foreign capital; balanced ratio of foreigners in comparison with the number of resident population; balanced ratio of total number of jobs in the economy in comparison with the number of the resident population; balanced geographic situation; balanced development of the national economy, between and within the sectors) exists. At least one member of the administration of a legal entity authorized to manage and represent it must be a Liechtenstein citizen domiciled in Liechtenstein and in possession of the professional licence to act as a lawyer, legal agent, trustee or auditor, or a government-recognized business qualification. From these obligations are excepted legal entities which on the basis of the law concerning trade have a qualified manager. The law concerning trade stipulates: The establishment of a commercial presence by an individual is subject to the requirement of prior residence during a certain period of time and of permanent domicile in Liechtenstein. He/she must possess sector specific government-recognized professional qualifications. The establishment of a commercial presence by a legal entity (including branches) is subject to the following requirements: At least one of the managers has to fulfil the requirements of prior residence during a certain period of time and of permanent domicile in Liechtenstein. He/She must possess sector specific government-recognized professional qualifications. The majority of the administrators (authorized to manage and represent the juridical person) must be resident in Liechtenstein and have either to be Liechtenstein citizens or have prior residence during a certain period of time in Liechtenstein. The general and the limited partnership have to fulfil the same conditions as corporations with limited liability (juridical person). In addition the majority of the associates have to be Liechtenstein citizens or to have prior residence during a certain period of time in Liechtenstein. The Liechtenstein company law does not prohibit joint stock companies from stipulating in their articles of incorporation the preclusion or limitation of the transfer of registered shares.	
	All acquisitions of real estate are subject to authorization. Such authorization is granted only if an actual and proven requirement for living or business	Investment

Sector or subsector	Reservations	Chapter to which reservations apply
	purposes is given and a certain period of residence has been completed. Non-residents are excluded from the acquisition of real estate.	
II. SECTOR-SPECIFIC RESERVATIONS		
1. BUSINESS SERVICES		
a) Legal services	Unbound except for consultancy on home country law (not Liechtenstein law) and international law. Unbound	Trade in services Investment
b) Accounting, auditing and book-keeping services - Accounting and auditing services, excluding auditing of banks (Part of 8621)	Unbound. Foreign equity ceiling of 49 per cent. Foreign voting rights may not exceed 49 per cent. At least one member of the administration body authorized to manage and represent must be a Liechtenstein citizen domiciled in Liechtenstein, be in possession of the professional licence to act as an auditor and must work full-time for the juridical person. The majority of the members of the administrative body must be in possession of the professional licence to act as an auditor.	Trade in services and Investment
- Auditing services related to banks	Unbound	Trade in services and Investment
c) Taxation services (CPC 863)	Unbound. Foreign equity ceiling of 49 per cent. Foreign voting rights may not exceed 49 per cent. At least one member of the administration body authorized to manage and represent must be a Liechtenstein citizen domiciled in Liechtenstein, be in possession of the professional licence to act as an auditor or trustee and must work full-time for the juridical person.	Investment
e) Engineering services (CPC 8672)	Liechtenstein nationality necessary for survey activities for official public purposes (however, foreign surveyors can work under the responsibility of a licensed Liechtenstein surveyor).	Trade in services and Investment
h) Medical and dental services (CPC 9312)	Unbound	Trade in services and Investment
i) Veterinary surgeons (CPC 932)	Unbound	Trade in services and

Sector or subsector	Reservations	Chapter to which reservations apply
		Investment
j) Services provided by midwives, nurses, physiotherapists and para-medical personnel	Unbound	Trade in services and Investment
k) Other	Unbound	Trade in services and Investment
C. Research and Development Services	Unbound for projects financed in whole or in part by public funds.	Trade in services and Investment
D. Real Estate Services	Unbound	Trade in services and Investment
E. Rental/Leasing without Operators		
a) Relating to ships	Unbound	Trade in services and Investment
e) Other	Unbound	Trade in services and Investment
F. Other Business Services		
a) Advertising services	Unbound for outdoor advertising, advertising for goods subject to import authorization and pharmaceutical products, alcohol, tobacco, toxics, explosives, weapons and ammunition.	Trade in services and Investment
j) Services incidental to energy distribution	Unbound	Trade in services and Investment
k) Placement and supply services of personnel	Unbound	Trade in services and Investment
l) Investigation and security	Unbound	Trade in services and Investment
o) Building cleaning	Unbound for other cleaning services (CPC 87409).	Trade in services and Investment
2. COMMUNICATION SERVICES		
A. Postal services	Unbound	Trade in services and

Sector or subsector	Reservations	Chapter to which reservations apply
		Investment
B. Courier Services	Unbound	Trade in services and Investment
C. Telecommunication services	General condition applicable to all telecommunication sectors: national monopoly on network infrastructure, services have to be provided over the public network or over leased lines; wireless networks subject to licensing, pricing of leased lines not volume-sensitive, connection with the public network possible. Unbound except for electronic mail, voice mail, on-line information and date base retrieval, electronic data interchange (EDI), enhanced/value-added facsimile services, code and protocol conversion, on-line information and/or date processing, videotext, enhanced/value added services based on licensed wireless networks including enhanced/value-added paging services, except for voice transmission.	Trade in services and Investment
D. Audio-visual services	Unbound	Trade in services and Investment
3.CONSTRUCTION AND RELATED ENGINEERING SERVICES	Unbound	Trade in services and Investment
DISTRIBUTION SERVICES services related to goods subject to import authorisation, to pharmaceutical products, toxic, explosives, weapons and ammunition, and precious metals	Unbound	Trade in services and Investment
- retailing services through mobile sales unit	Unbound	Trade in services and Investment
B. Wholesale trade services	Restrictions on sales area.	Investment
C. Retailing services	Restrictions on sales area.	Investment
5. EDUCATIONAL SERVICES		
- Compulsory education services	Unbound	Trade in services and

Sector or subsector	Reservations	Chapter to which reservations apply
(primary & secondary I)		Investment
- Non-compulsory secondary education services (secondary II), Higher education services, Adult education services, other education services	Foreigners may establish commercial presence only when organized as juridical person according to Liechtenstein law.	Investment
6. ENVIRONMENTAL SERVICES[1]		
B. Refuse Disposal Services (CPC 9402)	Unbound for garbage dump.	Investment
7. FINANCIAL SERVICES		
Commitments on banking, securities and insurance services in accordance with the "GATS Understanding on Commitments in Financial Services" (hereafter "Understanding") and subject to limitations and conditions as contained in Part I (horizontal commitments) and as listed below. It is understood that paragraph B.4 of the Understanding does not impose any obligation to allow non-resident financial services suppliers to solicit business.		
Insurance and Insurance-Related Services	Establishment of a commercial presence is required for the provision of insurance services in Liechtenstein. Residents may not purchase insurance services in the territory of another Member State.	Trade in services
	Permit for establishment of insurance companies from countries other than Liechtenstein is granted only to companies which are supervised by the Swiss insurance supervision authority; To be recognized for participation in the basic health insurance scheme, health insurance suppliers must be organized in the form of mutual associations (Genossenschaft, Verein: Versicherungsverein auf Gegenseitigkeit or Hilfskasse) or foundations (Stiftung); Duty of security for insurance services;	Investment

---

[1] Nothing in this commitment should be construed to include public work function whether owned and operated by municipalities or the Liechtenstein government or contracted out by them.

Sector or subsector	Reservations	Chapter to which reservations apply
	Economic need test for accident insurance services; Commercial presence does not cover the setting up of representative offices; Domestic legal entities and the branch or agency establishment of foreign legal entities whose managing or representing bodies, such as the board of directors and the administration, are comprised in the main of foreigners or foreign firms, shall appoint in Liechtenstein a Liechtenstein citizen who is permanently resident here either to represent the legal entity towards the authorities as a legal representative or, empowered as an authorized signatory (procurist), to exercise the representation, without the cooperation of others. Before setting up a commercial presence to provide specific classes of insurance services, a foreign insurer must have been authorised to operate in the same classes of insurance in its country of origin for at least three years.	
Banking and Other Financial Services (excluding insurance)	[2]Participation in settlement and clearing networks is subject to a commercial presence in Liechtenstein. Subvention for house building is only granted to Liechtenstein citizen, which have to take out the loan for the house building at a domestic bank. According to the practice in Liechtenstein, mutual funds (collective investments) have to be marketed through banks having a commercial presence in Liechtenstein. Swiss franc denominated issues can be lead-managed only by a bank having a commercial presence (registered office or branch office) in Liechtenstein.	Trade in services
	Licences granted to banks and financial companies according to the Liechtenstein Banking and Financial Companies Act have to be approved by the Liechtenstein parliament. One member of the board of directors and the administrators must have domicile in Liechtenstein. They must be duly authorized to fully represent their company. Banks and financial companies must be organized in the form of a limited company. Financial institutions other than banks and financial	Investment

---

[2] Covered are not only transactions indicated in paragraph B.3 of the 'Understanding' but the whole range of banking and other financial services transactions (excluding insurance).

Sector or subsector	Reservations	Chapter to which reservations apply
	companies according to the Liechtenstein Banking and Companies Act are subject to the following licensing requirements: foreign equity ceiling of 49 per cent; foreign voting rights may not exceed 49 per cent; at least one member of the administrative body authorized to manage and represent must be a Liechtenstein citizen domiciled in Liechtenstein, be in possession of the professional licence to act as an auditor or trustee and must work full-time for the juridical person. Commercial presence of foreign financial institutions is subject to licensing requirements relating to the name of firm, duties toward the Swiss national bank and regulations on financial institutions in the country of origin.	
8. HEALTH RELATED AND SOCIAL SERVICES	Unbound	Trade in services and Investment
9. TOURISM AND TRAVEL RELATED SERVICES		
A. Hotels and Restaurants (includes catering) (CPC 641 - 643)	Licence only granted if need for restaurants exists (assessment of economic needs is based on criteria such as population, degree of built-up area, type of neighbourhood, touristical interests, number of existing restaurants). Passing an examination may be required.	Investment
- catering	Unbound	Trade in services
10. RECREATIONAL, CULTURAL AND SPORTING SERVICES (other than audio-visual services)		
A. Entertainment services	Unbound	Trade in services and Investment
C. Libraries, archives, museums and other cultural services	Unbound	Trade in services and Investment

Sector or subsector	Reservations	Chapter to which reservations apply
11. TRANSPORT SERVICES		
D. Space Transport (CPC 733)	Unbound	Trade in services and Investment
G. Pipeline Transport	Unbound	Trade in services and Investment
12. ENERGY PRODUCTION AND DISTRIBUTION; INSTALLATION OF EQUIPMENT IN THE ENERGY SECTOR	Unbound	Trade in services and Investment

ANNEX N

RESERVATIONS BY NORWAY
(CHAPTER IX – INVESTMENT AND CHAPTER X – TRADE IN SERVICES)

The term "unbound" shall mean that Norway does not commit itself with respect to the specified item.

Sector or subsector	Reservations	Chapter to which reservation applies
I. HORIZONTAL RESERVATIONS		
The level of commitments in a particular sector shall not be construed to supersede the level of commitments taken with respect to any other sector to which such activity is an input or to which it is otherwise related. CPC numbers indicated in brackets are references to the UN Provisional Central Product Classification (Statistical Papers Series M No. 77, Provisional Central Product Classification, Department of International Economics and Social Affairs, Statistical Office of the United Nations, New York, 1991).		
All sectors: Company Law	The managing director and at least half of the members of the board of directors of several categories of companies, i.a. joint stock companies, must be domiciled in Norway. This does not apply to citizens of EEA Member States. As a main rule, in order to be considered a Norwegian	Investment

Sector or subsector	Reservations	Chapter to which reservation applies
	group, the parent company must be a Norwegian company. To some extent also foreign parent companies with Norwegian subsidiaries can be considered a group. This applies to a wider extent regarding parent companies from EEA Member States than companies outside the EEA area. A company is to a wider extent permitted to grant credits or pledge security for a parent company from an EEA Member State than for a shareholding company from other states.	
All sectors: Subsidies	Unbound Eligibility for subsidies may be limited to juridical persons established in Norway. Unbound for research and development subsidies.	Trade in services Investment
All sectors: Treatment of branches and agencies	Treatment accorded to subsidiaries of third country companies formed in accordance with the law of an EEA Member State and having their registered office, central administration or principal place of business within an EEA Member State may not be extended to branches or agencies established in an EEA Member State by a third-country company. Treatment less favourable may be accorded to subsidiaries of third-country companies formed in accordance with the law of an EEA Member State having only their registered office in the territory of an EEA Member State unless they show that they possess an effective and continuous link with the economy of one of the EEA Member States.	Investment
II. SECTOR-SPECIFIC RESERVATIONS		
1. BUSINESS SERVICES		
A. Professional services		
Legal services	The advocate is personally responsible for his activities. To have an interest (own shares and/or be a member of the board of the firm) in a firm of Norwegian advocates is only possible when taking active part in the business. Foreign advocates can give advice on foreign law and international law after application. Some restrictions on co-operation with Norwegian advocates as a consequence of legislation on how a firm of Norwegian advocates may be organized.	Investment
b) Accounting, auditing and book-keeping services		

Sector or subsector	Reservations	Chapter to which reservation applies
- Auditing services	Auditors who perform statutory audits must have a permanent place of business in Norway and reside within the European Economic Area. Auditing firms must have a permanent place of business in Norway.	Trade in services and Investment
- Accounting and bookkeeping services	Accounting shall take place in Norway. The King may decide that accounting takes place abroad.[1] Authorised accountants must have a permanent place of business in Norway, reside within the European Economic Area, and have a minimum of 2 years practice in Norway during the 5 preceding years. The managing director of an accounting firm must be an authorised accountant.	Trade in services
Medical and dental services (CPC 9312)	Unbound Must speak Norwegian and have passed certain national exams in different areas. Foreign exams giving equivalent competence may be recognized.	Trade in services Investment
i) Veterinary services	Unbound	Investment
j) Services provided by midwives, nurses, physiotherapists and para-medical personnel (CPC 93191)	Unbound	Investment
C. Research and development services		
a) R&D on natural science	Unbound	Trade in services and Investment
c) Interdisciplinary R&D services	Unbound	Trade in services and Investment
D. Real Estate Services a) involving own or leased property	Unbound	Trade in services and Investment
E. Rental/Leasing without operators b) relating to aircraft	To be registered in the aircraft register of Norway, the aircraft must be owned either by Norwegian natural persons or by Norwegian juridical persons.	Investment
c) relating to car-hiring	Unbound	Trade in

[1] This requirement continues to apply until changes in the Norwegian Accounting Act come into force.

Sector or subsector	Reservations	Chapter to which reservation applies
(CPC 83101)		services
F. Other business services h)services incidental to mining	Unbound	Trade in services and Investment
j) services incidental to energy distribution	Unbound	Trade in services and Investment
l) investigation and security - security and guarding	The manager must be an EEA-citizen. The members of the board in joint stock companies and partners in other company forms must be EEA-citizens.	Trade in services and Investment
s) convention services	Unbound	Trade in services and Investment
2. COMMUNICATION SERVICES A.Postal services	Unbound	Trade in services and Investment
D. Audiovisual services	Unbound	Trade in services and Investment
DISTRIBUTION SERVICES A. Commission Agents' services	Unbound	Trade in services and Investment
B. Wholesale trade services (import and trade in alcohol, arms, pharmaceuticals, fish and grain)	Unbound	Trade in services and Investment
C. Retailing services services (import and	Unbound	Trade in services and Investment

Sector or subsector	Reservations	Chapter to which reservation applies
trade in pharmaceutical products, alcohol and arms)		
5. EDUCATIONAL SERVICES - Educational services leading to the conferring of State recognized exams and/or degrees A. Primary and lower secondary education services B. Upper secondary education services Higher education services Adult education	Primary and secondary education are public service functions. Authorization may be given to foundations and other legal entities to offer additional parallel or specialized education on a commercial or non-commercial basis. Financial assistance to educational institutions or to students only available for studies at certified establishments.	Trade in services and Investment
6. ENVIRONMENTAL SERVICES[2] A. Sewage Services (CPC 9401)	Unbound	Trade in services
B. Refuse disposal services (CPC 9402)	For some categories of waste there exists a monopoly situation.	Trade in services and Investment
C. Sanitation and similar services (CPC 9403)	Unbound	Trade in services
D.Other - Noise abatement services (CPC 9405), Nature and landscape protection services (CPC 9406) other environmental protection services (CPC 9409) - Cleaning services of exhaust gases (CPC 9404)	Unbound Government owned monopoly for control services of exhaust-gas from cars and trucks. Such services must be offered on a non-profit basis.	Trade in services Trade in services and Investment
7.FINANCIAL		

[2] Nothing in this commitment should be construed to include public work function whether owned and operated by municipalities, cantons or federal government or contracted out by them.

Sector or subsector	Reservations	Chapter to which reservation applies
SERVICES		
Norway undertakes commitments on financial services in accordance with the "GATS Understanding on Commitments in Financial Services" (hereafter "the Understanding") and subject to limitations and conditions as contained in Part I (horizontal reservations) and as listed below. It is understood that paragraph B.4 of the Understanding does not impose any obligation to allow non-resident financial service suppliers to solicit business. The following restrictions and limitations apply:		
Insurance and Insurance-Related services	In addition to the services listed in paragraph B.3 (a) of the Understanding, non-resident insurance companies may supply insurance related to offshore exploration activities or insurance contracts regarding domestic companies with an activity of at least 10 man-years or annual sales of at least NOK 50 million. Non-resident insurance companies must supply the services listed above and in paragraph B.3 (a) of the Understanding through an insurance broker authorised in Norway.	Trade in services
	No single or coordinated group of investors may acquire or hold more than 10 per cent of the share capital in a Norwegian insurance company. The Ministry of Finance and Customs may in special circumstances make exemptions from these limitations on single investor ownership. Notwithstanding the foregoing, foreign insurance companies may establish partly or wholly owned subsidiaries in Norway. The other owners of such partly owned subsidiaries must be foreign insurance companies or Norwegian financial institutions. For subsidiaries or branches of financial institutions not incorporated within the European Economic Area, a separation requirement applies on a national treatment basis between life insurance, non-life insurance and credit risk insurance. Insurance companies incorporated in Norway must be organised as joint stock companies or mutual insurance companies. Insurance brokerage firms incorporated in Norway must be organised as joint stock companies. In Norwegian insurance companies, including	Investment

Sector or subsector	Reservations	Chapter to which reservation applies
	subsidiaries of foreign insurance companies, the manager, at least half the members of the board of directors and half the members of the corporate assembly must be permanent residents of Norway. This requirement does not apply to citizens of a State within the European Economic Area when residing in such State. The Ministry of Industry and Trade may grant exemptions from these rules. Foreign financial institutions other than insurance companies cannot own shares in a Norwegian insurance company, which is a partly owned subsidiary of a foreign insurance company.	
	Employers are obliged to have an insurance covering work-related injuries. The insurance company must as a rule have a permission from Norwegian authorities. However, this is not necessary if the head office of the company is established in an EEA Member State on the basis of a permission from the authorities of this state. Workers from EEA Member State are subject to some special rules regarding their rights. Producers and – on certain conditions – importers of medicines must have a specific kind of liability insurance. The insurance company must as a rule have a permission from Norwegian authorities. However, this is not necessary if the head office of the company is established in an EEAMember State on the basis of a permission from the authorities of this state. Import from EEAMember States is subject to some special rules regarding liability.	
Banking and Other Financial Services (excluding Insurance)	No single or coordinated group of investors may acquire or hold more than 10 per cent of the share capital of commercial banks or financing undertakings, or more than 10 per cent of the equity certificates of savings banks. The Ministry of Finance and Customs may in special circumstances make exemptions from these limitations on single investor ownership in such institutions. Notwithstanding the foregoing, foreign banks and financing undertakings may establish partly or wholly	Investment

---

[3] The act relating to the Norwegian Central Securities Depository is currently under revision. The legal monopoly is proposed to be abolished.

Sector or subsector	Reservations	Chapter to which reservation applies
	owned subsidiaries in Norway. The other owners of such partly owned subsidiaries must be banks or financial institutions respectively. Registration of securities, as stated in the act relating to the Norwegian Central Securities Depository regulating the book-entry registration system for paperless securities, is subject to a legal monopoly.[3] Commercial banks, securities firms and management companies for collective investment funds incorporated in Norway must be organised as joint stock companies. Branches in Norway of banks, securities firms and management companies for collective investment funds incorporated outside the European Economic Area cannot be account-operators in the Norwegian Central Securities Depository. In Norwegian commercial banks, financing undertakings, investment firms and management companies for collective investment funds, including subsidiaries of such foreign institutions, the manager, at least half the members of the board of directors and half the members of the corporate assembly must be permanent residents of Norway. This requirement does not apply to citizens of a State within the European Economic Area when residing in such State. The Ministry of Industry and Trade may grant exemptions from these rules. In savings banks and financing undertakings, which are not organised as joint stock companies, the members of decision-making bodies must be citizens of States within the European Economic Area and permanently residing in such States. The Ministry of Finance and Customs may grant exemptions from these rules.	
8. HEALTH RELATED AND SOCIAL SERVICES	Unbound	Trade in services and Investment
10. RECREATIONAL, CULTURAL AND SPORTING SERVICES (other than		

Sector or subsector	Reservations	Chapter to which reservation applies
audio-visual services)		
A. Entertainment services	Unbound	Trade in sevices and Investment
C. Libraries, archives museums and other cultural services	Unbound	Trade in services and Investment
D. Sporting and other recreational activities	Unbound	Trade in services Investment
11.TRANSPORT SERVICES		
A. Maritime transport services - International transport (freight and passengers) CPC 7211 and 7212 less cabotage[4] transport)	Ships on the Norwegian Ordinary Ship Register (NOR). Ships have to be owned by Norwegian citizens or by a Norwegian company where Norwegian citizens own at least 60 per cent of the capital. Exemptions from the 60 per cent rule may be granted. When the ship-owning company is a limited liability company, it must be headquartered in Norway. The majority of the members of the board, including the chairman, must be Norwegian citizens resident in Norway, having resided in Norway the preceding two years. Support scheme for parts of the NOR-fleet. Ships on the Norwegian International Ship Register (NIS): Ships with more than 40 per cent foreign ownership must be operated by a Norwegian ship-owning company with head office in Norway, or by Norwegian management company. If the ship is registered directly in the NIS by a foreign company, a Norwegian representative is required.	Investment
- Cabotage	Unbound	Trade in services and Investment
B. Internal Waterways Transport	Unbound	Trade in services and Investment
C. Space Transport (CPC 733)	Unbound	Trade in services and Investment

---

[4] "Cabotage" is defined as maritime transport of goods and passengers between ports in Norway, including locations on the continental shelf where petroleum is explored or produced.

Sector or subsector	Reservations	Chapter to which reservation applies
D. Pipeline Transport	Unbound	Trade in services and Investment
E. Services auxiliary to all modes of transport	Unbound except for maritime auxiliary services (maritime cargo handling services[5], Storage and warehousing services (CPC 742); customs clearance services[6]; container station and depot services[7], maritime agency services[8] ; freight forwarding services[9] and other supporting auxiliary transport services[10]).	Trade in services and Investment
III. OTHER EXCEPTIONS		
Fisheries	A concession to acquire a fishing vessel or share in a company which owns such vessels can only be given to a Norwegian citizen or a body that can be defined as a Norwegian citizen. A company is regarded as having equal rights with a Norwegian citizen when its main office is situated in Norway and the majority of the Board, including the Chair of the Board, are Norwegian	Investment

[5]   "Maritime cargo handling services" means activities exercised by stevedore companies, including terminal operators, but not including the direct activities of dockers, when this workforce is organized independently of the stevedoring or terminal operator companies. The activities covered include the organization and supervision of:

- the loading/discharging of cargo to/from a ship;

- the lashing/unlashing of cargo;

- the reception/delivery and safekeeping of cargoes before shipment or after discharge.

[6]   "Customs clearance services" (alternatively "customs house brokers' services") means activities consisting in carrying out on behalf of another party customs formalities concerning import, export or through transport of cargoes, whether this service is the main activity of the service provider or a usual complement of its main activity.

[7]   "Container station and depot services" means activities consisting in storing containers, whether in a port area or inland, with a view to their stuffing/stripping, repairing, and making them available for shipments.

[8]   "Maritime agency services" means the activities consisting in representing, within a given geographic area, as an agent the business interests of one or more shipping lines or shipping companies, for the following purposes:

    - marketing and sales of maritime transport and related services, from quotation to invoicing, and issuance of bills of lading on behalf of the companies; acquisition and resale of the necessary related services, preparation of documentation, and provision of business information;

- acting on behalf of the companies organizing the call of the ship or taking over cargoes when required.

[9]   "Freight forwarding services" means the activity consisting of organizing and monitoring shipment operations on behalf of shippers, through the acquisition of transport and related services, preparation of documentation and provision of business information.

[10]   "Other supporting and auxiliary transport services" means freight brokerage services; bill auditing and freight rate information services; transportation document preparation services; packing and crating and unpacking and de-crating services; freight inspection, weighing and sampling services; and freight receiving and acceptance services (including local pick-up and delivery).

Sector or subsector	Reservations	Chapter to which reservation applies
	citizens and have stayed in the country the last two years. Norwegian citizens also have to own a minimum of 60% of the shares and have to be authorised to vote for at least 60% of the votes. Ownership to the fishing fleet shall be reserved for professional fishermen. To obtain the right to own a fishing vessel, one has to have a record of active, professional fishing on a Norwegian fishing boat for at least three of the last five years. It is prohibited for others than Norwegian nationals or companies as specified above to process, pack or tranship fish, crustaceans and mollusc or parts and products of these inside the fishing limits of the Norwegain Economic zone. This applies to catches from both Norwegian and foreign vessels. Exceptions are granted under special circumstances.	
Real Estate	Acquisition or leasing of secondary residences by non-residents is subject to a concession.	Investment
Lotteries	There are special rules for persons from the EEA Member States regarding the right to provide services related to lotteries in Norway.	Trade in services
Debt collection	Persons and companies performing professional debt collecting in Norway are obligated to have a permanent place of business in Norway and must have a special authorisation from the Norwegian government.	Trade in services

ANNEX O

RESERVATIONS BY SWITZERLAND
(CHAPTER IX – INVESTMENT AND CHAPTER X - TRADE IN SERVICES)

In the reservations section, the term "unbound" shall mean that Switzerland does not commit itself with respect to the specified item.

Sector or subsector	Reservations	Chapter to which reservation applies
I. HORIZONTAL RESERVATIONS		
The level of commitments in a particular sector shall not be construed to supersede the level of commitments taken with respect to any other sector to which such activity is an input or to which it		

Sector or subsector	Reservations	Chapter to which reservation applies
	is otherwise related. CPC numbers indicated in brackets are references to the UN Provisional Central Product Classification (Statistical Papers Series M No. 77, Provisional Central Product Classification, Department of International Economics and Social Affairs, Statistical Office of the United Nations, New York, 1991). Unbound for privatisation as regards Articles 24 and 30 of the Convention. Unbound for measures taken by cantonal and communal authorities including by non-governmental bodies in the exercise of powers delegated by such authorities.	
All sectors	The majority of the board of directors of a "joint stock company" (société anonyme/Aktiengesellschaft or société en commandite par actions/ Kommanditaktiengesellschaft) must be Swiss citizens with domicile in Switzerland (except for holding companies). At least one manager of a "corporation with limited liability" (société à responsabilité limitée/Gesellschaft mit beschränkter Haftung) must have his domicile in Switzerland. The administrators of a "co-operative society" (société coopérative/Genossenschaft) must be composed of a majority of Swiss citizens with domicile in Switzerland. Joint stock companies are not prohibited to foresee in their articles of incorporation that shareholders can be denied registration in the shareholder register, inter alia in case federal law requires a certain composition of shareholders. The establishment of a branch requires a representative (natural person) with domicile in Switzerland who is duly authorized by the company to fully represent it. The establishment of a commercial presence by natural persons or in the form of an enterprise without juridical personality according to Swiss law (i.e. in a form other than "joint stock company", "cooperation with limited liability" or "co-operative society") is subject to the requirement of a permanent residency permit of the associate(s) by cantonal law.	Investment
	The acquisition of real estate by foreigners who are not permanently established in Switzerland and by enterprises with headquarters abroad and/or under foreign control is subject to authorization. For the purpose of personal housing needs (except the acquisition of holiday residences), professional use and business activities, authorization is granted upon verification of the purpose. Prohibited are purely financial investments, real estate business operations, acquisition, on a professional basis, of holiday apartments and facilities other than hotels (e.g. apartment houses, camps, sport areas) and acquisition of	Investment

Sector or subsector	Reservations	Chapter to which reservation applies
	agricultural real estate.	
	Unbound for subsidies, tax incentives and tax credits.	Trade in services and Investment
II. SECTOR-SPECIFIC RESERVATIONS		
1. BUSINESS SERVICES		
a) Legal services, except consultancy on home country law and international law	Unbound	Trade in services and Investment
b) Accounting, auditing and book-keeping services Auditing services, excluding auditing of banks (part of CPC 86211) Auditing services related to banks	At least one person supplying auditing services to a joint stock company (société anonyme/Aktiengesellschaft) or a société en commandite par actions/Kommanditaktiengesellschaft must have a commercial presence in Switzerland. Unbound	Trade in services Trade in services and Investment
Engineering services (CPC 8672)	Swiss nationality necessary for survey activities for official public purposes (however, foreign surveyors can work under the responsibility of a licensed Swiss surveyor).	Trade in services and Investment
h) Medical and dental services (CPC 9312)	Unbound	Investment
i) Veterinary surgeons (CPC 932)	Unbound	Investment
j) Services provided by midwives, nurses, physiotherapists and para-medical personnel	Unbound. None 5 years after the entry into force of the Agreement amending the Convention establishing the European Free Trade Association of 21 June 2001.	Trade in services and Investment
D. Real Estate Services	Unbound	Trade in services and Investment
E. Rental/Leasing without Operators		
a) Relating to ships		
- For maritime transport services (part of CPC 83103)	Unbound In order to sail under Swiss flag, vessels must be 100 per cent owned and controlled by Swiss nationals, 3/4 of which having residency in Switzerland.	Trade in services Investment

Sector or subsector	Reservations	Chapter to which reservation applies
	Board of directors and management of companies owning ships sailing under Swiss flag must be composed of Swiss nationals, the majority of which having residency in Switzerland.	Investment
- For internal waterways transport on the Rhine (part of CPC 83103)	Unbound In order to sail under Swiss flag, vessels must be owned by a company which is substantially influenced (66 per cent of capital and vote) by persons domiciled in Switzerland or in a State according to the Mannheim Convention and the protocols related to it. Traffic rights including cabotage are limited on the basis of the Mannheim Convention and the protocols related to it; owner of vessels must dispose of an appropriate managing agency in Switzerland.	Trade in services Investment Investment
F. Other Business Services j) Services incidental to energy distribution	Unbound	Trade in services and Investment
k) Placement and supply services of personnel	Unbound	Trade in services and Investment
l) Investigation and security	Unbound	Trade in services and Investment
2. COMMUNICATION SERVICES		
A. Postal services	Unbound	Trade in services and Investment
B. Courier Services	Unbound	Trade in services and Investment
D. Audio-visual services	Unbound	Trade in services and Investment
3. CONSTRUCTION AND RELATED ENGINEERING SERVICES		
C. Installation and Assembly Work (CPC 514 + 516)	Unbound for installations in the area of energy, heating, water, communications and elevators.	Investment

Sector or subsector	Reservations	Chapter to which reservation applies
DISTRIBUTION SERVICES Commission agents and retailing services related to goods subject to import authorisation, to pharmaceutical products, toxic, explosives, weapons and ammunition, and precious metals retailing services through mobile sales unit	Unbound	Trade in services and Investment
	Unbound	Trade in services and Investment
5. EDUCATIONAL SERVICES		
- Compulsory education services (primary & secondary I)	Unbound	Trade in services
6. ENVIRONMENTAL SERVICES[1]		
B. Refuse Disposal Services (CPC 9402)	Unbound for garbage dump.	Investment
7. FINANCIAL SERVICES		
Commitments on banking, securities and insurance services in accordance with the "GATS Understanding on Commitments in Financial Services" of the WTO (hereafter "Understanding") and subject to limitations and conditions as contained in Part I (horizontal commitments) and as listed below. It is understood that paragraph B.4 of the "Understanding" does not impose any obligation to allow non-resident financial services suppliers to solicit business.		
Insurance and Insurance-Related Services	Transactions as indicated in paragraph B.3 of the "Understanding": the underwriting of aircraft liability insurance requires a commercial presence in Switzerland.	Trade in services
	Acquisition of real estate by foreigners is limited as indicated in Part I; however, foreign or foreign-controlled insurance companies are granted authorisation	Trade in services and Investment

---

[1] Nothing in this commitment should be construed to include public work function whether owned and operated by municipalities, cantons or federal government or contracted out by them.

Sector or subsector	Reservations	Chapter to which reservation applies
	to invest in real estate, provided the total value of the buyer's property does not exceed the technical reserves required for the company's activities in Switzerland, as well as to acquire property that serves as a security for mortgage loans in case of bankruptcy or liquidation.	
	Transactions as indicated in paragraph B.4 of the "Understanding": the underwriting of aircraft liability insurance requires a commercial presence in Switzerland.	Trade in services
	Representative offices cannot conduct business or act as an agent; for insurance companies incorporated in Switzerland, the legal form of a joint-stock company (Aktiengesellschaft, société anonyme) or a mutual association (Genossenschaft, société cooperative) is required ; for branches of foreign insurance companies, the legal form of the insurance company in the head office State must be comparable to a Swiss joint-stock company or to a Swiss mutual association; participation in the basic health insurance scheme requires health insurance suppliers to be organized in one of the following legal entities: association (Verein, association), mutual association, foundation (Stiftung, fondation) or joint-stock company; participation in the statutory pension funds scheme (Berufsvorsorge / prévoyance professionnelle) requires pension funds to be organized in the form of a mutual association or a foundation.	Investment
	A minimum of three years of experience in the direct insurance business in the head office State is required.	Investment
Banking and Other Financial Services (excluding insurance)	Monopoly rights as indicated in paragraph B.1 of the "Understanding": two mortgage bonds issuance institutes have been granted an exclusive right for the issuance of specific mortgage bonds (Pfandbrief, lettre de gage); with regard to the first institute only Swiss cantonal banks are accepted as members; in the case of the second institute banks with head office in Switzerland whose national mortgage loan business amounts to at least 60 per cent of the balance sheet can be members; the issue of other mortgage-backed bonds is not affected by this regulation.	
	[1]Foreign investment funds can only be marketed or distributed through a licensed representative agent resident in Switzerland; Swiss franc denominated issues	Trade in services

---

[1] Not only transactions indicated in paragraph B.3 of the "Understanding" but the whole range of banking and other financial services transactions are covered (excluding insurance).

Sector or subsector	Reservations	Chapter to which reservation applies
	can be lead-managed only by a bank or a securities dealer having a commercial presence (except representative office) in Switzerland. Acquisition of real estate by foreigners is limited as indicated in Part I; however, foreign or foreign-controlled banks are granted authorisation to acquire property that serves as a security for mortgage loans in case of bankruptcy or liquidation; the issue of foreign collective investment funds is subject to stamp duty.	Trade in services and Investment
	Swiss franc denominated issues can be lead-managed only by a bank or a securities dealer having a commercial presence (except representative office) in Switzerland.	Trade in services
	Commercial presence of foreign financial service suppliers is subject to specific requirements relating to the name of firm and the regulations on financial institutions in the State of origin; commercial presence may be denied to financial service suppliers whose ultimate shareholders and/or beneficial owners are persons of a non-GATS Member; representative offices can neither conclude or deal business nor act as an agent.	Investment
8. HEALTH RELATED AND SOCIAL SERVICES	Unbound	Trade in services and Investment
9. TOURISM AND TRAVEL RELATED SERVICES		
Hotels and Restaurants (CPC 641 - 643) - Catering	Federal law enables cantons to grant licence for restaurants based on economic needs (assessment of economic needs is based on criteria such as population, degree of built-up area, type of neighbourhood, touristical interests, number of existing restaurants. Unbound	Investment Trade in Services
10. RECREATIONAL, CULTURAL AND SPORTING SERVICES (other than audio-visual services)		
A. Entertainment services	Unbound	Trade in services and Investment
C. Libraries, archives, museums and other cultural services	Unbound	Trade in services and Investment

Sector or subsector	Reservations	Chapter to which reservation applies
11.TRANSPORT SERVICES		
A. Maritime Transport Services	Unbound	Trade in services and Investment
B. Internal Waterways Transport	Unbound	Trade in services
Internal Waterways Transport on the Rhine: - Passenger and freight transportation (part of CPC 7221 and part of 7222)	In order to sail under Swiss flag, vessels must be owned by a company which is substantially influenced (66 per cent of capital and vote) by persons domiciled in Switzerland or in a State according to the Mannheim Convention and the protocols related to it. Traffic rights including cabotage are limited on the basis of the Mannheim Convention and the protocols related to it; owner of vessels must dispose of an appropriate managing agency in Switzerland.	Investment
- Rental of vessels with crew (part of CPC 7223)	In order to sail under Swiss flag, vessels must be owned by a company which is substantially influenced (66 per cent of capital and vote) by persons domiciled in Switzerland or in a State according to the Mannheim Convention and the protocols related to it.	Investment
	Traffic rights including cabotage are limited on the basis of the Mannheim Convention and the protocols related to it; owner of vessels must dispose of an appropriate managing agency in Switzerland.	Investment
D. Space Transport (CPC 733)	Unbound	Investment
G. Pipeline Transport	Unbound	Trade in services and Investment
12.ENERGY PRODUCTION AND DISTRIBUTION; INSTALLATION OF EQUIPMENT IN THE ENERGY SECTOR	Unbound	Trade in services and Investment

JOINT DECLARATION

Investment protection in relation to third States

The Member States will aim at agreeing on common guidelines in order to protect the investments of their respective investors in third States.

*

PART TWO

BILATERAL INSTRUMENTS

PARTNERSHIP AND COOPERATION AGREEMENT BETWEEN THE EUROPEAN COMMUNITIES AND THEIR MEMBER STATES AND THE REPUBLIC OF KAZAKHSTAN[*]
[excerpts]

The Partnership and Cooperation Agreement between the European Communities and Their Member States and the Republic of Kazakhstan was on 9 February 1995. It entered into force on 1 July 1999. The member States of the European Communities are: Austria, Belgium, Denmark, Finland, France, Germany, Greece, Ireland, Italy, Luxembourg, the Netherlands, Portugal, Spain, Sweden and the United Kingdom.

TITLE IV

PROVISIONS AFFECTING BUSINESS AND INVESTMENT

CHAPTER II

CONDITIONS AFFECTING THE ESTABLISHMENT AND OPERATION OF COMPANIES

Article 23

1. (a) The Community and its Member States shall grant for the establishment of Kazakh companies in their territories treatment no less favourable than that accorded to companies of any third country, and this in conformity with their legislation and regulations.

    (b) Without prejudice to the reservations listed in Annex II, the Community and its Member States shall grant to subsidiaries of Kazakh companies established in their territories a treatment no less favourable than that granted to any Community companies, in respect of their operation, and this in conformity with their legislation and regulations.

    (c) The Community and its Member States shall grant to branches of Kazakh companies established in their territories a treatment no less favourable than that accorded to branches of companies of any third country, in respect of their operation, and this in conformity with their legislation and regulations.

2. Without prejudice of the provisions of Articles 34 and 85, the Republic of Kazakhstan shall grant to Community companies and their branches treatment no less favourable than that

---

[*] *Source*: European Communities (1999). "Partnership and Cooperation Agreement between the European Communities and Their Member States and the Republic of Kazakhstan", *Official Journal of the European Communities*, L 196, 28 July 1999, pp. 3 - 45; available also on the Internet (http://www.europa.eu.int). [Note added by the editor.]

accorded to companies of the Republic of Kazakhstan and their branches or to any third-country companies and their branches, whichever is the better, in respect of their establishment and operations, as defined in Article 25, on its territory and this in conformity with its legislation and regulations.

Article 24

1.   The provisions of Article 23 shall not apply to air transport, inland waterways transport and maritime transport.

2.   However, in respect of activities undertaken by shipping agencies for the provision of international maritime transport services, including intermodal activities involving a sea leg, each Party shall permit to the companies of the other Party their commercial presence in its territory in the form of subsidiaries or branches, under conditions of establishment and operation no less favourable than those accorded to its own companies or to subsidiaries or branches of companies of any third country, whichever are the better.

Such activities include, but are not limited to:

(a)   marketing and sales of maritime transport and related services through direct contact with customers, from quotation to invoicing, whether these services are operated or offered by the service supplier itself or by service suppliers with which the service seller has established standing business arrangements;

(b)   purchase and use, on their own account or on behalf of their customers (and to resale to their customers) of any transport and related services, including inward transport services by any mode, particularly inland waterways, road and rail, necessary for the supply of an integrated service;

(c)   preparation of documentation concerning transport documents, customs documents, or other documents related to the origin and character of the goods transported;

(d)   provision of business information by any means, including computerised information systems and electronic data interchange (subject to any non-discriminatory restrictions concerning telecommunications);

(e)   setting up of any business arrangement, including participation in the company's stock and the appointment of personnel recruited locally (or, in the case of foreign personnel, subject to the relevant provisions of this Agreement), with any locally established shipping agency;

(f)   acting on behalf of the companies, organising the call of the ship or taking over cargoes when required.

Article 25

For the purpose of this Agreement:

(a)   a "Community company" or a "Kazakh company" respectively shall mean a company set up in accordance with the laws of a Member State or of the Republic of Kazakhstan respectively and having its registered office or central administration, or principal place of business in the territory of the Community or the Republic of Kazakhstan respectively. However, should the company be set up in accordance with the laws of a Member State or the Republic of Kazakhstan respectively, the company shall be considered a Community or Kazakh company respectively if its operations possess a real and continuous link with the economy of one of the Member States or the Republic of Kazakhstan respectively;

(b) "subsidiary" of a company shall mean a company which is effectively controlled by the first company;

(c)   "branch" of a company shall mean a place of business not having legal personality which has the appearance of permanency, such as the extension of a parent body, has a management and is materially equipped to negotiate business with third parties so that the latter, although knowing that there will if necessary be a legal link with the parent body, the head office of which is abroad, do not have to deal directly with such parent body but may transact business at the place of business constituting the extension;

(d)   "establishment" shall mean the right of Community or Kazakh companies as referred to in point (a) to take up economic activities by means of the setting up of subsidiaries and branches in the Republic of Kazakhstan or in the Community respectively;

(e)   "operation" shall mean the pursuit of economic activities;

(f)   "economic activities" shall mean activities of an industrial, commercial and professional character;

(g)   With regard to international maritime transport, including intermodal operations involving a sea leg, nationals of the Member States or of the Republic of Kazakhstan established outside the Community or the Republic of Kazakhstan respectively, and shipping companies established outside the Community or the Republic of Kazakhstan and controlled by nationals of a Member State or nationals of the Republic of Kazakhstan respectively, shall also be beneficiaries of the provisions of this Chapter and Chapter III if their vessels are registered in that Member State or in the Republic of Kazakhstan respectively in accordance with their respective legislation.

Article 26

1.   Notwithstanding any other provisions of the Agreement, a Party shall not be prevented from taking measures for prudential reasons, including for the protection of investors, depositors, policy holders or persons to whom a fiduciary duty is owed by a financial service supplier, or to ensure the integrity and stability of the financial system. Where such measures do not conform with the provisions of the Agreement, they shall not be used as a means of avoiding the obligations of a Party under the Agreement.

2.   Nothing in the Agreement shall be construed to require a Party to disclose information relating to the affairs and accounts of individual customers or any confidential or proprietary information in the possession of public entities.

Article 27

The provisions of this Agreement shall not prejudice the application by each Party of any measure necessary to prevent the circumvention of its measures concerning third-country access to its market, through the provisions of this Agreement.

Article 28

1.   Notwithstanding the provisions of Chapter I of this Title, a Community company or a Kazakh company established in the territory of the Republic of Kazakhstan or the Community respectively shall be entitled to employ, or have employed by one of its subsidiaries or branches, in accordance with the legislation in force in the host country of establishment, in the territory of the Republic of Kazakhstan and the Community respectively, employees who are nationals of Community Member States and the Republic of Kazakhstan respectively, provided that such employees are key personnel as defined in paragraph 2, and that they are employed exclusively by companies, or branches. The residence and work permits of such employees shall only cover the period of such employment.

2.   Key personnel of the abovementioned companies herein referred to as "organisations" are "intra-corporate transferees" as defined in (c) in the following categories, provided that the organisation is a legal person and that the persons concerned have been employed by it or have been partners in it (other than majority shareholders), for at least the year immediately preceding such movement:

(a)   persons working in a senior position with an organisation, who primarily direct the management of the establishment, receiving general supervision or direction principally from the board of directors or stockholders of the business or their equivalent, including:

- directing the establishment or a department or subdivision of the establishment,

- supervising and controlling the work of other supervisory, professional or managerial employees,

- having the authority personally to hire and fire or recommend hiring, firing or other personnel actions;

(b)   persons working within an organisation who possess uncommon knowledge essential to the establishment's service, research equipment, techniques or management. The assessment of such knowledge may reflect, apart from knowledge specific to the establishment, a high level of qualification referring to a type of work or trade requiring specific technical knowledge, including membership of an accredited profession;

(c)   an "intra-corporate transferee" is defined as a natural person working within an organisation in the territory of a Party, and being temporarily transferred in the context of pursuit of economic activities in the territory of the other Party; the organisation concerned must have its principal place of business in the territory of a Party and the transfer to be an establishment (branch, subsidiary) of that organisation, effectively pursuing like economic activities in the territory of the other Party.

Article 29

1.   The Parties shall use their best endeavours to avoid taking any measures or actions which render the conditions for the establishment and operation of each other's companies more restrictive than the situation existing on the day preceding the date of signature of the Agreement.

2.   The provisions of this Article are without prejudice to those of Article 37: the situations covered by such Article 37 shall be solely governed by its provisions to the exclusion of any other.

3.   Acting in the spirit of partnership and cooperation and in the light of the provisions of Article 43 the Government of the Republic of Kazakhstan shall inform the Community of its intentions to submit new legislation or adopt new regulations which may render the conditions for the establishment or operation in the Republic of Kazakhstan of subsidiaries and branches of Community companies more restrictive than the situation existing on the day preceding the date of signature of the Agreement. The Community may request the Republic of Kazakhstan to communicate the drafts of such legislation or regulations and to enter into consultations about those drafts.

4.   Where new legislation or regulations introduced in the Republic of Kazakhstan would result in rendering the conditions for operation of subsidiaries and branches of Community companies established in the Republic of Kazakhstan more restrictive than the situation existing on the day of signature of the Agreement, such legislation or regulations shall not apply during three years following the entry into force of the relevant act to those subsidiaries and branches already established in the Republic of Kazakhstan at the time of entry into force of the relevant act.

CHAPTER III

CROSS BORDER SUPPLY OF SERVICES BETWEEN THE COMMUNITY AND THE REPUBLIC OF KAZAKHSTAN

Article 30

1.   The Parties undertake in accordance with the provisions of this Chapter to take the necessary steps to allow progressively the supply of services by Community or Kazakh companies who are established in a Party other than that of the person for whom the services are intended taking into account the development of the services sectors in the Parties.

2.   The Cooperation Council shall make recommendations for the implementation of paragraph 1.

Article 31

The Parties shall cooperate with the aim of developing a market-oriented service sector in the Republik of Kazakhstan.

Article 32

1.   The Parties undertake to apply effectively the principle of unrestricted access to the international maritime market and traffic on a commercial basis:

(a)   the above provision does not prejudice the rights and obligations arising from the United Nations Convention on a Code of Conduct for Liner Conferences, as applicable to one or other Contracting Party to this Agreement. Non-conference lines will be free to operate in competition with a conference line as long as they adhere to the principle of fair competition on a commercial basis;

(b)   the Parties affirm their commitment to a freely competitive environment as being an essential feature of the dry and liquid bulk trade.

2.   In applying the principles of paragraph 1, the Parties shall:

(a)   not apply, as from entry into force of this agreement, any cargo sharing provisions of bilateral agreements between any Member States of the Community and the former Soviet Union;

(b)   not introduce cargo sharing clauses into future bilateral agreements with third countries, other than in those exceptional circumstances where liner shipping companies from one or other Party to this Agreement would not otherwise have an effective opportunity to ply for trade to and from the third country concerned;

(c)   prohibit cargo sharing arrangements in future bilateral agreements concerning dry and liquid bulk trade;

(d)   abolish upon entry into force of this Agreement, all unilateral measures, administrative, technical and other obstacles which could have restrictive or discriminatory effects on the free supply of services in international maritime transport.

Each Party shall grant, inter alia, no less favourable treatment, for the ships operated by nationals or companies of the other Party, than that accorded to a Party's own ships, with regard to access to ports open to international trade, the use of infrastructure and auxiliary maritime services of the ports, as well as related fees and charges, customs facilities and the assignment of berths and facilities for loading and unloading.

3.   Nationals and companies of the Community providing international maritime transport services shall be free to provide international sea-river services in the inland waterways of the Republic of Kazakhstan and vice versa.

Article 33

With a view to assuring a coordinated development of transport between the Parties, adapted to their commercial needs, the conditions of mutual market access and provision of services in transport by road, rail and inland waterways and, if applicable, in air transport may be dealt with by specific agreements where appropriate negotiated between the Parties after entry into force of this Agreement.

CHAPTER IV

GENERAL PROVISIONS

Article 34

1.   The provisions of this Title shall be applied subject to limitations justified on grounds of public policy, public security or public health.

2.   They shall not apply to activities which in the territory of either Party are connected, even occasionally, with the exercise of official authority.

Article 35

For the purpose of this Title, nothing in the Agreement shall prevent the Parties from applying their laws and regulations regarding entry and stay, work, labour conditions and establishment of natural persons and supply of services, provided that, in so doing, they do not apply them in a manner as to nullify or impair the benefits accruing to any Party under the terms of a specific provision of the Agreement. The above provision does not prejudice the application of Article 34.

Article 36

Companies which are controlled and exclusively owned by Kazakh companies and Community companies jointly shall also be beneficiaries of the provisions of Chapters II, III and IV.

Article 37

Treatment granted by either Party to the other hereunder shall, as from the day one month prior to the date of entry into force of the relevant obligations of the General Agreement on Trade in Services (GATS), in respect of sectors or measures covered by the GATS, in no case be more favourable than that accorded by such first Party under the provisions of GATS and this in respect of each service sector, sub-sector and mode of supply.

Article 38

For the purposes of Chapters II, III and IV, no account shall be taken of treatment accorded by the Community, its Member States or the Republic of Kazakhstan pursuant to commitments entered into in economic integration agreements in accordance with the principles of Article V of GATS.

Article 39

1.   The most-favoured-nation treatment granted in accordance with the provisions of this Title shall not apply to the tax advantages which the Parties are providing or will provide in the future on the basis of agreements to avoid double taxation, or other tax arrangements.

2.   Nothing in this Title shall be construed to prevent the adoption or enforcement by the Parties of any measure aimed at preventing the avoidance or evasion of taxes pursuant to the tax provisions of agreements to avoid double taxation and other tax arrangements, or domestic fiscal legislation.

3.   Nothing in this Title shall be construed to prevent Member States or the Republic of Kazakhstan from distinguishing, in the application of the relevant provisions of their fiscal legislation, between tax payers who are not in identical situations, in particular as regards their place of residence.

Article 40

Without prejudice to Article 28, no provision of Chapters II, III and IV shall be interpreted as giving the right to:

- nationals of the Member States or of the Republic of Kazakhstan respectively to enter, or stay in, the territory of the Republic of Kazakhstan or the Community respectively in any capacity whatsoever, and in particular as a shareholder or partner in a company or manager or employee thereof or supplier or recipient of services,

- Community subsidiaries or branches of Kazakh companies to employ or have employed in the territory of the Community nationals of the Republic of Kazakhstan,

- Kazakh subsidiaries or branches of Community companies to employ or have employed in the territory of the Republic of Kazakhstan nationals of the Member States,

- Kazakh companies or Community subsidiaries or branches of Kazakh companies to supply Kazakh persons to act for and under the control of other persons by temporary employment contracts,

- Community companies or Kazakh subsidiaries or branches of Community companies to supply workers who are nationals of the Member States by temporary employment contracts.

CHAPTER V

CURRENT PAYMENTS AND CAPITAL

Article 41

1.   The Parties undertake to authorise in freely convertible currency, any payments on the current account of balance of payments between residents of the Community and of the Republic

of Kazakhstan connected with the movement of goods, services or persons made in accordance with the provisions of this Agreement.

2.   With regard to transactions on the capital account of balance of payments, from entry into force of this Agreement, the free movement of capital relating to direct investments made in companies formed in accordance with the laws of the host country and investments made in accordance with the provisions of Chapter II, and the liquidation or repatriation of these investments and of any profit stemming therefrom shall be ensured.

3.   Without prejudice to paragraph 2 or to paragraph 5, as from entry into force of this Agreement, no new foreign exchange restrictions on the movement of capital and current payments connected therewith between residents of the Community and the Republic of Kazakhstan shall be introduced and the existing arrangements shall not become more restrictive.

4.   The Parties shall consult each other with a view to facilitating the movement of forms of capital other than those referred to in paragraph 2 between the Community and the Republic of Kazakhstan in order to promote the objectives of this Agreement.

5.   With reference to the provisions of this Article, until a full convertibility of the Kazakh currency within the meaning of Article VIII of the Articles of Agreement of the International Monetary Fund (IMF) is introduced, the Republic of Kazakhstan may in exceptional circumstances apply exchange restrictions connected with the granting or taking up of short and medium-term financial credits to the extent that such restrictions are imposed on the Republic of Kazakhstan for the granting of such credits and are permitted according to the Republic of Kazakhstan's status under the IMF. The Republic of Kazakhstan shall apply these restrictions in a non-discriminatory manner. They shall be applied in such a manner as to cause the least possible disruption to this Agreement. The Republic of Kazakhstan shall inform the Cooperation Council promptly of the introduction of such measures and of any changes therein.

6.   Without prejudice to paragraphs 1 and 2, where, in exceptional circumstances, movements of capital between the Community and the Republic of Kazakhstan cause, or threaten to cause, serious difficulties for the operation of exchange rate policy or monetary policy in the Community or the Republic of Kazakhstan, the Community and the Republic of Kazakhstan, respectively, may take safeguard measures with regard to movements of capital between the Community and the Republic of Kazakhstan for a period not exceeding six months if such measures are strictly necessary.

CHAPTER VI

INTELLECTUAL, INDUSTRIAL AND COMMERCIAL PROPERTY PROTECTION

Article 42

1.   Pursuant to the provisions of this Article and of Annex III, the Republic of Kazakhstan shall continue to improve the protection of intellectual, industrial and commercial property rights in order to provide, by the end of the fifth year after the entry into force of the Agreement, for a level of protection similar to that existing in the Community, including effective means of enforcing such rights.

2.   By the end of the fifth year after entry into force of the Agreement, the Republic of Kazakhstan shall accede to the multilateral conventions on intellectual, industrial and commercial property rights referred to in paragraph 1 of Annex III to which Member States are parties or which are de facto applied by Member States, according to the relevant provisions contained in these conventions.

TITLE V

LEGISLATIVE COOPERATION

Article 43

1.   The Parties recognise that an important condition for strengthening the economic links between the Republic of Kazakhstan and the Community is the approximation of the Republic of Kazakhstan's existing and future legislation to that of the Community. The Republic of Kazakhstan shall endeavour to ensure that its legislation will be gradually made compatible with that of the Community.

2.   The approximation of laws shall extend to the following areas in particular: customs law, company law, banking law, company accounts and taxes, intellectual property, protection of workers at the workplace, financial services, rules on competition including any related issues and practices affecting trade, public procurement, protection of health and life of humans, animals and plants, the environment, consumer protection, indirect taxation, technical rules and standards, nuclear laws and regulations, transport.

3.   The Community shall provide the Republic of Kazakhstan with technical assistance for the implementation of these measures, which may include, inter alia:

- the exchange of experts,
- the provision of early information especially on relevant legislation,
- organisation of seminars,
- training activities,
- aid for translation of Community legislation in the relevant sectors.

4.   The Parties agree to examine ways to apply their respective competition laws on a concerted basis in such cases where trade between them is affected.

TITLE VI

ECONOMIC COOPERATION

Article 44

1.   The Community and the Republic of Kazakhstan shall establish economic cooperation aimed at contributing to the process of economic reform and recovery and sustainable development of the Republic of Kazakhstan. Such cooperation shall strengthen existing economic links, to the benefit of both Parties.

2.   Policies and other measures will be designed to bring about economic and social reforms and restructuring of the economic system in the Republic of Kazakhstan and will be guided by the requirements of sustainability and harmonious social development; they will also fully incorporate environmental considerations.

3.   To this end the cooperation will concentrate, in particular, on economic and social development, human resources development, support for enterprises (including privatisation, investment and development of financial services), agriculture and food, energy and civil nuclear safety, transport, tourism, environmental protection and regional cooperation.

4.   Special attention shall be devoted to measures capable of fostering cooperation between the Independent States with a view to stimulating a harmonious development of the region.

5.   Where appropriate, economic cooperation and other forms of cooperation provided for in this Agreement may be supported by technical assistance from the Community, taking into account the Community's relevant Council regulation applicable to technical assistance in the Independent States, the priorities agreed upon in the indicative programme related to Community technical assistance to the Republic of Kazakhstan and its established coordination and implementation procedures.

Article 45
Industrial cooperation

1.   Cooperation shall aim at promoting the following in particular:

- the development of business links between economic operators of both sides,
- Community participation in Kazakhstan's efforts to restructure its industry,
- the improvement of management,
- the improvement of the quality of industrial products,
- the development of efficient production and processing capacity in the raw materials sector,
- the development of appropriate commercial rules and practices including product marketing,
- environmental protection,
- defence conversion.

2.   The provisions of this Article shall not affect the enforcement of Community competition rules applicable to undertakings.

Article 46
Investment promotion and protection

1.   Bearing in mind the respective powers and competences of the Community and the Member States, cooperation shall aim to establish a favourable climate for private investment, both domestic and foreign, especially through better conditions for investment protection, the transfer of capital and the exchange of information on investment opportunities.

2.   The aims of cooperation shall be in particular:

- the conclusion, where appropriate, between the Member States and the Republic of Kazakhstan of agreements for the promotion and protection of investment,

- the conclusion, where appropriate, between the Member States and the Republic of Kazakhstan of agreements to avoid double taxation,

- the creation of favourable conditions for attracting foreign investments into the Kazakh economy,

- to establish stable and adequate business law and conditions, and to exchange information on laws, regulations and administrative practices in the field of investment,

- to exchange information on investment opportunities in the form of, inter alia, trade fairs, exhibitions, trade weeks and other events.

Article 47
Public procurement

The Parties shall cooperate to develop conditions for open and competitive award of contracts for goods and services in particular through calls for tenders.

Article 49
Mining and raw materials

1.   The Parties shall aim at increasing investment and trade in mining and raw materials.

2.   The cooperation shall focus in particular on the following areas:

- exchange of information on the prospects of the mining and non-ferrous metals sectors,
- the establishment of a legal framework for cooperation,
- trade matters,
- the adoption and implementation of environmental legislation,
- training,
- safety in the mining industry.

Article 50
Cooperation in science and technology

1.   The Parties shall promote cooperation in civil scientific research and technological development (RTD) on the basis of mutual benefit and, taking into account the availability of resources, adequate access to their respective programmes and subject to appropriate levels of effective protection of intellectual, industrial and commercial property rights (IPR).

2.   Science and technology cooperation shall cover:

- the exchange of scientific and technical information,

- joint RTD activities,

- training activities and mobility programmes for scientists, researchers and technicians engaged in RTD in both sides.

Where such cooperation takes the form of activities involving education and/or training, it should be carried out in accordance with the provisions of Article 51.

The Parties, on the basis of mutual agreement, can engage in other forms of cooperation in science and technology.

In carrying out such cooperation activities, special attention shall be devoted to the redeployment of scientists, engineers, researchers and technicians which are or have been engaged in research on/and production of weapons of mass destruction.

3.   The cooperation covered by this Article shall be implemented according to specific arrangements to be negotiated and concluded in accordance with the procedures adopted by each Party, and which shall set out, inter alia, appropriate IPR provisions.

Article 52
Agriculture and the agro-industrial sector

The purpose of cooperation in this area shall be the pursuance of agrarian reform, the modernisation, privatisation and restructuring of agriculture, the agro-industrial and services sectors in the Republic of Kazakhstan, development of domestic and foreign markets for the Kazakh products, in conditions that ensure the protection of the environment, taking into account the necessity to improve security of food supply as well as the development of agri-business, the processing and distribution of agricultural products. The Parties shall also aim at the gradual approximation of Kazakh standards to Community technical regulations concerning industrial and agricultural food products including sanitary and phytosanitary standards.

Article 53
Energy

1.   Cooperation shall take place within the principles of the market economy and the European Energy Charter, against a background of the progressive integration of the energy markets in Europe.

2.   The cooperation shall include among others the following areas:

- the environmental impact of energy production supply and consumption, in order to prevent or minimise the environmental damage resulting from these activities,

- improvement of the quality and security of energy supply, including diversification of supply, in an economic and environmentally sound manner,

- formulation of energy policy,

- improvement in management and regulation of the energy sector in line with a market economy,

- the introduction of the range of institutional, legal, fiscal and other conditions necessary to encourage increased energy trade and investment,

- promotion of energy saving and energy effectiveness,

- modernisation of energy infrastructure,

- improvement of energy technologies in supply and end use across the range of energy types,

- management and technical training in the energy sector,

- security in energy supply, transportation and transit of energy and energy materials.

Article 57
Postal services and telecommunications

Within their respective powers and competencies the Parties shall expand and strengthen cooperation in the following areas:

- the establishment of policies and guidelines for the development of the telecommunications sector and postal services,

- development of principles of a tariff policy and marketing in telecommunications and postal services,

- encouraging the development of projects for telecommunications and postal services and attracting investment,

- enhancing efficiency and quality of the provision of telecommunications and postal services, amongst others through liberalisation of activities of sub-sectors,

- advanced application of telecommunications, notably in the area of electronic funds transfer,

- management of telecommunications networks and their "optimisation",

- an appropriate regulatory basis for the provision of telecommunication and postal services and for the use of the radio frequency spectrum,

- training in the field of telecommunications and postal services for operations in market conditions.

Article 58
Financial services

Cooperation shall in particular aim at facilitating the involvement of the Republic of Kazakhstan in universally accepted systems of mutual settlements. Technical assistance shall focus on:

- the development of banking and financial services, the development of a common market of credit resources, the involvement of the Republic of Kazakhstan in a universally accepted system of mutual settlements,

- the development of the fiscal system, fiscal institutions in the Republic of Kazakhstan and the exchange of experience and personnel training in fiscal matters,

- the development of insurance services, which would, inter alia, create a favourable framework for Community companies participation in the establishment of joint ventures in the insurance sector in the Republic of Kazakhstan, as well as the development of export credit insurance.

This cooperation shall in particular contribute to foster the development of relations between the Republic of Kazakhstan and the Member States in the financial services sector.

Article 59
Money laundering

1.   The Parties agree on the necessity of making efforts and cooperating in order to prevent the use of their financial systems for laundering of proceeds from criminal activities in general and drug offences in particular.

2.   Cooperation in this area shall include administrative and technical assistance with the purpose of establishing suitable standards against money laundering equivalent to those adopted by the Community and international forums in this field, including the Financial Action Task Force (FATF).

Article 63
Small and medium-sized enterprises

1.   The Parties shall aim to develop and strengthen small and medium-sized enterprises and their associations and cooperation between SMEs in the Community and the Republic of Kazakhstan.

2.   Cooperation shall include technical assistance, in particular in the following areas:

- the development of a legislative framework for SMEs,

- the development of an appropriate infrastructure (an agency to support SMEs communications, assistance to the creation of a fund for SMEs),

- the development of technology parks.

ANNEX III

INTELLECTUAL, INDUSTRIAL AND COMMERCIAL PROPERTY CONVENTIONS REFERRED TO IN ARTICLE 42

1.   Paragraph 2 of Article 42 concerns the following multilateral conventions:

- Berne Convention for the Protection of Literary and Artistic Works (Paris Act, 1971),

- International Convention for the Protection of Performers, Producers of Phonograms and Broadcasting Organisations (Rome, 1961),

- Protocol relating to the Madrid Agreement concerning the International Registration of Marks (Madrid, 1989),

- Nice Agreement concerning the International Classification of Goods and Services for the purposes of the Registration of Marks (Geneva 1977 and amended in 1979),

- Budapest Treaty on the International Recognition of the Deposit of Microorganisms for the purposes of Patent Procedures (1977, modified in 1980),

- International Convention for the Protection of New Varieties of Plants (UPOV) (Geneva Act, 1991).

2.   The Cooperation Council may recommend that paragraph 2 of Article 42 shall apply to other multilateral conventions. If problems in the area of intellectual, industrial and commercial property affecting trading conditions were to occur, urgent consultations will be undertaken, at the request of either Party, with a view to reaching mutually satisfactory solutions.

3.   The Parties confirm the importance they attach to the obligations arising from the following multilateral conventions:

- Paris Convention for the Protection of Industrial Property (Stockholm Act, 1967 and amended in 1979),

- Madrid Agreement concerning the International Registration of Marks (Stockholm Act, 1967 and amended in 1979),

- Patent Cooperation Treaty (Washington, 1970, amended in 1979 and modified in 1984).

4.   From the entry into fource of this Agreement, the Republic of Kazakhstan shall grant to Community companies and nationals, in respect of the recognition and protection of intellectual, industrial and commercial property, treatment no less favourable than that granted by it to any third country under bilateral agreements.

5.   The provisions of paragraph 4 shall not apply to advantages granted by the Republic of Kazakhstan to any third country on an effective reciprocal basis and to advantages granted by the Republic of Kazakhstan to another country of the former USSR.

*

AGREEMENT BETWEEN THE REPUBLIC OF SINGAPORE AND JAPAN FOR A NEW-AGE ECONOMIC PARTNERSHIP[*]

The Agreement between the Republic of Singapore and Japan for a New-Age Economic Partnership was signed in Singapore on 13 January 2002.

PREAMBLE

The Republic of Singapore and Japan (hereinafter referred to in this Agreement as "the Parties"),

Conscious of their warm relations and strong economic and political ties, including shared perceptions on various issues, that have developed through many years of fruitful and mutually beneficial co-operation;

Recognising that a dynamic and rapidly changing global environment brought about by globalisation and technological progress presents many new economic and strategic challenges and opportunities to the Parties;

Acknowledging that encouraging innovation and competition and improving their attractiveness to capital and human resources can enhance their ability to respond to such new challenges and opportunities;

Recognising that the economic partnership of the Parties would create larger and new markets, and would improve their economic efficiency and consumer welfare, enhancing the attractiveness and vibrancy of their markets, and expanding trade and investment not only between them but also in the region;

Reaffirming that such partnership will provide a useful framework for enhanced regulatory co-operation between the Parties to meet new challenges posed by emerging market developments and to improve their market infrastructure;

Bearing in mind their rights and obligations under other international agreements to which they are parties, in particular those of the Marrakesh Agreement Establishing the World Trade Organization (hereinafter referred to in this Agreement as "the WTO Agreement");

Reaffirming the importance of the multilateral trading system embodied by the World Trade Organization (hereinafter referred to in this Agreement as "the WTO");

Recognising the catalytic role which regional and bilateral trade agreements that are consistent with the rules of the WTO can play in accelerating global and regional trade and investment liberalisation and rule-making;

---

[*] *Source*: The Government of Japan and The Government of Singapore (2002). "Agreement between the Republic of Singapore and Japan for a New-Age Economic Partnership", available on the Internet (http://www.mti.gov.sg/public/PDF/CMT/FTA_JSEPA_Agreement.pdf) and (http://www.mofa.go.jp/region/asia-paci/singapore/jsepa.html). [Note added by the editor.]

<u>Realising</u> that enhancing economic ties between the Parties would strengthen Japan's involvement in Southeast Asia;

<u>Observing</u> in particular that such ties would help catalyse trade and investment liberalisation in Asia-Pacific;

<u>Convinced</u> that stronger economic linkages between them would provide greater opportunities, larger economies of scale and a more predictable environment for economic activities not only for Japanese and Singapore businesses but also for other businesses in Asia;

<u>Determined</u> to create a legal framework for an economic partnership between the Parties;

HAVE AGREED as follows:

CHAPTER 1
GENERAL PROVISIONS

Article 1
Objectives

The objectives of this Agreement are:

(a)   to facilitate, promote, liberalise and provide a stable and predictable environment for economic activity between the Parties through such means as:

    (i)   reducing or eliminating customs duties and other barriers to trade in goods between the Parties;

    (ii)   improving customs clearance procedures with a view to facilitating bilateral trade in goods;

    (iii)   promoting paperless trading between the Parties;

    (iv)   facilitating the mutual recognition of the results of conformity assessment procedures for products or processes;

    (v)   removing barriers to trade in services between the Parties;

    (vi)   mutually enhancing investment opportunities and strengthening protection for investors and investments;

    (vii)   easing the movement of business people including professionals;

    (viii)   developing co-operation between the Parties in the field of intellectual property;

    (ix)   enhancing opportunities in the government procurement market; and encouraging effective control of and promoting co-operation in the field of anti-competitive activities; and

(b)   to establish a co-operative framework for further strengthening the economic relations between the Parties through such means as:

(i)   promoting regulatory co-operation in the field of financial services, facilitating development of financial markets, including capital markets in the Parties and in Asia, and improving the financial market infrastructure of the Parties;

(ii)   promoting the development and use of information and communications technology (hereinafter referred to in this Agreement as "ICT") and ICT-related services;

(iii)   developing and encouraging co-operation in the field of science and technology;

(iv)   developing and encouraging co-operation in the field of human resource development;

(v)   promoting trade and investment activities of private enterprises of the Parties through facilitating their exchanges and collaboration;

(vi)   promoting, particularly, trade and investment activities of small and medium enterprises of the Parties through facilitating their close co-operation;

(vii)   developing and encouraging co-operation in the field of broadcasting; and

(viii)   promoting and developing tourism in the Parties.

Article 2
Transparency

1.   Each Party shall promptly make public, or otherwise make publicly available, its laws, regulations, administrative procedures and administrative rulings and judicial decisions of general application as well as international agreements which pertain to or affect the operation of this Agreement.

2.   Each Party shall, upon request by the other Party, promptly respond to specific questions from, and provide information to, the other Party with respect to matters referred to in paragraph 1 above

Article 3
Confidential Information

1.   Nothing in this Agreement shall be construed to require a Party to provide confidential information, the disclosure of which would impede law enforcement, or otherwise be contrary to the public interest, or which would prejudice legitimate commercial interests of particular enterprises, public or private.

2.   Nothing in this Agreement shall be construed to require a Party to provide information relating to the affairs and accounts of customers of financial institutions.

3.   Each Party shall, in accordance with its laws and regulations, maintain the confidentiality of information provided in confidence by the other Party pursuant to this Agreement, including business-confidential information.

Article 4
Security and General Exceptions

1.   Nothing in this Agreement shall be construed:

    (a)   to require a Party to furnish any information the disclosure of which it considers contrary to its essential security interests;

    (b)   to prevent a Party from taking any action which it considers necessary for the protection of its essential security interests:

        (i)   relating to fissionable and fusionable materials or the materials from which they are derived;

        (ii)   relating to the traffic in arms, ammunition and implements of war and to such traffic in other goods and materials as is carried on directly or indirectly for the purpose of supplying a military establishment;

        (iii)   relating to the supply of services as carried out directly or indirectly for the purpose of provisioning a military establishment;

        (iv)   relating to the procurement of arms, ammunition or war materials, or to procurement indispensable for national security or for national defence purposes; or

        (v)   taken in time of war or other emergency within that Party or in international relations; or

    (c)   to prevent a Party from taking any action in pursuance of its obligations under the United Nations Charter for the maintenance of international peace and security.

2.   In the application of paragraph 1 above, the relevant interpretations and operation of the WTO Agreement shall, where appropriate, be taken into account.

3.   Nothing in this Agreement shall be construed to prevent a Party from taking any action necessary to protect communications infrastructure of critical importance from unlawful acts against such infrastructure.

Article 5
Taxation

1.   Unless otherwise provided for in this Agreement, its provisions shall not apply to any taxation measures.

2.   Articles 2, 3 and 4 above shall apply to taxation measures, to the extent that the provisions of this Agreement are applicable to such taxation measures.

Article 6
Relation to Other Agreements

1.   In the event of any inconsistency between this Agreement and any other agreement to which both Parties are parties, the Parties shall immediately consult with each other with a view to finding a mutually satisfactory solution, taking into consideration general principles of international law.

2.   For the purposes of this Agreement, references to articles in the General Agreement on Tariffs and Trade 1994 in Annex 1A to the WTO Agreement (hereinafter referred to in this Agreement as "GATT 1994") include the interpretative notes, where applicable.

Article 7
Implementing Agreement

The Parties shall conclude a separate agreement setting forth the details and procedures for the implementation of this Agreement (hereinafter referred to in this Agreement as "the Implementing Agreement").

Article 8
Supervisory Committee

1.   A Supervisory Committee shall be established to ensure the proper implementation of this Agreement, to review the economic relationship and partnership between the Parties, and to consider the necessity of amending this Agreement for furthering its objectives.

2.   The functions of the Supervisory Committee shall include:

   (a)   reviewing the implementation of this Agreement;

   (b)   discussing any issues concerning trade-related and investment-related measures which are of interest to the Parties;

   (c)   encouraging each other to take appropriate measures which will lead to significant improvement of business environment between the Parties;

   (d)   considering and recommending further liberalisation and facilitation of trade in goods and services, and investment;

   (e)   considering and recommending ways of furthering the objectives of this Agreement through more extensive co-operation; and

   (f)   considering and recommending, at any time and whether or not in the context of the general review provided for in Article 10, any amendment to this Agreement or modification to the commitments herein.

3.   Where there are any amendments to the provisions of the WTO Agreement on which provisions of this Agreement are based, the Parties shall, through the Supervisory Committee, consider the possibility of incorporating such amendments to this Agreement.

4.   The Supervisory Committee:

(a)   shall be composed of representatives of the Parties;

(b)   shall be co-chaired by Ministers or senior officials of the Parties as may be delegated by them for this purpose; and

(c)   may establish and delegate responsibilities to working groups.

5.   To promote dialogue between the government, academia and business communities of the Parties, for the purpose of developing and enhancing the economic partnership between the Parties, the working groups may, where necessary, invite academics and business persons with the relevant expertise to participate in the discussions of the working groups.

6.   The Supervisory Committee shall convene once a year in regular session alternately in each Party. Special meetings of the Supervisory Committee shall also convene, within 30 days, at the request of either Party.

Article 9
Communications

Each Party shall designate a contact point to facilitate communications between the Parties on any matter relating to this Agreement.

Article 10
General Review

The Parties shall undertake a general review of the operation of this Agreement in 2007 and every five years thereafter.

CHAPTER 7
TRADE IN SERVICES

Article 58
Scope of and Definitions under Chapter 7

1.   This Chapter shall apply to measures by the Parties affecting trade in services.

2.   In respect of air transport services, this Agreement shall not apply to measures affecting traffic rights, however granted; or to measures affecting services directly related to the exercise of traffic rights, other than measures affecting:

(a)   aircraft repair and maintenance services;

(b)   the selling and marketing of air transport services; and

(c)   computer reservation system services.

3.   This Chapter shall not apply to cabotage in maritime transport services.

4.   Annexes IVA and IVB provide supplementary provisions to this Chapter with respect to measures affecting the supply of financial services and of telecommunications services respectively.

5.   Government procurement of services shall be governed by Chapter 11.

6.   For the purposes of this Chapter:

(a)   the term "measure" means any measure by a Party, including those of taxation, whether in the form of a law, regulation, rule, procedure, decision, administrative action or any other form;

(b)   the term "supply of a service" includes the production, distribution, marketing, sale and delivery of a service;

(c)   the term "measures by a Party affecting trade in services" includes measures in respect of:

   (i)   the purchase, payment or use of a service;

   (ii)   the access to and use of, in connection with the supply of a service, services which are required by a Party to be offered to the public generally;

   (iii)   the presence, including commercial presence, of persons of a Party for the supply of a service in the territory of the other Party;

(d)   the term "commercial presence" means any type of business or professional establishment, including through:

   (i)   the constitution, acquisition or maintenance of a juridical person; or

   (ii)   the creation or maintenance of a branch or a representative office; within the territory of a Party for the purpose of supplying a service;

(e)   the term "sector" of a service means:

   (i)   with reference to a specific commitment, one or more, or all, subsectors of that service, as specified in a Party's Schedule of specific commitments in Annex IVc; or

   (ii)   otherwise, the whole of that service sector, including all of its subsectors;

(f)   the term "service supplier" means any person that supplies a service; [Note]

   Note: Where the service is not supplied directly by a juridical person but through other forms of commercial presence such as a branch or a representative office, the service supplier (i.e. the juridical person) shall, nonetheless, through such presence be accorded the treatment provided for service suppliers. Such treatment shall be extended to the presence through which the service is supplied and need not be extended to any other parts of the supplier located outside the territory where the service is supplied.

(g)   the term "service consumer" means any person that receives or uses a service;

(h)   the term "service of the other Party" means a service which is supplied:

    (i)   from or in the territory of the other Party, or in the case of maritime transport, by a vessel registered under the laws of the other Party, or by a person of the other Party which supplies the service through the operation of a vessel or its use in whole or in part; or

    (ii)   in the case of the supply of a service through commercial presence or through the presence of natural persons, by a service supplier of the other Party;

(i)   the term "person" means either a natural person or a juridical person;

(j)   the term "service supplier of the other Party" means any natural person of the other Party or juridical person of the other Party, that supplies a service;

(k)   the term "natural person of the other Party" means a natural person who resides in the territory of the other Party or elsewhere and who under the law of the other Party:

    (i)   in respect of Japan, is a national of Japan; and

    (ii)   in respect of Singapore, is a national of Singapore or has the right of permanent residence in Singapore;

(l)   the term "juridical person" means any legal entity duly constituted or otherwise organised under applicable law, whether for profit or otherwise, and whether privately-owned or governmentally-owned, including any corporation, trust, partnership, joint venture, sole proprietorship or association;

(m)   the term "juridical person of the other Party" means a juridical person which is either:

    (i)   constituted or otherwise organised under the law of the other Party and, if it is owned or controlled by natural persons of non-Parties or juridical persons constituted or otherwise organised under the law of non-Parties, is engaged in substantive business operations in the territory of either Party; or

    (ii)   in the case of the supply of a service through commercial presence, owned or controlled by:
        (A)   natural persons of the other Party; or

        (B)   juridical persons of the other Party identified under sub-paragraph (i) above;

(n)   a juridical person is:

(i)   "owned" by persons of a Party if more than 50 percent of the equity interest in it is beneficially owned by persons of that Party;

(ii)   "controlled" by persons of a Party if such persons have the power to name a majority of its directors or otherwise to legally direct its actions;

(iii)   "owned by natural persons of non-Parties" if more than 50 percent of the equity interest in it is beneficially owned by natural persons of non-Parties;

(iv)   "controlled by natural persons of non-Parties" if such natural persons have the power to name a majority of its directors or otherwise to legally direct its actions;

(v)   "affiliated" with another person when it controls, or is controlled by, that other person; or when it and the other person are both controlled by the same person;

(o)   the term "trade in services" means the supply of a service:

(i)   from the territory of one Party into the territory of the other Party ("cross-border mode");

(ii)   in the territory of one Party to the service consumer of the other Party ("consumption abroad mode");

(iii)   by a service supplier of one Party, through commercial presence in the territory of the other Party ("commercial presence mode");

(iv)   by a service supplier of one Party, through presence of natural persons of that Party in the territory of the other Party ("presence of natural persons mode");

(p)   the term "measures by a Party" means measures taken by:

(i)   central or local governments; and

(ii)   non-governmental bodies in the exercise of powers delegated by central or local governments;

in fulfilling its obligations and commitments under this Chapter, each Party shall take such reasonable measures as may be available to it to ensure observance of the provisions of this Chapter by its local governments and non-governmental bodies in the exercise of powers delegated by its central or local governments within its territory;

(q)   the term "services" includes any service in any sector except services supplied in the exercise of governmental authority;

(r)   the term "a service supplied in the exercise of governmental authority" means any service which is supplied neither on a commercial basis nor in competition with one or more service suppliers;

(s)   the term "aircraft repair and maintenance services" means such activities when undertaken on an aircraft or a part thereof while it is withdrawn from service and does not include so-called line maintenance;

(t)   the term "selling and marketing of air transport services" means opportunities for the air carrier concerned to sell and market freely its air transport services including all aspects of marketing such as market research, advertising and distribution. These activities do not include the pricing of air transport services nor the applicable conditions;

(u)   the term "computer reservation system services" means services provided by computerised systems that contain information about air carriers' schedules, availability, fares and fare rules, through which reservations can be made or tickets may be issued;

(v)   the term "traffic rights" means the rights for scheduled and non-scheduled services to operate or to carry passengers, cargo and mail for remuneration or hire from, to, within, or over the territory of a Party, including points to be served, routes to be operated, types of traffic to be carried, capacity to be provided, tariffs to be charged and their conditions, and criteria for designation of airlines, including such criteria as number, ownership and control;

(w)   the term "monopoly supplier of a service" means any person, public or private, which in the relevant market of the territory of a Party is authorised or established formally or in effect by that Party as the sole supplier of that service; and

(x)   the term "direct taxes" comprises all taxes on total income, on total capital or on elements of income or of capital, including taxes on gains from the alienation of property, taxes on estates, inheritances and gifts, and taxes on the total amounts of wages or salaries paid by enterprises, as well as taxes on capital appreciation.

Article 59
Market Access

1.   With respect to market access through the modes of supply defined in sub-paragraph (o) of paragraph 6 of Article 58 above, each Party shall accord services and service suppliers of the other Party treatment no less favourable than that provided for under the terms, limitations and conditions agreed and specified in its Schedule of specific commitments in Annex IVc. [Note]

> Note: If a Party undertakes a market-access commitment in relation to the supply of a service through the mode of supply referred to in (i) of sub-paragraph (o) of paragraph 6 of Article 58 above and if the cross-border movement of capital is an essential part of the service itself, that Party is thereby committed to allow such movement of capital. If a Party undertakes a market-access commitment in relation to the supply of a service through the mode of supply referred to in (iii) of sub-paragraph (o) of paragraph 6 of Article 58 above, it is thereby committed to allow related transfers of capital into its territory.

2.   In sectors where market-access commitments are undertaken, the measures which a Party shall not maintain or adopt either on the basis of a regional subdivision or on the basis of its entire territory, unless otherwise specified in its Schedule of specific commitments in Annex IVc, are defined as:

(a)   limitations on the number of service suppliers whether in the form of numerical quotas, monopolies, exclusive service suppliers or the requirements of an economic needs test;

(b)   limitations on the total value of service transactions or assets in the form of numerical quotas or the requirement of an economic needs test;

(c)   limitations on the total number of service operations or on the total quantity of service output expressed in terms of designated numerical units in the form of quotas or the requirement of an economic needs test; (Note)

   Note: Sub-paragraph (c) of paragraph 2 of Article 59 does not cover measures of a Party which
            limit inputs for the supply of services.

(d)   limitations on the total number of natural persons that may be employed in a particular service sector or that a service supplier may employ and who are necessary for, and directly related to, the supply of a specific service in the form of numerical quotas or the requirement of an economic needs test;

(e)   measures which restrict or require specific types of legal entity or joint venture through which a service supplier may supply a service; and

(f)   limitations on the participation of foreign capital in terms of maximum percentage limit on foreign shareholding or the total value of individual or aggregate foreign investment.

Article 60
National Treatment under Chapter 7

1.   In the sectors inscribed in its Schedule of specific commitments in Annex IVc, and subject to any conditions and qualifications set out therein, each Party shall accord to services and service suppliers of the other Party, in respect of all measures affecting the supply of services, treatment no less favourable than that it accords to its own like services and service suppliers. [Note]

   Note: Specific commitments assumed under Article 60 shall not be construed to require either Party to
            compensate for any inherent competitive disadvantages which result from the foreign character of
            the relevant services or service suppliers.

2.   A Party may meet the requirement of paragraph 1 above by according to services and service suppliers of the other Party, either formally identical treatment or formally different treatment to that it accords to its own like services and service suppliers.

3.   Formally identical or formally different treatment shall be considered to be less favourable if it modifies the conditions of competition in favour of services or service suppliers of a Party compared to like services or service suppliers of the other Party.

4.   A Party may not invoke paragraphs 1, 2 and 3 above under Chapter 21 with respect to a measure of the other Party that falls within the scope of an international agreement between them relating to the avoidance of double taxation.

Article 61
Additional Commitments

The Parties may negotiate commitments with respect to measures affecting trade in services not subject to scheduling under Articles 59 and 60 above, including those regarding qualifications, standards or licensing matters. Such commitments shall be inscribed in a Party's Schedule of specific commitments in Annex IVc.

Article 62
Service Suppliers of Any Non-Party

Each Party shall also accord treatment granted under this Chapter to a service supplier other than those of the Parties, that is a juridical person constituted under the laws of either Party, and who supplies a service through commercial presence, provided that it engages in substantive business operations in the territory of either Party.

Article 63
Schedule of Specific Commitments under Chapter 7

1.   Each Party shall set out in a schedule the specific commitments it undertakes under Articles 59, 60 and 61. With respect to sectors where such commitments are undertaken, each Schedule of specific commitments in Annex IVc shall specify:

(a)   terms, limitations and conditions on market access;

(b)   conditions and qualifications on national treatment;

(c)   undertakings relating to additional commitments; and

(d)   where appropriate, the time-frame for implementation of such commitments.

2.   Measures inconsistent with both Articles 59 and 60 shall be inscribed in the column relating to Article 59. This inscription will be considered to provide a condition or qualification to Article 60 as well. 3. Schedules of specific commitments shall be annexed to this Agreement as Annex IVc.

4.   (a)   If a Party has entered into an international agreement on trade in services with a non-Party, or enters into such an agreement after this Agreement comes into force, it shall favourably consider according to services and service suppliers of the other Party, treatment no less favourable than the treatment that it accords to like services and service suppliers of that non-Party pursuant to such an agreement.

(b)   An international agreement referred to in sub-paragraph (a) above shall not include an agreement on the avoidance of double taxation or provisions on the avoidance of double taxation in any other international agreement or arrangement by which the Party is bound.

Article 64
Domestic Regulation

1.　In sectors where specific commitments are undertaken, each Party shall ensure that all measures of general application affecting trade in services are administered in a reasonable, objective and impartial manner.

2.　Each Party shall maintain or institute as soon as practicable judicial, arbitral or administrative tribunals or procedures which provide, at the request of an affected service supplier of the other Party, for the prompt review of, and where justified, appropriate remedies for, administrative decisions affecting trade in services. Where such procedures are not independent of the agency entrusted with the administrative decision concerned, the Party shall ensure that the procedures in fact provide for an objective and impartial review.

3.　The provisions of paragraph 2 above shall not be construed to require a Party to institute such tribunals or procedures where this would be inconsistent with its constitutional structure or the nature of its legal system.

4.　Where authorisation is required for the supply of a service on which a specific commitment has been made, the competent authorities of a Party shall, within a reasonable period of time after the submission of an application considered complete under that Party's domestic laws and regulations, inform the applicant of the decision concerning the application. At the request of the applicant, the competent authorities of the Party shall provide, without undue delay, information concerning the status of the application.

5.　In sectors where a Party has undertaken specific commitments subject to any terms, limitations, conditions or qualifications set out therein, the Partyshall not apply licensing and qualification requirements and technical standards that nullify or impair such specific commitments in a manner which:

(a)　does not comply with the following criteria:

(i)　based on objective and transparent criteria, such as competence and the ability to supply the service;

(ii)　not more burdensome than necessary to ensure the quality of the service; or

(iii)　in the case of licensing procedures, not in themselves a restriction on the supply of the service; and

(b)　could not reasonably have been expected of that Party at the time the specific commitments in those sectors were made.

6.　In determining whether a Party is in conformity with its obligations under paragraph 5 above, account shall be taken of international standards of relevant international organisations [Note] applicable to that Party.

> Note:　The term "relevant international organisations" refers to international bodies whose membership is open to the relevant bodies of both Parties.

Article 65
Monopolies and Exclusive Service Suppliers

1.   Each Party shall ensure that any monopoly supplier of a service in its territory does not, in the supply of the monopoly service in the relevant market, act in a manner inconsistent with the Party's specific commitments.

2.   Where a Party's monopoly supplier competes, either directly or through an affiliated company, in the supply of a service outside the scope of its monopoly rights and which is subject to that Party's specific commitments, the Party shall ensure that such a supplier does not abuse its monopoly position to act in its territory in a manner inconsistent with such commitments.

3.   If a Party has reason to believe that a monopoly supplier of a service of the other Party is acting in a manner inconsistent with paragraph 1 or 2 above, it may request the other Party to provide specific information concerning the relevant operations.

4.   The provisions of this Article shall also apply to cases of exclusive service suppliers, where a Party, formally or in effect:

       (a)   authorises or establishes a small number of service suppliers; and

       (b)   substantially prevents competition among those suppliers in its territory.

Article 66
Business Practices

1.   The Parties recognise that certain business practices of service suppliers, other than those falling under Article 65 above, may restrain competition and thereby restrict trade in services.

2.   A Party shall, at the request of the other Party, enter into consultations with a view to eliminating practices referred to in paragraph 1 above. The Party addressed shall accord full and sympathetic consideration to such a request and shall co-operate through the supply of publicly available non-confidential information of relevance to the matter in question. The Party addressed shall also provide other information available to the requesting Party, subject to its domestic law and to the conclusion of a satisfactory agreement concerning the safeguarding of its confidentiality by the requesting Party.

Article 67
Payments and Transfers

1.   Except under the circumstances envisaged in Article 68 below, a Party shall not apply restrictions on international transfers and payments for current transactions relating to its specific commitments.

2.   Nothing in this Chapter shall affect the rights and obligations of the Parties as members of the International Monetary Fund (hereinafter referred to in this Chapter as "the Fund") under the Articles of Agreement of the Fund, including the use of exchange actions which are in conformity with the Articles of Agreement of the Fund, provided that a Party shall not impose restrictions on any capital transactions inconsistently with its specific commitments regarding such transactions, except under Article 68 below, or at the request of the Fund.

Article 68
Restrictions to Safeguard the Balance of Payments under Chapter 7

1.   In the event of serious balance-of-payments and external financial difficulties or threat thereof, a Party may adopt or maintain restrictions on trade in services on which it has undertaken specific commitments, including on payments or transfers for transactions related to such commitments.

2.   The restrictions referred to in paragraph 1 above:

   (a)   shall not discriminate between the Parties;

   (b)   shall ensure that the other Party is treated as favourably as any non-Party;

   (c)   shall be consistent with the Articles of Agreement of the Fund;

   (d)   shall avoid unnecessary damage to the commercial, economic and financial interests of the other Party;

   (e)   shall not exceed those necessary to deal with the circumstances described in paragraph 1 above; and

   (f)   shall be temporary and be phased out progressively as the situation specified in paragraph 1 above improves.

3.   In determining the incidence of such restrictions, a Party may give priority to the supply of services which are more essential to their economic or development programmes. However, such restrictions shall not be adopted or maintained for the purpose of protecting a particular service sector.

4.   Any restrictions adopted or maintained under paragraph 1 of this Article, or any changes therein, shall be promptly notified to the other Party.

5.   Where a Party has adopted restrictions pursuant to paragraph 1 of this Article:

   (a)   that Party shall commence consultations with the other Party promptly in order to review the restrictions adopted by the former Party;

   (b)   the restrictions shall be subjected to annual review through further consultations, beginning one year after the date that the consultations referred to in sub-paragraph (a) above commenced. At these consultations, all restrictions applied for balance-of-payments purposes shall be reviewed. The Partiesmay also agree to a different frequency of such consultations;

   (c)   such consultations shall assess the balance-of-payments situation of the Party concerned and the restrictions adopted or maintained under this Article, taking into account, inter alia, such factors as:

      (i)   the nature and extent of the balance-of-payments and the external financial difficulties;

(ii)   the external economic and trading environment of the consulting Party; and

(iii)   alternative corrective measures which may be available;

(d)   the consultations shall address the compliance of the restrictions with paragraph 2 of this Article, in particular the progressive phaseout of restrictions in accordance with sub-paragraph (f) of paragraph 2 of this Article; and

(e)   in such consultations, all findings of statistical and other facts presented by the Fund relating to foreign exchange, monetary reserves and balance-of-payments, shall be accepted and conclusions shall be based on the assessment by the Fund of the balance-of-payments and the external financial situation of the consulting Party.

Article 69
General Exceptions under Chapter 7

1.   Subject to the requirement that such measures are not applied in a manner which would constitute a means of arbitrary or unjustifiable discrimination against the other Party, or a disguised restriction on trade in services between the Parties, nothing in this Chapter shall be construed to prevent the adoption or enforcement by either Party of measures:

(a)   necessary to protect public morals or to maintain public order; (Note)

> Note: The public order exception may be invoked only where a genuine and sufficiently serious threat is posed to one of the fundamental interests of society.

(b)   necessary to protect human, animal or plant life or health;

(c)   necessary to secure compliance with laws or regulations which are not inconsistent with the provisions of this Chapter including those relating to:

(i)   the prevention of deceptive and fraudulent practices or to deal with the effects of a default on services contracts;

(ii)   the protection of the privacy of individuals in relation to the processing and dissemination of personal data and the protection of confidentiality of individual records and accounts;

(iii)   safety;

d)   inconsistent with Article 60, provided that the difference in treatment is aimed at ensuring the equitable or effective [Note] imposition or collection of direct taxes in respect of services or service suppliers of the other Party.

> Note: Measures that are aimed at ensuring the equitable or effective imposition or collection of direct taxes include measures taken by a Party under its taxation system which:

(i)   apply to non-resident service suppliers in recognition of the fact that the tax obligation of non-residents is determined with respect to taxable items sourced or located in the Party's territory;

(ii)   apply to non-residents in order to ensure the imposition or collection of taxes in the Party's territory;

(iii)   apply to non-residents or residents in order to prevent the avoidance or evasion of taxes, including compliance measures;

(iv)   apply to consumers of services supplied in or from the territory of the other Party in order to ensure the imposition or collection of taxes on such consumers derived from sources in the Party's territory;

(v)   distinguish service suppliers subject to tax on worldwide taxable items from other service suppliers, in recognition of the difference in the nature of the tax base between them; or

(vi)   determine, allocate or apportion income, profit, gain, loss, deduction or credit of resident persons or branches, or between related persons or branches of the same person, in order to safeguard the Party's tax base.

Tax terms or concepts in sub-paragraph (d) of paragraph 1 of Article 69 and in this note are determined according to tax definitions and concepts, or equivalent or similar definitions and concepts, under the domestic law of the Party taking the measure.

2.   In the application of paragraph 1 above, the relevant interpretations and operation of the WTO Agreement shall, where appropriate, be taken into account.

Article 70
Denial of Benefits

A Party may deny the benefits of this Chapter:

(a)   to the supply of any service, if it establishes that the service is supplied from or in the territory of a non-Party;

(b)   in the case of the supply of a maritime transport service, if it establishes that the service is supplied:

(i)   by a vessel registered under the laws of a non-Party, and

(ii)   by a person which operates or uses the vessel in whole or in part but which is of a non-Party:

(c)   to any service supplier that is a juridical person, if it establishes that the service supplier is neither a "service supplier of the other Party" as defined in sub-paragraph (j) of paragraph 6 of Article 58 nor a "service supplier other than those of the Parties" granted benefits under Article 62.

CHAPTER 8
INVESTMENT

Article 71
Scope of Chapter 8

1.   This Chapter shall apply to measures adopted or maintained by a Party relating to:

    (a)   investors of the other Party in the territory of the former Party; and

    (b)   investments of investors of the other Party in the territory of the former Party.

2.   This Chapter shall not apply to government procurement.

3.   Movement of natural persons who are investors shall be governed by Chapter 9.

Article 72
Definitions under Chapter 8

For the purposes of this Chapter:

(a)   the term "investments" means every kind of asset owned or controlled, directly or indirectly, by an investor, including:

    (i)   an enterprise;

    (ii)   shares, stocks or other forms of equity participation in an enterprise, including rights derived therefrom;

    (iii)   bonds, debentures, and loans and other forms of debt, (Note) including rights derived therefrom;

    (iv)   rights under contracts, including turnkey, construction, management, production or revenue-sharing contracts;

    (v)   claims to money and claims to any performance under contract (Note) having a financial value;

        Note: For the purposes of this Chapter, "loans and other forms of debt" described in (iii) of sub-paragraph (a) of Article 72 and "claims to money and claims to any performance under contract" described in (v) of sub-paragraph (a) of Article 72 refer to assets which relate to a business activity and do not refer to assets which are of a personal nature, unrelated to any business activity.

    (vi)   intellectual property rights, including trademarks, industrial designs, layout-designs of integrated circuits, copyrights, patents, trade names, indications of source or geographical indications and undisclosed information;

    (vii)   rights conferred pursuant to laws and regulations or contracts such as concessions, licences, authorisations, and permits; and

(viii)   any other tangible and intangible, movable and immovable property, and any related property rights, such as leases, mortgages, liens and pledges;

(b)   the term "investments" also includes amounts yielded by investments, in particular, profit, interest, capital gains, dividends, royalties and fees. A change in the form in which assets are invested does not affect their character as investments;

(c)   the term "investor" means any person that seeks to make, is making, or has made, investments;

(d)   the term "person" means either a natural person or an enterprise;

(e)   the term "investor of the other Party" means any natural person of the other Party or any enterprise of the other Party;

(f)   the term "natural person of the other Party" means a natural person who resides in the territory of the other Party or elsewhere and who under the law of the other Party:

(i)   in respect of Japan, is a national of Japan; and

(ii)   in respect of Singapore, is a national of Singapore or has the right of permanent residence in Singapore;

(g)   the term "enterprise" means any legal person or any other entity duly constituted or otherwise organised under applicable law, whether for profit or otherwise, and whether privately-owned or controlled or governmentally-owned or controlled, including any corporation, trust, partnership, joint venture, sole proprietorship, association, organisation, company or branch;

(h)   the term "enterprise of the other Party" means any enterprise duly constituted or otherwise organised under applicable law of the other Party, except an enterprise owned or controlled by persons of non-Parties and not engaging in substantive business operations in the territory of the other Party; and

(i)   an enterprise is:

(i)   "owned" by persons of non-Parties if more than 50 percent of the equity interest in it is beneficially owned by persons of non-Parties; and

(ii)   "controlled" by persons of non-Parties if such persons have the power to name a majority of its directors or otherwise to legally direct its actions.

Article 73
National Treatment under Chapter 8

Each Party shall within its territory accord to investors of the other Party and to their investments in relation to the establishment, acquisition, expansion, management, operation, maintenance, use, possession, liquidation, sale, or other disposition of investments, treatment no less favourable than the treatment which it accords in like circumstances to its own investors and investments (hereinafter referred to in this Chapter as "national treatment").

Article 74
Access to the Courts of Justice

Each Party shall within its territory accord to investors of the other Party treatment no less favourable than the treatment which it accords in like circumstances to its own investors, with respect to access to its courts of justice and administrative tribunals and agencies in all degrees of jurisdiction both in pursuit and in defence of such investors' rights.

Article 75
Prohibition of Performance Requirements

1.   Neither Party shall impose or enforce any of the following requirements as a condition for the establishment, acquisition, expansion, management, operation, maintenance, use or possession of investments in its territory of an investor of the other Party:

(a)   to export a given level or percentage of goods or services;

(b)   to achieve a given level or percentage of domestic content;

(c)   to purchase or use goods produced or services provided in the territory of the former Party, or to purchase goods or services from natural or legal persons in the territory of the former Party;

(d)   to relate the volume or value of imports to the volume or value of exports or to the amount of foreign exchange inflows associated with such investments;

(e)   to restrict sales of goods or services in the territory of the former Party that such investments produce or provide by relating such sales to the volume or value of its exports or foreign exchange earnings;

(f)   to transfer technology, a production process or other proprietary knowledge to a natural or legal person of the former Party, except when the requirement:

    (i)   is imposed or enforced by a court, administrative tribunal or competition authority to remedy an alleged violation of competition laws; or

    (ii)   concerns the transfer of intellectual property which is undertaken in a manner not inconsistent with the Agreement on Trade-Related Aspects of Intellectual Property Rights in Annex 1C to the WTO Agreement;

(g)   to locate its headquarters for a specific region or the world market in the territory of the former Party;

(h)   to achieve a given level or value of research and development in the territory of the former Party; or

(i)   to supply one or more of the goods that it produces or the services that it provides to a specific region outside the territory of the former Party exclusively from the territory of the former Party.

2.   Each Party is not precluded by paragraph 1 above from conditioning the receipt or continued receipt of an advantage, in connection with investments in its territory of an investor of the other Party, on compliance with any of the requirements set forth in sub-paragraphs (f) through (i) of paragraph 1 above.

3.   Nothing in this Article shall be construed so as to derogate from the obligations of the Parties under the Agreement on Trade Related Investment Measures in Annex 1A to the WTO Agreement.

Article 76
Specific Exceptions

1.   Articles 73 and 75 shall not apply to investors and investments, in respect of:

    (a)   any exception specified by the Parties in Annexes VA and VB; and

    (b)   an amendment or modification to any exception referred to in sub-paragraph (a) above, provided that the amendment or modification does not decrease the level of conformity of the exception with Articles 73 and 75.

2.   The exceptions referred to in sub-paragraph (a) of paragraph 1 above shall include the following elements, to the extent that these elements are applicable:

    (a)   sector or matter;

    (b)   obligation or article in respect of which the exception is taken;

    (c)   legal source or authority of the exception; and

    (d)   succinct description of the exception.

3.   If a Party makes an amendment or modification referred to in sub-paragraph (b) of paragraph 1 of this Article, that Party shall, prior to the implementation of the amendment or modification, or in exceptional circumstances, as soon as possible thereafter:

    (a)   notify the other Party of the elements set out in paragraph 2 above; and

    (b)   provide to the other Party, upon request, particulars of the amended or modified exception.

4.   Each Party shall endeavour, where appropriate, to reduce or eliminate the exceptions specified in Annexes VA and VB respectively.

Article 77
Expropriation and Compensation

1.   Each Party shall accord to investments in its territory of investors of the other Party fair and equitable treatment and full protection and security.

2.   Neither Party shall expropriate or nationalise investments in its territory of an investor of the other Party or take any measure equivalent to expropriation or nationalisation (hereinafter referred to in this Chapter as "expropriation") except for a public purpose, on a non-discriminatory basis, in accordance with due process of law, and upon payment of compensation in accordance with this Article.

3.   Compensation shall be equivalent to the fair market value of the expropriated investments. The fair market value shall not reflect any change in market value occurring because the expropriation had become publicly known earlier, but may, insofar as such expropriation relates to land, reflect the market value before the expropriation occurred, the trend in the market value, and adjustments to the market value in accordance with the laws of the expropriating Party concerning expropriation.

4.   The compensation shall be paid without delay and shall carry an appropriate interest taking into account the length of time from the time of expropriation until the time of payment. It shall be effectively realisable and freely transferable and shall be freely convertible, at the market exchange rate prevailing on the date of the expropriation, into the currency of the Party of the investors concerned and freely usable currencies defined in the Articles of Agreement of the International Monetary Fund.

5.   The investors affected by expropriation shall have a right of access to the courts of justice or the administrative tribunals or agencies of the Party making the expropriation to seek a prompt review of the investor's case or the amount of compensation that has been assessed in accordance with the principles set out in this Article.

Article 78
Repurchase of Leases

If an agency of the government of a Party responsible for leasing industrial land repurchases a leasehold interest in land owned by an investor of the other Party, that agency shall take into consideration the following matters:

(a)   the value attributable to the remaining period of such leasehold interest;

(b)   priority allocation by the agency of a suitable, alternative property for the investor; and

(c)   reasonable relocation costs that would be incurred by the investor in relocating to the alternative property within the territory of the Party.

Article 79
Protection from Strife

1.   Each Party shall accord to investors of the other Party that have suffered loss or damage relating to their investments in the territory of the former Party due to armed conflict, or state of emergency such as revolution, insurrection and civil disturbance, treatment, as regards restitution, indemnification, compensation or any other settlement, that is no less favourable than that which it accords to its own investors.

2.   Any payments made pursuant to paragraph 1 above shall be effectively realisable, freely convertible and freely transferable.

Article 80
Transfers

1.   Each Party shall allow all payments relating to investments in its territory of an investor of the other Party to be freely transferred into and out of its territory without delay. Such transfers shall include:

(a)   the initial capital and additional amounts to maintain or increase investments;

(b)   profits, capital gains, dividends, royalties, interests and other current incomes accruing from investments;

(c)   proceeds from the total or partial sale or liquidation of investments;

(d)   payments made under a contract including loan payments in connection with investments;

(e)   earnings of investors of a Party who work in connection with investments in the territory of the other Party;

(f)   payments made in accordance with Articles 77 and 79; and

(g)   payments arising out of the settlement of a dispute under Article 82.

2.   Each Party shall allow transfers to be made without delay in a freely usable currency at the market rate of exchange prevailing on the date of transfer.

3.   Notwithstanding paragraphs 1 and 2 above, a Party may delay or prevent a transfer through the equitable, non-discriminatory and good-faith application of its laws relating to:

(a)   bankruptcy, insolvency or the protection of the rights of creditors;
(b)   the issuing, trading or dealing in securities;

(c)   criminal matters;

(d)   ensuring compliance with orders or judgements in adjudicatory proceedings; or

(e)   obligations of investors arising from social security and public retirement plans.

Article 81
Subrogation

1.   If a Party or its designated agency makes a payment to any of its investors pursuant to an indemnity, guarantee or contract of insurance, arising from or pertaining to an investment of that investor within the territory of the other Party, the other Party shall:

(a)   recognise the assignment, to the former Party or its designated agency, of any right or claim of such investor that formed the basis of such payment; and

(b)   recognise the right of the former Party or its designated agency to exercise by virtue of subrogation any such right or claim to the same extent as the original right or claim of the investor.

2.   Paragraphs 2 to 5 of Article 77, and Articles 79 and 80, shall apply <u>mutatis mutandis</u> as regards payment to be made to the Party or its designated agency first mentioned in paragraph 1 above by virtue of such assignment of right or claim, and the transfer of such payment.

Article 82
Settlement of Investment Disputes between a Party and an investor of the other Party

1.   For the purposes of this Chapter, an investment dispute is a dispute between a Party and an investor of the other Party that has incurred loss or damage by reason of, or arising out of, an alleged breach of any right conferred by this Chapter with respect to the investments of the investor of that other Party.

2.   In the event of an investment dispute, such investment dispute shall, as far as possible, be settled amicably through consultations between the parties to the investment dispute.

3.   If an investment dispute cannot be settled through such consultations within five months from the date on which the investor requested for the consultations in writing, and if the investor concerned has not submitted the investment dispute for resolution (i) under administrative or judicial settlement, or (ii) in accordance with any applicable, previously agreed dispute settlement procedures, that investor may either:

(a)   request the establishment of an arbitral tribunal in accordance with the procedures set out in Annex Vc and submit the investment dispute to that tribunal;

(b)   submit the investment dispute to conciliation or arbitration in accordance with the provisions of the Convention on the Settlement of Investment Disputes between States and Nationals of Other States done at Washington, March 18, 1965 (hereinafter referred to in this Chapter as "the ICSID Convention"), so long as the ICSID Convention is in force between the Parties, or conciliation or arbitration under the Additional Facility Rules of the International Centre for Settlement of Investment Disputes (hereinafter referred to in this Chapter as "ICSID") so long as the ICSID Convention is not in force between the Parties; or

(c)   submit the investment dispute to arbitration under the Arbitration Rules of the United Nations Commission on International Trade Law, adopted by the United Nations Commission on International Trade Law on April 28, 1976.

4.   Each Party hereby consents to the submission of investment disputes to international conciliation or arbitration as provided for in paragraph 3 above, in accordance with the provisions of this Article, provided that:

(a)   less than three years have elapsed since the date the investor knew or ought to have known, whichever is the earlier, of the loss or damage which, it is alleged, has been incurred by the investor; and

(b)   in the case of arbitration in accordance with the provisions of the ICSID Convention referred to in sub-paragraph (b) of paragraph 3 above, if the Chairman of ICSID is asked to appoint an arbitrator or arbitrators pursuant to Article 38 or 56(3) of the ICSID Convention, the Chairman:

(i)   allows both the Party and the investor to each indicate up to three nationalities, the appointment of arbitrators of which pursuant to Article 38 or 56(3) of the ICSID Convention is unacceptable to it; and

(ii)   does not appoint as arbitrator any person who is, by virtue of sub-paragraph (i) above, excluded by either the Party or the investor or both the Party and the investor.

5.   When the condition set out in sub-paragraph (a) of paragraph 4 above is not met, the consent given in paragraph 4 above shall be invalidated.

6.   When the conditions set out in sub-paragraph (b) of paragraph 4 of this Article are not met, the consent to arbitration by ICSID given in paragraph 4 of this Article shall be invalidated. In such circumstances, a different method of dispute settlement can be chosen from among those methods provided for in paragraph 3 of this Article other than ICSID arbitration.

7.   Paragraphs 3 and 4 of this Article shall not apply if an investor which is an enterprise of a Party owned or controlled by persons of non-Parties submits an investment dispute with respect to its investments in the territory of the other Party, unless the investments concerned have been established, acquired or expanded in the territory of that other Party.

8.   An investor to an investment dispute who intends to submit an investment dispute pursuant to paragraph 3 of this Article shall give to the Party that is a party to the investment dispute written notice of intent to do so at least 90 days before the claim is submitted. The notice of intent shall specify:

(a)   the name and address of the investor concerned;

(b)   the specific measures of that Party at issue and a brief summary of the factual and legal basis of the dispute sufficient to present the problem clearly, including the provisions of this Chapter alleged to have been breached; and

(c)   the dispute settlement procedures set forth in sub-paragraph (a), (b) or (c) of paragraph 3 of this Article which the investor will seek.

9.   When an investor of a Party submits an investment dispute pursuant to paragraph 3 of this Article and the disputing Party invokes Article 84 or 85, the arbitrators to be selected shall, on the request of the disputing Party or investor, have the necessary expertise relevant to the specific financial matters under dispute.

10.   (a)   The award shall include:

(i)   a judgement whether or not there has been a breach by a Party of any rights conferred by this Chapter in respect of the investor of the other Party and its investments; and

(ii)   a remedy if there has been such breach.

(b)   The award rendered in accordance with sub-paragraph (a) above shall be final and binding upon the Party and the investor, except to the extent provided for in sub-paragraphs (c) and (d) below.

(c)   Where an award provides that there has been a breach by a Party of any rights conferred by this Chapter in respect of the investor of the other Party and its investments, the Party to the dispute is entitled to implement the award through one of the following remedies, in lieu of the remedy indicated pursuant to (ii) of sub-paragraph (a) of this paragraph:

(i)   pecuniary compensation, including interest from the time the loss or damage was incurred until time of payment;

(ii)   restitution in kind; or

(iii)   pecuniary compensation and restitution in combination, provided that:

(A)   the Party notifies the investor, within 30 days after the date of the award, that it will implement the award through one of the remedies indicated in (i), (ii) or (iii) of this sub-paragraph; and

(B)   where the Party chooses to implement the award in accordance with (i) or (iii) of this sub-paragraph, the Party and the investor agree as to the amount of pecuniary compensation, or in lieu of such agreement, a decision pursuant to sub-paragraph (d) below is made.

(d)   If the Party and the investor are unable to agree, within 60 days after the date of the award, as to the amount of pecuniary compensation as provided for in (B) of sub-paragraph (c) above, the matter may be referred, by either the Party or the investor, to the arbitral tribunal that rendered the award. The award on the amount of pecuniary compensation in accordance with this paragraph is final and binding on both the Party and the investor.

(e)   The award shall be executed by the applicable laws and regulations concerning the execution of such awards in force in the Party in whose territory such execution is sought.

11.   Nothing in this Article shall be construed so as to prevent an investor to an investment dispute from seeking administrative or judicial settlement within the territory of the Party that is a party to the investment dispute.

12.   Neither Party shall give diplomatic protection, or bring an international claim, in respect of an investment dispute which one of its investors and the other Party shall have consented to

submit or shall have submitted to arbitration under this Article, unless such other Party shall have failed to abide by and comply with the award rendered in such dispute. Diplomatic protection, for the purposes of this paragraph, shall not include informal diplomatic exchanges for the sole purpose of facilitating a settlement of the dispute.

Article 83
General Exceptions under Chapter 8

1.   Subject to the requirement that such measures are not applied in a manner which would constitute a means of arbitrary or unjustifiable discrimination against the other Party, or a disguised restriction on investments of investors of a Party in the territory of the other Party, nothing in this Chapter shall be construed to prevent the adoption or enforcement by either Party of measures:

(a)   necessary to protect public morals or to maintain public order; [Note]

> Note: The public order exception may be invoked only where a genuine and sufficiently serious threat is posed to one of the fundamental interests of society.

(b)   necessary to protect human, animal or plant life or health;

(c)   necessary to secure compliance with the laws or regulations which are not inconsistent with the provisions of this Agreement including those relating to:

(i)   the prevention of deceptive and fraudulent practices or to deal with the effects of a default on contract;

(ii)   the protection of the privacy of the individual in relation to the processing and dissemination of personal data and the protection of confidentiality of personal records and accounts;

(iii)   safety;

(d)   relating to prison labour;

(e)   imposed for the protection of national treasures of artistic, historic, or archaeological value;

(f)   to conserve exhaustible natural resources if such measures are made effective in conjunction with restrictions on domestic production or consumption.

2.   In cases where a Party takes any measure pursuant to paragraph 1 above or Article 4, which it implements after this Agreement comes into force, such Party shall make reasonable effort to notify the other Party of the description of the measure either before such measure is taken or as soon as possible thereafter, if such measure could affect investments or investors of the other Party in respect of obligations made under this Chapter.

Article 84
Temporary Safeguard

1.   A Party may adopt or maintain measures inconsistent with its obligations provided for in Article 73 relating to cross-border capital transactions or Article 80:

(a)   in the event of serious balance-of-payments or external financial difficulties or threat thereof; or

(b)   where, in exceptional circumstances, movements of capital result in serious economic and financial disturbance in the Party concerned.

2.   The measures referred to in paragraph 1 above:

(a)   shall be consistent with the Articles of Agreement of the International Monetary Fund;

(b)   shall not exceed those necessary to deal with the circumstances described in paragraph 1 above;

(c)   shall be temporary and shall be eliminated as soon as conditions permit;

(d)   shall promptly be notified to the other Party;

(e)   shall not discriminate between the Parties;

(f)   shall ensure that the other Party is treated as favourably as any non-Party; and

(g)   shall avoid unnecessary damage to the commercial, economic and financial interests of the other Party.

3.   Nothing in this Chapter shall be regarded as affecting the rights enjoyed and obligations undertaken by a Party as a party to the Articles of Agreement of the International Monetary Fund.

Article 85
Prudential Measures

1.   Notwithstanding any other provisions of this Chapter, a Party shall not be prevented from taking measures for prudential reasons, including measures for the protection of investors, depositors, policy holders or persons to whom a fiduciary duty is owed by an enterprise supplying financial services, or to ensure the integrity and stability of the financial system.

2.   Where such measures do not conform with the provisions of this Chapter, they shall not be used as a means of avoiding the Party's commitments or obligations under this Chapter.

Article 86
Intellectual Property Rights

Notwithstanding the provisions of Article 73, the Parties agree in respect of intellectual property rights that national treatment as provided for in that Article shall apply only to the extent as provided for in the Agreement on Trade-RelatedAspects of Intellectual Property Rights in Annex 1C to the WTO Agreement.

Article 87
Taxation Measures as Expropriation

1.   Article 77 shall apply to taxation measures, to the extent that such taxation measures constitute expropriation as provided for in paragraph 2 of Article 77.

2.   Where paragraph 1 above applies, Articles 74, 82, 88 and paragraph 1 of Article 89 shall also apply in respect of taxation measures.

Article 88
Joint Committee on Investment

1.   For the purposes of effective implementation of this Chapter, a Joint Committee on Investment (hereinafter referred to in this Article as "the Committee") shall be established. The functions of the Committee shall be:

(a)   reviewing and discussing the implementation and operation of this Chapter;

(b)   reviewing the specific exceptions under paragraph 1 of Article 76 for the purpose of contributing to the reduction or elimination, where appropriate, of such exceptions, and encouraging favourable conditions for investors of both Parties; and

(c)   discussing other investment related issues concerning this Chapter.

2.   The Committee may decide to hold a joint meeting with the private sector.

Article 89
Application of Chapter 8

1.   In fulfilling the obligations under this Chapter, each Party shall take such reasonable measures as are available to it to ensure observance by its local governments and non-governmental bodies in the exercise of power delegated by central or local governments within its territory.

2.   If a Party has entered into an international agreement on investment with a non-Party, or enters into such an agreement after this Agreement comes into force, it shall favourably consider according to investors of the other Party and to their investments, treatment, in relation to the establishment, acquisition, expansion, management, operation, maintenance, use, possession, liquidation, sale, or other disposition of investments, no less favourable than the treatment that it accords in like circumstances to investors of that non-Party and their investments pursuant to such an agreement.

CHAPTER 9

MOVEMENT OF NATURAL PERSONS

Article 90
Scope of Chapter 9

1.   This Chapter applies to measures affecting the movement of natural persons of a Party who enter the territory of the other Party for business purposes.

2.   This Agreement shall not apply to measures regarding nationality or citizenship, residence on a permanent basis or employment on a permanent basis.

Article 91
Definitions under Chapter 9

The term "natural person of the other Party" means a natural person who resides in the territory of the other Party or elsewhere and who under the law of the other Party:

(a)   in respect of Japan, is a national of Japan; and

b)   in respect of Singapore, is a national of Singapore or has the right of permanent residence in Singapore.

Article 92
Specific Commitments under Chapter 9

1.   Each Party shall set out in Part A of Annex VI the specific commitments it undertakes for:

    (a)   short-term business visitors of the other Party; and

    (b)   intra-corporate transferees of the other Party.

2.   Each Party shall set out in Part B of Annex VI the specific commitments it undertakes, to be implemented in accordance with its laws and regulations, for:

    (a)   investors of the other Party; and

    (b)   natural persons of the other Party who engage in work on the basis of a personal contract with public or private organisations in its territory.

3.   Natural persons covered by a specific commitment referred to in paragraphs 1 and 2 above shall be granted entry and stay in accordance with the terms and conditions of the specific commitment.

4.   The specific commitments referred to in paragraphs 1 and 2 of this Article shall apply only to sectors where specific commitments referred to in Article 63 are undertaken under Chapter 7 and no specific exceptions are made under Chapter 8.

Article 93
Mutual Recognition of Professional Qualifications

1.   A Party may recognise the education or experience obtained, requirements met, or licences or certifications granted in the territory of the other Party for the purposes of the fulfilment, in whole or in part, of its standards or criteria for the authorisation, licensing or certification of natural persons with professional qualifications.

2.   Recognition referred to in paragraph 1 above, which may be achieved through harmonisation or otherwise, may be based upon an agreement or arrangement between the Parties or may be accorded unilaterally.

3. Where a Party recognises, by agreement or arrangement or unilaterally, the education or experience obtained, requirements met or licences or certifications granted in the territory of a non-Party, the Party shall accord the other Party an adequate opportunity to demonstrate that the education or experience obtained, requirements met or licences or certifications granted in the territory of the other Party should also be recognised.

Article 94

Joint Committee on Mutual Recognition of Professional Qualifications

1.   For the purposes of effective implementation of Article 93 above, a Joint Committee on Mutual Recognition of Professional Qualifications (hereinafter referred to in this Article as "the Committee") shall be established.

The functions of the Committee shall be:

(a)   reviewing and discussing the issues concerning the effective implementation of Article 93 above;

(b)   identifying and recommending areas for and ways of furthering co-operation between the Parties; and

(c)   discussing other issues relating to the implementation of Article 93 above.

2.   The composition of the Committee shall be specified in the Implementing Agreement.

Article 95
General Provisions for Chapter 9

1.   Subject to the requirement that such measures are not applied in a manner which would constitute a means of arbitrary or unjustifiable discrimination against the other Party, or a disguised restriction on trade in services between the Parties or on investments of investors of a Party in the territory of the other Party, nothing in this Chapter shall be construed to prevent the adoption or enforcement by either Party of measures:

(a)   necessary to protect public morals or to maintain public order; [Note]

> Note: The public order exception may be invoked only where a genuine and sufficiently serious threat is posed to one of the fundamental interests of society.

(b)   necessary to protect human, animal or plant life or health;

(c)   necessary to secure compliance with laws or regulations which are not inconsistent with the provisions of this Chapter including those relating to:

    (i)   the prevention of deceptive and fraudulent practices or to deal with the effects of a default on services contracts;

    (ii)   the protection of the privacy of individuals in relation to the processing and dissemination of personal data and the protection of confidentiality of individual records and accounts;

    (iii)   safety.

2.   This Chapter shall not prevent a Party from applying measures to regulate the entry of natural persons of the other Party into, or their temporary stay in, its territory, including those measures necessary to protect the integrity of, and to ensure the orderly movement of natural persons across, its borders, provided that such measures are not applied in such a manner as to nullify or impair the benefits accruing to the other Party under the terms of a specific commitment. (Note)

    Note: The sole fact of requiring a visa for natural persons of a certain nationality or citizenship and not for those of others shall not be regarded as nullifying or impairing benefits under a specific commitment.

CHAPTER 10
INTELLECTUAL PROPERTY

Article 96
Areas and Forms of Co-operation under Chapter 10

1.   The Parties, recognising the growing importance of intellectual property (hereinafter referred to in this Chapter as "IP") as a factor of economic competitiveness in the knowledge-based economy, and of IP protection in this new environment, shall develop their co-operation in the field of IP.

2.   The areas of the co-operation pursuant to paragraph 1 above may include:

(a)   patents, trade secrets and related rights;

(b)   trade marks and related rights;

(c)   repression of unfair competition;

(d)   copyright, designs and related rights;

(e)   IP brokerage or licensing, IP management, registration and exploitation, and patent mapping;

(f)   IP protection in the digital environment and the growth and development of e-commerce;

(g)   technology and market intelligence; and

(h)   IP education and awareness programmes.

3.   The forms of the co-operation under paragraph 1 of this Article may include:

(a)   exchanging information and sharing experiences on IP and on relevant IP events, activities and initiatives organised in their respective territories;

(b)   jointly undertaking training and exchanging of experts in the field of IP for the purposes of contributing to a better understanding of each Party's IP policies and experiences; and

(c)   disseminating information, sharing experiences and conducting training on IP enforcement.

Article 97
Joint Committee on Intellectual Property

1.   For the purposes of effective implementation of this Chapter, a Joint Committee on IP (hereinafter referred to in this Article as "the Committee") shall be established. The functions of the Committee shall be:

(a)   overseeing and reviewing the co-operation and implementation of this Chapter;

(b)   providing advice to the Parties with regard to the implementation of this Chapter;

(c)   considering and recommending new areas of co-operation under this Chapter; and

(d)   discussing other issues relating to IP.

2.   The composition of the Committee shall be specified in the Implementing Agreement.

Article 98
Facilitation of Patenting Process

1.   Singapore shall, in accordance with its laws and regulations, take appropriate measures to facilitate the patenting process of an application filed in Singapore that corresponds to an application filed in Japan.

2. The details of such measures taken by Singapore pursuant to paragraph 1 above shall be specified in the Implementing Agreement.

Article 99
Facilitation of the Use of IP Databases

The Parties shall take appropriate measures, as set out in the Implementing Agreement, to facilitate the use of the Parties' IP databases open to the public.

Article 100
Costs of Co-operative Activities under Chapter 10

Costs of co-operative activities shall be borne in such manner as may be mutually agreed.

CHAPTER 11
GOVERNMENT PROCUREMENT

Article 101
Scope of Chapter 11

1.   Paragraph 2 of Article I, and Article II to Article XXIII of the Agreement on Government Procurement in Annex 4 to the WTO Agreement (hereinafter referred to in this Agreement as "the GPA") (except for sub-paragraph (b) of paragraph 1 of Article III, Article V, paragraph 2 of Article XVI, paragraph 5 of Article XIX, Article XXI, Article XXII and paragraph 1 of Article XXIII) shall apply mutatis mutandis to procurement of goods and services specified in Annex VIIA, by entities specified in Annex VIIB. The threshold for a procurement covered by the provisions of this Chapter is SDR 100,000.

2.   Where entities specified in Annex VIIB, in the context of procurement covered under this Agreement, require enterprises not included in Annex VIIB to award contracts in accordance with particular requirements, Article III of the GPA (except for sub-paragraph (b) of paragraph 1) shall apply mutatis mutandis to such requirements.

3.   When an entity listed in Annex VIIB is privatised, this Chapter shall no longer apply to that entity. A Party shall notify the other Party of the name of such entity before it is privatised or as soon as possible thereafter.

4.   For the purposes of paragraph 3 above, a government entity is construed as privatised if it has been re-constituted to be a legal person operating commercially and is no longer entitled to exercise governmental authority, even though the government possesses holdings thereof or appoints members of the board of directors thereto.

5.   Nothing in this Chapter shall be construed so as to derogate from the obligations of the Parties as parties to the GPA.

Article 102
Exchange of Information on Government Procurement

The government officials of the Parties responsible for procurement policy shall meet upon the request of either Party and, subject to the laws and regulations of each Party, exchange information in respect of government procurement.

CHAPTER 12
COMPETITION

Article 103
Anti-competitive Activities

1.   Each Party shall, in accordance with its applicable laws and regulations, take measures which it considers appropriate against anti-competitive activities, in order to facilitate trade and investment flows between the Parties and the efficient functioning of its markets.

2.   Each Party shall, when necessary, endeavour to review and improve or to adopt laws and regulations to effectively control anti-competitive activities.

Article 104
Co-operation on Controlling Anti-competitive Activities

1.   The Parties shall, in accordance with their respective laws and regulations, co-operate in the field of controlling anti-competitive activities subject to their available resources.

2.   The sectors, details and procedures of co-operation under this Chapter shall be specified in the Implementing Agreement.

3.   Pursuant to paragraph 1 of this Article, the Parties shall exchange information as provided for in the Implementing Agreement with respect to the implementation of this Chapter. Article 3 shall not apply to such exchange of information.

Article 105
Dispute Settlement

The dispute settlement procedures provided for in Chapter 21 shall not apply to this Chapter.

CHAPTER 13
FINANCIAL SERVICES CO-OPERATION

Article 106
Co-operation in the Field of Financial Services

The Parties shall co-operate in the field of financial services with a view to:

(a)   promoting regulatory co-operation in the field of financial services;

(b)   facilitating development of financial markets, including capital markets, in the Parties and in Asia; and

c)   improving financial market infrastructure of the Parties.

Article 107
Regulatory Co-operation

1.   The Parties shall promote regulatory co-operation in the field of financial services, with a view to:

(a)   implementing sound prudential policies, and enhancing effective supervision of financial institutions of either Party operating in the territory of the other Party;

(b)   responding properly to issues relating to globalisation in financial services, including those provided by electronic means;

(c)   maintaining an environment that does not stifle legitimate financial market innovations; and

(d)   conducting oversight of global financial institutions to minimise systemic risks and to limit contagion effects in the event of crises.

2.   As a part of regulatory co-operation as set out in paragraph 1 above, the Parties shall, in accordance with their respective laws and regulations, co-operate in sharing information on securities markets and securities derivatives markets of the respective Parties as provided for in the Implementing Agreement, for the purposes of contributing to the effective enforcement of the securities laws of each Party.

3.   Articles 2 and 3 and Chapter 21 shall not apply to the co-operation between the Parties in sharing information on securities markets and securities derivatives markets as set out in paragraph 2 above.

Article 108
Capital Market Development

The Parties, recognising a growing need to enhance the competitiveness of their capital markets and to preserve and strengthen their stability in rapidly evolving global financial transactions, shall co-operate in facilitating the development of the capital markets in the Parties with a view to fostering sound and progressive capital markets and improving their depth and liquidity.

Article 109
Improvement of Financial Market Infrastructure

The Parties, recognising that efficient and reliable financial market infrastructure will facilitate trade and investment, shall co-operate in strengthening their financial market infrastructure.-

Article 110
Development of Regional Financial Markets including Capital Markets

The Parties, recognising the importance of stable and well-functioning financial markets, including capital markets, shall co-operate with a view to contributing to further development of cross-border financial activities in Asia and to regional financial stability.

Article 111
Joint Committee on Financial Services Co-operation

1.   For the purposes of effective implementation of this Chapter, a Joint Committee on Financial Services Co-operation (hereinafter referred to in this Article as "the Committee") shall be established. The functions of the Committee shall include:

(a)   reviewing and discussing issues concerning the effective implementation of this Chapter;

(b)   identifying and recommending to the Parties areas for further co-operation; and

(c)   discussing other issues relating to financial services co-operation between the Parties.

2.   The Committee may establish expert working groups to examine specific issues and initiatives in detail.

3.   The composition of the Committee shall be specified in the Implementing Agreement.

CHAPTER 14
INFORMATION AND COMMUNICATIONS TECHNOLOGY

Article 112
Co-operation in the Field of ICT

The Parties, recognising the rapid development, led by the private sector, of ICT and of business practices concerning ICT-related services both in the domestic and the international contexts, shall co-operate to promote the development of ICT and ICT-related services with a view to obtaining the maximum benefit of the use of ICT for the Parties.

Article 113
Areas and Forms of Co-operation under Chapter 14

1.   The areas of co-operation pursuant to Article 112 above may include the following:

(a)   promotion of electronic commerce;

(b)   promotion of the use by consumers, the public sector and the private sector, of ICT-related services, including newly emerging services; and

(c)   human resource development relating to ICT.

2.   The Parties may set out, in the Implementing Agreement, specific areas of co-operation which they deem important.

3.   The forms of co-operation pursuant to Article 112 above may include the following:

(a)   promoting dialogue on policy issues;

(b)   promoting co-operation between the private sectors of the Parties;

(c)   enhancing co-operation in international fora relating to ICT; and

(d)   undertaking other appropriate co-operative activities.

Article 114
Joint Committee on ICT

1.   For the purposes of effective implementation of this Chapter, a Joint Committee on ICT (hereinafter referred to in this Article as "the Committee") shall be established. The functions of the Committee shall be:

(a)   reviewing and discussing issues concerning the effective implementation of this Chapter;

(b)   identifying ways of further co-operation between the Parties in the field of ICT; and

(c)   discussing other issues relating to ICT.

2.   The composition of the Committee shall be specified in the Implementing Agreement.

CHAPTER 15
SCIENCE AND TECHNOLOGY

Article 115
Co-operation in the Field of Science and Technology

1.   The Parties, recognising that science and technology, particularly in advanced areas, will contribute to the continued expansion of their respective economies in the medium and long term, shall develop and promote co-operative activities between the governments of the Parties (hereinafter referred to in this Chapter as "Co-operative Activities") for peaceful purposes in the field of science and technology on the basis of equality and mutual benefit.

2.   The Parties shall also encourage, where appropriate, other co-operative activities between parties, one or both of whom are entities in their respective territories other than the governments of the Parties (hereinafter referred to in this Chapter as "Other Co-operative Activities").

Article 116
Areas and Forms of Co-operative Activities under Chapter 15

The Parties may agree on the areas and forms of Co-operative Activities, which are to be specified in the Implementing Agreement.

Article 117
Joint Committee on Science and Technology

1.   For the purposes of effective implementation of this Chapter, a Joint Committee on Science and Technology (hereinafter referred to in this Article as "the Committee") shall be established. The functions of the Committee shall be:

(a)   reviewing and discussing the co-operative relationship in the field of scientific and technological development of the Parties and the progress of Co-operative Activities and Other Co-operative Activities;

(b)   exchanging views and information on scientific and technological policy issues;

(c)   providing advice to the Parties with regard to the implementation of this Chapter, which may include identification and recommendation of Co-operative Activities and encouragement of their implementation;

(d)   discussing ways of encouraging Other Co-operative Activities, especially in the areas that the Parties consider important; and

(e)   discussing other issues relating to science and technology.

2.   The composition of the Committee shall be specified in the Implementing Agreement.

Article118
Protection and Distribution of Intellectual Property Rights
and other Rights of a Proprietary Nature

1.   Scientific and technological information of a non-proprietary nature arising from Co-operative Activities may be made available to the public by the government of either Party.

2.   In accordance with the applicable laws and regulations of the Parties and with relevant international agreements to which the Parties are, or may become parties, the Parties shall ensure the adequate and effective protection, and give due consideration to the distribution, of intellectual property rights or other rights of a proprietary nature resulting from the Co-operative Activities undertaken pursuant to this Chapter. The Parties shall consult for this purpose as necessary.

Article 119
Costs of Co-operative Activities under Chapter 15

1.   The implementation of this Chapter shall be subject to the availability of appropriated funds and the applicable laws and regulations of each Party.

2.   Costs of Co-operative Activities shall be borne in such manner as may be mutually agreed.

Article 120
Implementing Arrangements

Implementing arrangements setting forth the details and procedures of Co-operative Activities under this Chapter may be made between the government agencies of the Parties.

CHAPTER 17
TRADE AND INVESTMENT PROMOTION

Article 126
Co-operation in the Field of Trade and Investment Promotion

The Parties shall co-operate in promoting trade and investment activities by private enterprises of the Parties, recognising that efforts of the Parties to facilitate exchange and collaboration between private enterprises of the Parties will act as a catalyst to promote trade and investment in Japan, Singapore and Asia.

Article 127
Review and Recommendation under Chapter 17

1.   The Parties recognise that certain co-operation between parties, one or both of whom are entities in their respective territories other than the governments of the Parties, could contribute to trade and investment promotion between the Parties. Such co-operation shall be specified in the Implementing Agreement.

2.   The Parties shall review the co-operation set forth in paragraph 1 above and, where appropriate, recommend ways or areas of further co-operation between the parties to such co-operation.

Article 128
Joint Committee on Trade and Investment Promotion

1.   For the purposes of effective implementation of this Chapter, a JointCommittee on Trade and Investment Promotion (hereinafter referred to in this Article as "the Committee") shall be established. The functions of the Committee shall be:

   (a)   exchanging views and information on trade and investment promotion;

   (b)   reviewing and discussing issues concerning the effective implementation of this Chapter;

   (c)   identifying and recommending ways of further co-operation between the Parties; and

   (d)   discussing other issues relating to co-operation in trade and investment promotion.

2.   The composition of the Committee shall be specified in the Implementing Agreement.

CHAPTER 18
SMALL AND MEDIUM ENTERPRISES

Article 129
Co-operation in the Field of Small and Medium Enterprises

The Parties, recognising the fundamental role of small and medium enterprises (hereinafter referred to in this Chapter as "SMEs") in maintaining the dynamism of their respective national economies, shall co-operate in promoting close co-operation between SMEs of the Parties.

Article 130
Review and Recommendation under Chapter 18

1. The Parties recognise that certain co-operation between parties, one or both of whom are entities in their respective territories other than the governments of the Parties, could contribute to close co-operation between SMEs of the Parties. Such co-operation shall be specified in the Implementing Agreement.

2.   The Parties shall review the co-operation set forth in paragraph 1 above and, where appropriate, recommend ways or areas of further co-operation between the parties to such co-operation.

Article 131
Facilitation of SMEs Investment

The Parties, recognising the geographical position of Singapore in Southeast Asia, shall co-operate in facilitating investments of Japanese SMEs in Singapore, with a view to enabling SMEs of both Parties to co-operate in their businesses, especially in Southeast Asia. The Parties shall likewise co-operate to facilitate investments of Singapore SMEs in Japan.

Article 132
Joint Committee on SMEs

1.   For the purposes of effective implementation of this Chapter, a Joint Committee on SMEs (hereinafter referred to in this Article as "the Committee") shall be established. The functions of the Committee shall be:

   (a)   reviewing and discussing issues concerning the effective implementation of this Chapter;

   (b)   exchanging views and information on the promotion of SMEs co-operation;

   (c)   identifying and recommending ways of further co-operation between the Parties; and

   (d)   discussing other issues relating to SMEs co-operation.

2.   The composition of the Committee shall be specified in the Implementing Agreement.

CHAPTER 21
DISPUTE AVOIDANCE AND SETTLEMENT

Article 139
Scope of Chapter 21

1.   This Chapter shall apply with respect to the avoidance and settlement of disputes between the Parties concerning the interpretation or application of this Agreement or the Implementing Agreement.

2.   Nothing in this Chapter shall prejudice any rights of the Parties to have recourse to dispute settlement procedures available under any other international agreement to which they are parties.

3.   Notwithstanding paragraph 2 above, once a dispute settlement procedure has been initiated under this Chapter or under any other international agreement to which the Parties are parties with respect to a particular dispute, that procedure shall be used to the exclusion of any other procedure for that particular dispute. However, this does not apply if substantially separate and distinct rights or obligations under different international agreements are in dispute.

4.   Paragraph 3 above shall not apply where the Parties expressly agree to the use of more than one dispute settlement procedure in respect of a particular dispute.

Article 140
General Consultations for the Avoidance and Settlement of Disputes

1.   For the purpose of avoiding disputes, a Party may request consultations with the other Party with regard to any matter on the interpretation or application of this Agreement or the Implementing Agreement.

2.   When a Party requests consultations pursuant to paragraph 1 above, the other Party shall afford adequate opportunity for consultations and shall reply promptly to the request and enter into consultations in good faith.

3.   If the Parties fail to resolve any matter through consultations, either Party may request a meeting of the Consultative Committee established pursuant to paragraph 4 below. The Consultative Committee shall convene within 30 days after the date of receipt of the request, with a view to a prompt and satisfactory resolution of the matter.

4.   To facilitate the implementation of this Chapter, the Parties establish the Consultative Committee, which shall consist of representatives of each Party, including one legal expert designated by each Party.

5.   The procedure provided for in this Article shall not be applicable if, in respect of the same dispute, the procedure provided for in Article 142 has already been initiated.

Article 141
Good Offices, Conciliation or Mediation

1.   Good offices, conciliation or mediation may be requested at any time by either Party. They may begin at any time if the Parties agree. The use of good offices, conciliation or mediation may be terminated at any time at the request of either Party.

2.   If the Parties agree, good offices, conciliation or mediation may continue while procedures of the arbitral tribunal provided for in this Chapter are in progress.

Article 142
Special Consultations for Dispute Settlement

1.   For the purpose of settling disputes, either Party may make a request in writing for consultations to the other Party if the requesting Party considers that any benefit accruing to it directly or indirectly under this Agreement or the Implementing Agreement is being nullified or impaired, as a result of failure of the requested Party to carry out its obligations, or as a result of the application by the requested Party of measures which conflict with its obligations, under this Agreement or the Implementing Agreement.

2.   Unless the Parties agree otherwise, the requested Party shall:

   (a)   enter into consultations within 30 days after the date of receipt of the request for consultations made pursuant to paragraph 1 above; or

   (b)   enter into consultations within 10 days after the date of receipt of the request for consultations made pursuant to paragraph 1 above if the procedure provided for in Article 140 was utilised in respect of the same dispute and 60 days or more have elapsed from the date of the initiation of consultations under that Article.

3.   The Parties shall make every effort to reach a mutually satisfactory resolution through consultations.

4.   Where there is an infringement of the obligations assumed under this Agreement or the Implementing Agreement, such infringement is considered prima facie to constitute a case of nullification or impairment.

Article 143
Establishment of Arbitral Tribunals

1.   Unless otherwise agreed by the Parties, if the Parties fail to resolve a dispute through consultations provided for in Article 142 above, either Party may request the establishment of an arbitral tribunal in respect of that dispute:

   (a)   after 60 days from the date on which the requested Party receives the request for consultations made pursuant to subparagraph (a) of paragraph 2 of Article 142 above; or

(b)   after 30 days from the date on which the requested Party receives the request for consultations made pursuant to subparagraph (b) of paragraph 2 of Article 142 above.

2.   Any request to establish an arbitral tribunal pursuant to this Article shall identify:

(a)   the legal basis of the complaint including the provisions of this Agreement or the Implementing Agreement alleged to have been breached and any other relevant provisions; and

(b)   the factual basis for the complaint.

3.   The Parties shall, within 30 days after the date of receipt of the request for the establishment of an arbitral tribunal, appoint one arbitrator each. If one Party fails to so appoint an arbitrator, the legal expert designated by that Party pursuant to paragraph 4 of Article 140 shall be appointed as an arbitrator.

4.   The Parties shall agree on and designate a third arbitrator, who shall chair the arbitral tribunal. If the Parties fail to agree on the third arbitrator, each Party shall prepare and exchange with the other Party, a list of five persons whom that Party can accept as the third arbitrator. The third arbitrator shall be chosen in the following manner:

(a)   if only one name is common to both lists, that person, if available, will be chosen as the third arbitrator;

(b)   if more than one name appears on both lists, the Parties shall consult for the purpose of agreeing on the third arbitrator from such names;

(c)   if the Parties are not able to reach agreement in accordance with sub-paragraph (b) above or if there is no name common to both lists, or the arbitrator agreed upon or chosen is not available and the Parties cannot decide on a replacement for the arbitrator that is not available, then the two arbitrators appointed pursuant to paragraph 3 above shall agree on the third arbitrator; and

(d)   if the arbitrators are not able to reach agreement on the third arbitrator, the third arbitrator shall be chosen by random drawing in accordance with the procedure agreed to by the Parties for this purpose in the Implementing Agreement.

5.   The third arbitrator shall be appointed within 40 days after the date of appointment of the second arbitrator.

6.   The third arbitrator shall not, unless the Parties agree otherwise, be a national of either of the Parties, nor have his or her usual place of residence in the territory of either of the Parties, nor be employed by either Party, nor have dealt with the dispute in any capacity.

7.   The arbitral tribunal should be composed of arbitrators with relevant technical or legal expertise.

Article 144
Functions of Arbitral Tribunals

1.   The arbitral tribunal established pursuant to Article 143 above:

(a)   should consult with the Parties as appropriate and provide adequate opportunities for the development of a mutually satisfactory resolution;

(b)   shall make its award in accordance with this Agreement, the Implementing Agreement, and applicable rules of international law;

(c)   shall set out, in its award, its findings of law and fact, together with the reasons therefor; and

(d)   may, apart from giving its findings, include in its award suggested implementation options for the Parties to consider in conjunction with Article 147.

2.   The Parties agree that the award of the arbitral tribunal shall be final and binding on the Parties.

3.   The arbitral tribunal may seek, from the Parties, such relevant information as it considers necessary and appropriate. The Parties shall respond promptly and fully to any request by an arbitral tribunal for such information as the arbitral tribunal considers necessary and appropriate.

4.   The arbitral tribunal may seek information from any relevant source and may consult experts to obtain their opinion on certain aspects of the matter. With respect to factual issues concerning a scientific or other technical matter raised by a Party, the arbitral tribunal may request advisory reports in writing from an expert or experts. The arbitral tribunal may, at the request of a Party or proprio motu, select, in consultation with the Parties, no fewer than two scientific or technical experts who shall assist the arbitral tribunal throughout its proceedings, but who shall not have the right to vote in respect of any decision to be made by the arbitral tribunal, including its award.

5.   The deliberations of the arbitral tribunal shall be confidential. The award of the arbitral tribunal shall be drafted without the presence of the Parties, and in the light of the information provided and the statements made.

6.   The arbitral tribunal shall issue its award within 120 days of its establishment, unless the dispute is settled otherwise or the proceeding of the arbitral tribunal is terminated in accordance with Article 146. When the arbitral tribunal is unable to issue its award within 120 days, the arbitral tribunal may, in consultation with the Parties, agree to delay the issuance of its award by no more than 30 days.

7.   The arbitral tribunal shall accord equal opportunity to the Parties to review the award in draft form.

8.   The arbitral tribunal shall attempt to make its decisions, including its award, by consensus but may also make such decisions, including its award, by majority vote.

Article 145
Proceedings of Arbitral Tribunals

1. The arbitral tribunal shall meet in closed session.

2. The deliberations of the arbitral tribunal and the documents submitted to it shall be kept confidential.

3. Notwithstanding paragraph 2 above, either Party may make public statements as to its views regarding the dispute, but shall treat as confidential, information and written submissions submitted by the other Party to the arbitral tribunal which that other Party has designated as confidential. Where a Party has provided information or written submissions designated to be confidential, the other Party may request a non-confidential summary of the information or written submissions which may be disclosed publicly. The Party to whom such a request is made may agree to such a request and submit such a summary, or refuse the request without needing to ascribe any reasons or justification.

4. The Parties shall be given the opportunity to attend any of the presentations, statements or rebuttals in the proceeding. Any information or written submissions submitted by a Party to the arbitral tribunal, including any comments on the descriptive part of the draft award and responses to questions put by the arbitral tribunal, shall be made available to the other Party.

Article 146
Termination of Proceedings

Even if the arbitral tribunal has been established and is proceeding with the procedure provided for in Article 145 above, the Parties may agree to terminate the proceedings at any time by jointly so notifying the chair of the arbitral tribunal.

Article 147
Implementation of Chapter 21

1. The award of the arbitral tribunal made pursuant to Article 144 (hereinafter referred to in this Chapter as "the original award") shall be complied with promptly. A Party which is required by the arbitral tribunal to comply with its award (hereinafter referred to in this Chapter as "the implementing Party") shall, within 20 days after the date of issuance of the original award, notify the other Party (hereinafter referred to in this Chapter as "the other Party") as to the period which it assesses to be reasonable and necessary in order to implement the original award. Such period may:

   (a) extend to 12 months only if administrative or legislative measures have to be undertaken;

   (b) be extended or shortened if the Parties agree that special circumstances so justify; or

   (c) give rise to a request for consultations if the other Party considers the period notified to be unacceptable, in which case the Parties shall enter into consultations within 10 days after the date of receipt of the request.

2.   If the implementing Party considers that compliance with the original award is impracticable, it shall, instead of notifying the period for implementing the award in accordance with paragraph 1 above, promptly enter into consultations with the other Party, with a view to developing a mutually acceptable resolution, through compensation or any alternative arrangement, and agreeing on a reasonable period to implement such resolution.

3.   If the other Party considers that the measures taken by the implementing Party to comply with the original award do not comply with the original award, it may request consultations.

4.   Either Party may refer matters arising from the implementation of the original award to an arbitral tribunal if:

(a)   consultations were initiated under sub-paragraph (c) of paragraph 1 of this Article, and the Parties fail to reach agreement on the period for implementation within 20 days after the date of receipt of the request;

(b)   consultations were initiated under paragraph 2 of this Article, and the Parties fail to reach agreement on a mutually acceptable resolution or the period for its implementation within 30 days after the date of the initiation of consultations;

(c)   consultations were initiated under paragraph 3 above, and the Parties fail to resolve the matter, and at least 30 days have elapsed since the date of the expiration of the period for implementation provided for in paragraph 1 of this Article; or

(d)   the Party that is requested to enter into consultations refuses to do so where required pursuant to paragraph 1, 2 or 3 above.

5.   If the arbitral tribunal convened pursuant to sub-paragraph (c) of paragraph 4 above confirms that the implementing Party has failed to comply with the original award within the implementation period as determined pursuant to paragraph 1 or sub-paragraph (a) of paragraph 4 above, the other Party may, within 30 days from the date of such confirmation by the arbitral tribunal, notify the implementing Party that it intends to suspend the application to the implementing Party of the obligations of the other Party under this Agreement or the Implementing Agreement.

6.   If the implementing Party has failed to implement the compensation or other alternative arrangement within the implementation period as determined pursuant to paragraph 2 or sub-paragraph (b) of paragraph 4 of this Article, the other Party may, within 30 days from the date of the expiration of such implementation period, notify the implementing Party that it intends to suspend the application to the implementing Party of the obligations of the other Party under this Agreement or the Implementing Agreement.

7.   Suspension pursuant to paragraphs 5 and 6 above may only be implemented at least 30 days after the date of the notification in accordance with that paragraph. Such suspension:

(a)   shall not be effected if, in respect of the dispute to which the suspension relates, consultations, or proceedings before an arbitral tribunal are in progress;

(b)   shall be temporary, and shall be discontinued when the Parties reach a mutually satisfactory resolution or where compliance with the original award is effected;

(c)   shall be restricted to the level of nullification or impairment that is attributable to the failure to comply with the original award; and

(d)   shall be restricted to the same sector or sectors to which the nullification or impairment relates, unless it is not practicable or effective to suspend obligations in such sector or sectors.

8.   If the implementing Party considers that the requirements in paragraph 5, 6 or 7 above have not been met, it may request consultations with the other Party. The other Party shall enter into consultations within 10 days after the date of receipt of the request. If the Parties fail to resolve matters within 30 days after the date of receipt of the request for consultations pursuant to this paragraph, either Party may refer the matter to an arbitral tribunal.

9.   The arbitral tribunal that is convened for the purpose of this Article shall, wherever possible, have as its members, the members of the original arbitral tribunal. If this is not possible, then the members to the arbitral tribunal shall be appointed pursuant to paragraphs 3 to 7 of Article 143.

Unless the Parties agree to a different period, such arbitral tribunal shall issue its award within 60 days after the date when the matter is referred to it.

Article 148
Expenses

Unless the Parties agree otherwise, the expenses of the arbitral tribunal, including the remuneration of its members, shall be borne by the Parties in equal shares.

ANNEX IVA
FINANCIAL SERVICES

I.   Scope and Definitions

1.   This Annex applies to measures affecting the supply of financial services. Reference to the supply of a financial service in this Annex shall mean the supply of a service as defined in sub-paragraph (o) of paragraph 6 of Article 58.

2.   (a)   For the purposes of this Annex:

(i)   the term "financial service" means any service of a financial nature offered by a financial service supplier of a Party. Financial services include all insurance and insurance-related services, and all banking and other financial services (excluding insurance). Financial services include the following activities:

(A)   Insurance and Insurance-Related Services

(AA)   direct insurance (including co-insurance):

       (aa)   life

       (bb)   non-life

  (BB) reinsurance and retrocession;

  (CC) insurance intermediation, such as brokerage and agency;

  (DD) services auxiliary to insurance, such as consultancy, actuarial, risk assessment and claim settlement services;

(B)   Banking and Other Financial Services (Excluding Insurance)

  (AA) acceptance of deposits and other repayable funds from the public;

  (BB) lending of all types, including consumer credit, mortgage credit, factoring and financing of commercial transaction;

  (CC) financial leasing;

  (DD) all payment and money transmission services, including credit, charge and debit cards, travellers cheques and bankers drafts;

  (EE) guarantees and commitments;

  (FF) trading for own account or for account of customers, whether on an exchange, in an over-the- counter market or otherwise, the following:

      (aa)   money market instruments (including cheques, bills, certificates of deposits);

      (bb)   foreign exchange;

      (cc)   derivative products including, but not limited to, futures and options;

      (dd)   exchange rate and interest rate instruments, including products such as swaps, forward rate agreements;

      (ee)   transferable securities;

      (ff)   other negotiable instruments and financial assets, including bullion;

(GG) participation in issues of all kinds of securities, including underwriting and placement as agent (whether publicly or privately) and provision of services related to such issues;

(HH) money broking;

(II) asset management, such as cash or portfolio management, all forms of collective investment management, pension fund management, custodial, depository and trust services;

(JJ) settlement and clearing services for financial assets, including securities, derivative products, and other negotiable instruments;

(KK) provision and transfer of financial information, and financial data processing and related software by suppliers of other financial services; and

(LL) advisory, intermediation and other auxiliary financial services on all the activities listed in sub-paragraphs (AA) through (KK) above, including credit reference and analysis, investment and portfolio research and advice, advice on acquisitions and on corporate restructuring and strategy;

(ii) the term "financial service supplier" means any natural or juridical person of a Party wishing to supply or supplying financial services, but the term "financial service supplier" does not include a public entity;

(iii) the term "public entity" means:

(A) a government, a central bank or a monetary authority of a Party, or an entity owned or controlled by a Party, that is principally engaged in carrying out governmental functions or activities for governmental purposes, not including an entity principally engaged in supplying financial services on commercial terms; or

(B) a private entity, performing functions normally performed by a central bank or monetary authority, when exercising those functions;

(iv) for the purposes of sub-paragraph (q) of paragraph 6 of Article 58, the term "services supplied in the exercise of governmental authority" means the following:

(A) activities conducted by a central bank or monetary authority or by any other public entity in pursuit of monetary or exchange rate policies;

        (B)   activities forming part of a statutory system of social security or public retirement plans; and

        (C)   other activities conducted by a public entity for the account or with the guarantee or using the financial resources of the Government.

(b)   For the purposes of sub-paragraph (q) of paragraph 6 of Article 58, if a Party allows any of the activities referred to in (iv)(B) of sub-paragraph (a) or (iv)(C) of sub-paragraph (a) above to be conducted by its financial service suppliers in competition with a public entity or a financial service supplier, the term "services" shall include such activities.

(c)   Sub-paragraph (r) of paragraph 6 of Article 58 shall not apply to services covered by this Annex.

II.   Domestic Regulation

1.   Notwithstanding any provisions of Chapter 7, a Party shall not be prevented from taking measures for prudential reasons, including measures for the protection of investors, depositors, policy holders or persons to whom a fiduciary duty is owed by a financial service supplier, or to ensure the integrity and stability of the financial system. Where such measures do not conform with the provisions of Chapter 7, they shall not be used as a means of avoiding the Party's commitments or obligations under Chapter 7.

2.   Nothing in Chapter 7 shall be construed to require a Party to disclose information relating to the affairs and accounts of individual customers or any confidential or proprietary information in the possession of public entities.

III.   Recognition

1.   A Party may recognise the prudential measures of any international regulatory body or non-Party in determining how the Party's measures relating to financial services shall be applied. Such recognition, which may be achieved through harmonisation or otherwise, may be based upon an agreement or arrangement with the international regulatory body or non-Party concerned or may be accorded autonomously.

2.   A Party that is a party to such an agreement or arrangement referred to in paragraph 1 above, whether future or existing, shall afford adequate opportunity for the other Party to negotiate its accession to such agreements or arrangements, or to negotiate comparable ones with it, under circumstances in which there would be equivalent regulation, oversight, implementation of such regulation, and if appropriate, procedures concerning the sharing of information between the parties to the agreement or arrangement. Where a Party accords recognition autonomously, it shall afford adequate opportunity for the other Party to demonstrate that such circumstances exist.

IV.   Dispute Settlement

Arbitral tribunals established under Article 143 for disputes on prudential issues and other financial matters shall have the necessary expertise relevant to the specific financial service under dispute.

V.   New Financial Services

1.   Each Party shall give due consideration to applications by financial service suppliers of the other Party to offer in the territory of the former Party any new financial service that is regulated by the other Party within the territory of the other Party. Where an application is approved, the provision of the new financial service is subject, on a non-discriminatory basis, to relevant licensing, institutional and juridical form requirements of the former Party.

2.   For the purposes of paragraph 1 above, the term "new financial service" shall include services related to existing and new products or services, or the manner in which such products or services are delivered, that are not supplied in the territory of a Party but are supplied in the territory of the other Party.

VI.   Modification of Schedules

The Parties shall, on the request in writing by either Party, hold consultations to consider any modification or withdrawal of a commitment in the Schedule of specific commitments on trade in financial services. Such consultations shall be held within three months after the requesting Party makes such a request.

In such consultations, the Parties shall aim to ensure that a general level of mutually advantageous commitments not less favourable to trade than that provided for in the Schedule of specific commitments in Annex IVC prior to such consultations is maintained.

ANNEX IVB
TELECOMMUNICATIONS SERVICES

I.   Scope and Definitions

1.   This Annex applies to measures affecting telecommunications services where specific commitments are undertaken.

2.   For the purposes of this Annex:

   (a)   the term "telecommunications" means the transmission and reception of signals by any electromagnetic means;

   (b)   the term "public telecommunications transport service" means any telecommunications transport service required, explicitly or in effect, by a Party to be offered to the public generally. Such services may include, inter alia, telegraph, telephone, telex, and data transmission typically involving the real-time transmission of customer-supplied information between two or more points without any end-to-end change in the form or content of the customer's information;

   (c)   the term "public telecommunications transport network" means the public telecommunications infrastructure which permits telecommunications between and among defined network termination points;

(d)   the term "essential facilities" means facilities of a public telecommunications transport network or service that:

(i)   are exclusively or predominantly provided by a single or limited number of suppliers; and

(ii)   cannot feasibly be economically or technically substituted in order to provide a service;

(e)   the term " major supplier" means a supplier that has the ability to materially affect the terms of participation having regard to price and supply in the relevant market for basic telecommunications services as a result of:

(i)   control over essential facilities; or

(ii)   use of its position in the market;

(f)   the term "facilities-based suppliers" means:

(i)   for Japan, Type 1 Telecommunications Carriers provided for in Article 12 of the Telecommunications Business Law (Law No. 86, 1984); or

(ii)   for Singapore, Facilities-Based Operators; and

(g)   the term "services-based suppliers" means:

(i)   for Japan, Type 2 Telecommunications Carriers provided for in Articles 22 and 27 of the Telecommunications Business Law (Law No. 86, 1984); or

(ii)   for Singapore, Services-Based Operators.

II.   Competitive Safeguards

Prevention of Anti-competitive Practices in Telecommunications

1.   Each Party shall maintain appropriate measures for the purpose of preventing suppliers, who alone or together are a major supplier, from engaging in or continuing anti-competitive practices.

Safeguards

2.   The anti-competitive practices referred to in paragraph 1 above shall include in particular:

(a)   engaging in anti-competitive cross-subsidisation or pricing services in a manner that gives rise to unfair competition;

(b)   discriminating unfairly in providing telecommunications services;

(c)   using information obtained from competitors with anti-competitive results; and

(d)   not making available to other service suppliers on a timely basis technical information about essential facilities and commercially relevant information which are necessary for them to provide services.

Asymmetric Regulation

3.   Each Party may, in accordance with its laws and regulations, determine the appropriate level of regulation required to promote fair competition.

III.   Public Availability of Licensing Criteria

1.   Where a licence is required, each Party shall make publicly available the following:

(a)   all the licensing criteria and the period of time normally required to reach a decision concerning an application for a licence; and

(b)   the terms and conditions of individual licences.

2.   Each Party shall make known to the applicant the reasons for the denial of a licence upon request.

IV.   Interconnection

Interconnection to be ensured

1.   Each Party shall ensure interconnection between a facilities-based supplier and any other facilities-based supplier or a services-based supplier to the extent provided for in its laws and regulations.

Interconnection with Major Suppliers

2.   Each Party shall ensure that a major supplier is required to provide interconnection at any technically feasible point in the network. Such interconnection is provided:

(a)   under non-discriminatory terms, conditions (including technical standards and specifications) and rates and of a quality no less favourable than that provided for its own like services, for like services of non-affiliated service suppliers or for like services of its subsidiaries or other affiliates;

(b)   in a timely fashion, on terms, conditions (including technical standards and specifications) and cost-oriented rates that are transparent, reasonable, having regard to economic feasibility, and sufficiently unbundled [Note] so that the supplier need not pay for network components or facilities that it does not require for the services to be provided; and

Note: "Sufficiently unbundled" network components or facilities include unbundled local loop (including line sharing).

(c)   upon request, at points in addition to the network termination points offered to the majority of users, subject to charges that reflect the cost of construction of necessary additional facilities.

3.   Each Party shall ensure that a major supplier is required to allow other suppliers who interconnect with the major supplier:

(a)   to locate their equipment which is essential for interconnection within the major supplier's buildings; [Note 1] or

(b)   to install their cables and lines which are essential for interconnection within the major supplier's buildings, [Note 1] conduits, [Note 2] cable tunnels or telephone poles;

where physically feasible and where no practical or viable alternatives exist, in order to interconnect smoothly with the essential facilities of the major supplier.

Note 1: Buildings used for communications that house a point of interconnection.

Note 2: Underground communications facilities installed to accommodate or protect underground cables and to connect manholes, etc.

Interconnection Pursuant to an Approved Reference Interconnection Offer

4.   Each Party shall ensure that major suppliers are required to provide a reference interconnection offer for approval by the relevant regulatory authorities. The reference interconnection offer shall be consistent with the principles of II of this Annex and shall contain written statements of the charges and conditions on which a major supplier will interconnect with suppliers. At a minimum, the reference interconnection offer shall be required to contain the following:

(a)   a list and description of the interconnection-related services offered, the terms and conditions for such services, the operational and technical requirements, and the procedures or processes that will be used to order and provide such services;

(b)   a list of cost-based prices that a major supplier offers for all its interconnection-related services. Where feasible, the major supplier shall be required to use an established methodology based on incremental forward-looking economic cost;

(c)   standard periods between the dates of request and commencement which are stipulated in a clear manner and are reasonable; and

(d)   a statement regarding the duration of the proposed interconnection agreement, if it is fixed.

5.   Paragraphs 2, 3 and 4 of IV of this Annex are applied only to a major supplier which has control over essential facilities.

Public Availability of the Procedures for Interconnection Negotiations

6.   Each Party shall ensure that the procedures applicable for interconnection to a major supplier are made publicly available.

Transparency of Interconnection Arrangements

7.   Each Party shall ensure that a major supplier makes publicly available either its interconnection agreements or reference interconnection offer.

V.   Interconnection Dispute Settlement

A service supplier requesting interconnection with a major supplier shall have recourse, either:

(a)   at any time; or

(b)   after a reasonable period of time which has been made publicly known;

to an independent domestic body, which may be a regulatory body as referred to in VII of this Annex, to resolve disputes regarding appropriate terms, conditions and rates for interconnection within a reasonable period of time, to the extent that these have not been established previously.

VI.   Universal Service

Each Party shall have the right to define the kind of universal service obligation it wishes to maintain. Such obligations shall not be regarded as anti-competitive per se, provided that they are administered in a transparent, non-discriminatory and competitively neutral manner and are not more burdensome than necessary for the kind of universal service defined by the Party.

VII.   Independent Regulators

The regulatory body shall be separate from, and not accountable to, any supplier of telecommunications services. The decisions of and the procedures used by regulators shall be impartial with respect to all market participants.

VIII.   Allocation and Use of Scarce Resources

Any procedures for the allocation and use of scarce resources, including frequencies, numbers and rights of way, shall be carried out in an objective, timely, transparent and non-discriminatory manner. Each Party shall make publicly available the current state of allocated frequency bands.

Each Party shall not be required to make publicly available detailed identification of frequencies allocated for specific government uses.

ANNEX VA

LIST OF EXCEPTIONS IN THE AREA OF INVESTMENT
(Japan)

Horizontal Exceptions

1.	(a)	Matter:	Land Transaction
	(b)	Legal Source or Authority:	Alien Land Law (Law No. 42, 1925)

(c)   Relevant Obligation: National Treatment (Article 73)

(d)   Description: With respect to acquisition or lease of land properties in Japan, prohibitions or restrictions may be imposed by Cabinet Ordinances on Singapore nationals or entities, where Japanese nationals or entities are placed under identical or similar prohibitions or restrictions in Singapore.

2.   (a)   Matter: Prior Notification

    (b)   Legal Source or Authority :   Foreign Exchange and Foreign Trade Law (Law No. 228, 1949)

    (c)   Relevant Obligation: National Treatment (Article 73)

    (d)   Description:

The prior notification requirement under Article 27 of the Foreign Exchange and Foreign Trade Law (Law No. 228, 1949) shall apply to the following sectors:

- Primary Industry related to Agriculture, Forestry and Fisheries
- Oil Industry
- Leather and Leather Products Manufacturing Industry
- Heat Supply Industry
-Biological Preparations Manufacturing Industry
- Water Supply and Water Works Industry
- Railway Transport Industry
- Omnibus Industry
- Water Transport Industry
- Telecommunications Industry
- Security Industry.

Note 1: All organic chemicals such as ethylene, ethylene glycol and polycarbonates are outside the scope of the "Oil Industry". Therefore, prior notification under the Foreign Exchange and Foreign Trade Law (Law No. 228, 1949) is not required for the investment in manufacturing these products.

Note 2: Biological Preparations Manufacturing Industry deals with establishments which mainly produce vaccine, serum, toxoid, antitoxin and some preparations similar to the aforementioned products, or blood products.

Note 3: Freight Forwarding Industry is not included in any of Railway Transport, Omnibus or Water Transport Industry.

Note 4: The manufacture of vehicles, parts and components for the Railway Transport Industry is not included in Railway Transport Industry and is exempted from prior notification requirements.

Note 5: The manufacture of vehicles, parts and components is not included in Omnibus Industry and is exempted from prior notification requirements.

> Note 6: Water Transport Industry refers to Oceangoing/Seagoing Transport, Coastwise Transport (i.e. maritime transport between ports in Japan), Inland Water Transport and Ship Leasing Industry. However, Oceangoing/Seagoing Transport Industry and Ship Leasing Industry excluding Coastwise Ship Leasing Industry are exempted from prior notification requirements.

3.   (a)   Matter: Formalities

    (b)   Legal Source or Authority: N/A

    (c)   Relevant Obligation: National Treatment (Article 73)

    (d)   Description:

Formalities may be prescribed in connection with the investment-related activities of Singapore investors, provided that such formalities:

(i)   only require the notification of facts or the submission of documents for proof;

(ii) do not impair the substance of the rights provided for in this Chapter;

(iii) do not entail any discretionary approval; and

(iv) are not implemented in an arbitrary or discriminatory manner.

Such formalities include:

(A)   Article 479 and paragraph 1 of Article 481 of the Commercial Code (Law No. 48, 1899)

According to the Commercial Code (Law No. 48, 1899), if a foreign company intends to engage in commercial transactions as a continuing business in Japan, it shall appoint a representative in Japan and establish an office of business at the residence of such representative or at any other place. The foreign company has to register its office of business in accordance with the same procedures as those required for the registration of a branch office of a company established in Japan which is either of the same nature or of the kind which it most closely resembles. The full name and permanent residence of its representative in Japan must also be registered.

(B)   Article 55-5 of the Foreign Exchange and Foreign Trade Law (Law No. 228, 1949)

Article 55-5 of the Foreign Exchange and Foreign Trade Law (Law No. 228, 1949) requires foreign investors to submit ex post facto reports to the Minister of Finance and the Minister(s) in charge of the industry involved after implementing a foreign investment in Japan. (This shall not apply to the foreign investment for which prior notification is required.)

4.   (a)   Matter :   Public Monopoly and State Enterprise

        (b)   Legal Source or Authority: N/A

        (c)   Relevant Obligation: National Treatment (Article 73)

        (d)   Description:

National treatment shall not apply to:

          (i)   the disposal of a public monopoly or a state enterprise either at one time or in stages; (Note) and

               Note: Paragraph (i) above includes the liberalising of certain activities restricted to that public monopoly or that state enterprise by laws and regulations.

         (ii)   the establishment of successor public monopolies or successor state enterprises in the same sector as the public monopoly or state enterprise which has been disposed of.

5.   (a)   Matter: Subsidies

        (b)   Legal Source or Authority: N/A

        (c)   Relevant Obligation: National Treatment (Article 73)

        (d)   Description: National treatment may not be accorded in the case of subsidies designed for research and development investments.

6.   (a)   Matter :   Permanent Residents

        (b)   Legal Source or Authority: N/A

        (c)   Relevant Obligation: National Treatment (Article 73)

        (d)   Description:

There may be limitations on the treatment accorded to the investors who have the right of permanent residence in Singapore, where Japan adopts or maintains measures pursuant to its domestic laws and regulations whose implementation would be prejudiced if the treatment accorded to the investors who have the right of permanent residence in Singapore is equivalent to the treatment accorded to the investors who are nationals of Singapore.

Such measures include those pursuant to Article 27 of the Foreign Exchange and Foreign Trade Law (Law No. 228, 1949).

In respect of the investors who have the right of permanent residence in Singapore, to whom sub-paragraph 2 of paragraph 3 of Article 27 of the Foreign Exchange and Foreign Trade Law (Law No. 228, 1949) is applicable on the basis of their nationality, the notification to competent authorities is required prior to investment in all sectors.

(e)   Others:

  (i)   In cases where Japan takes any measures mentioned above, Japan will notify Singapore of the description of the measure before such measure is taken;

  (ii)   with reference to the Foreign Exchange and Foreign Trade Law (Law No. 228, 1949), Japan will notify Singapore before any new country is added to the list of countries to which sub-paragraph 2 of paragraph 3 of Article 27 of the above Law applies; and

  (iii)   Japan will receive the views of Singapore on such measure in writing before implementing the measure in question and will take such views into consideration. Japan will promptly notify Singapore if Japan thereafter intends to proceed with the implementation of the measure in question.

Sectoral Exceptions

7.   (a)   Sector: Agriculture, Plant Breeder's Right

      (b)   Legal Source or Authority: Seeds and Seedlings Law (Law No. 83, 1998), Seeds and Seedlings Law Enforcement Regulation

      (c)   Relevant Obligation: National Treatment (Article 73)

      (d)   Description:

  (i)   According to Article 10 of the Seeds and Seedlings Law (Law No. 83, 1998), a foreigner who has neither a domicile nor residence (nor establishment, in the case of a legal person) in Japan cannot enjoy a breeder's right except in any of the following cases:

    (A)   where the State of which the person is a national or the State in which the person has a domicile or residence (or its establishment, in the case of a legal person) is a contracting party to the International Convention for the Protection of New Varieties of Plants of December 2, 1961, as Revised at Geneva on November 10, 1972 on October 23, 1978 and on March 19, 1991 (hereinafter referred to in this Annex as "the 1991 UPOV Convention");

    (B)   where the State of which the person is a national or the State in which the person has a domicile or residence (or its establishment, in the case of a legal person) is a contracting party to the

International Convention for the Protection of New Varieties of Plants of December 2, 1961, as Revised at Geneva on November 10, 1972 and on October 23, 1978 (hereinafter referred to in this Annex as "the 1978 UPOV Convention") and further provides the protection for plant genus and species to which the person's applied variety belongs; or

(C)   where the State of which the person is a national provides Japanese nationals with the protection of varieties under the same condition as its own nationals and further provides the protection for plant genus and species to which the person's applied variety belongs.

Since Singapore is not a contracting party to either the 1991 UPOV Convention or to the 1978 UPOV Convention, and does not provide Japanese nationals with the protection of varieties, the person who is a national of Singapore or has a domicile or residence (or its establishment, in the case of a legal person) in Singapore (excluding the cases provided for in (i)(A), (i)(B) and (i)(C)) cannot enjoy plant breeder's right in Japan. This paragraph shall cease to apply if Singapore becomes a contracting party to the 1991 UPOV Convention or provides Japanese nationals with the protection of varieties under the same conditions as its own nationals and further provides the protection for plant genus and species to which the person's applied variety belongs.

(ii)   The Seeds and Seedlings Law Enforcement Regulation requires foreign applicants to attach a document certifying his or her nationality and any one of the documents set out below:

(A)   a document certifying the fact that the applicant has a domicile or residence (or its establishment, in the case of a legal person) in Japan; or

(B)   a document certifying the fact that the applicant has a domicile or residence (or its establishment, in the case of a legal person) in the territory of a contracting party to the 1991 UPOV Convention or to the 1978 UPOV Convention, other than Japan..

8.   (a)   Sector: Mining Industry including Oil and Natural Gas Exploration and Development

(b)   Legal Source or Authority: Mining Law (Law No. 289, 1950)

(c)   Relevant Obligation: National Treatment (Article 73)

(d)   Description:

Persons other than Japanese nationals and Japanese legal persons are not allowed to have mining rights or mining lease rights.

9.   (a)   Sector: Water Transport Industry [Note]

(b) Legal Source or Authority: Ship Law (Law No. 46, 1899)

(c) Relevant Obligation: National Treatment (Article 73)

(d) Description:

In accordance with the Ship Law (Law No. 46, 1899), the Japanese nationality shall be given to a ship whose owner is a natural person with Japanese nationality, or a legal person established under Japanese law, with all representatives ("daihyosha") and not less than two-thirds of executives administering the affairs of the legal person ("gyomu-wo-shikkosuru-yakuin") having Japanese nationality. This law prevents ships not flying the Japanese flag from entering Japanese ports which are not open to foreign commerce and from carrying cargoes or passengers between Japanese ports.

Note: Water Transport Industry refers to Oceangoing/Seagoing Transport, Coastwise Transport (i.e. maritime transport between ports in Japan), Inland Water Transport and Ship Leasing Industry.

10. (a) Sector: Telecommunications Industry

(b) Legal Source or Authority: Law concerning Nippon Telegraph and Telephone Corporation, etc. (Law No. 85, 1984)

(c) Relevant Obligation: National Treatment (Article 73)

(d) Description:

(i) Nippon Telegraph and Telephone Corporation (NTT) shall not enter the name and address in its register of shareholders if the aggregate of the ratio of the voting rights directly and/or indirectly held by the person set forth in item (A) through (C) below reaches or exceeds one third:

(A) a person who does not have Japanese nationality;

(B) a foreign government or its representative; or

(C) a foreign legal person or association;

(ii) NTT shall always hold all shares of the Regional Companies; and

(iii) any person who does not have Japanese nationality shall not assume the office of director or auditor of NTT and the Regional Companies.

11. (a) Sector: Financial Services

(b) Legal Source or Authority: Deposit Insurance Law (Law No. 34, 1971)

(c) Relevant Obligation: National Treatment (Article 73)

(d)   Description:

The deposit insurance system only covers financial institutions which have their head offices within the jurisdiction of Japan.

12.   (a)   Sector: Investment in specific sectors

        (b)   Legal Source or Authority: N/A

        (c)   Relevant Obligation: National Treatment (Article 73), Prohibition of Performance Requirements (Article 75)

        (d)   Description:

National treatment and prohibition of performance requirements shall not apply to the following sectors:

        - Fisheries within the territorial sea, internal waters and Exclusive Economic Zones
        - Explosive Manufacturing Industry
        - Nuclear Energy Industry
        - Aircraft Industry
        - Arms Industry
        - Space Industry
        - Electric Utility Industry, Gas Utility Industry
        - Broadcasting Industry.

ANNEX VB

LIST OF EXCEPTIONS IN THE AREA OF INVESTMENT

(Singapore)

Horizontal Exceptions

1.   (a)   Matter: Subsidies/Incentives for all sectors

        (b)   Legal Source or Authority: Economic Expansion Incentives (Relief from Income Tax) Act (Cap. 86), Income Tax Act (Cap.134), Relevant Government Agencies

        (c)   Relevant Obligation: National Treatment (Article 73), Prohibition of Performance Requirements (Article 75)

        (d)   Description: National Treatment
                                           National treatment may not be accorded in the provision of the following:

(A) subsidies/incentives or programmes to help develop local entrepreneurs and to assist local companies to expand and upgrade their operations;

(B) subsidies/incentives pertaining to the supply of service.

Prohibition of Performance Requirements

(i) Conditions that are inconsistent with sub-paragraphs (a) through (e) of paragraph 1 of Article 75 may be imposed for the receipt or continued receipt of any advantage in connection with an investment in the services sector in Singapore.

(ii) For the avoidance of doubt, conditions or requirements that are not listed in Article 75 may be imposed for the receipt or continued receipt of any advantage in connection with an investment in Singapore.

2. (a) Matter: Company registration formalities for all sectors

(b) Legal Source or Authority: Companies Act (Cap. 50)

(c) Relevant Obligation: National Treatment (Article 73), Prohibition of Performance Requirements (Article 75)

(d) Description: Compliance by foreign companies with the Companies Act in their establishment, and reporting and filing of accounts

(i) Commercial presence, right of establishment and movement of legal persons are subject to compliance with the following provisions:

(A) a foreigner who wishes to register a business firm must have a local manager who should be:

(AA) a Singapore citizen;

(BB) a Singapore permanent resident; or

(CC) a Singapore employment pass holder.

However, a foreigner who is a Singapore permanent resident or a Singapore employment pass holder can register a business without appointing a local manager;

    (B)   at least one director of the company must be locally resident;

    (C)   all branches of foreign companies registered in Singapore must have at least two locally resident agents. (To qualify as locally resident, a person should be either a Singapore citizen or a Singapore permanent resident or a Singapore employment pass holder).

    (ii)   Establishment of a foreign company's branch is subject to the filing of necessary documents.

3.   (a)   Matter: Ownership of Residential Land/Property

    (b)   Legal Source or Authority: Residential Property Act (Cap. 274), Banking Act (Cap. 19), Finance Companies Act (Cap. 108), Monetary Authority of Singapore Act (Cap. 186)

    (c)   Relevant Obligation: National Treatment (Article 73)

    (d)   Description: (i)   Ownership of residential land: non-citizens cannot own residential land.

    (ii)   Ownership of residential property:

    (A)   non-citizens are restricted from purchasing landed residential property and residential property in a building of less than 6 levels;

    (B)   non-citizens and non-Singapore permanent residents cannot own residential property under government public housing schemes.

    (iii)   Housing loans: banks, finance companies and merchant banks are:

    (A)   not allowed to extend Singapore Dollar (S$) loans to non-Singapore citizens (excluding Singapore permanent residents) and non-Singapore companies for the purpose of purchasing residential properties in

Singapore. A company is considered a Singapore company only if it is incorporated in Singapore and majority-owned by Singapore citizens.

Any company which is incorporated outside Singapore is considered a non-Singapore company. A company incorporated in Singapore and majority-owned by non-Singapore citizens and/or Singapore permanent residents is considered a non-Singapore company;

(B) allowed to grant Singapore permanent residents only one S$ loan each for the purchase of a residential property in Singapore which must be for owner-occupation.

4. (a) Matter: Regulation on Singapore dollar transactions

    (b) Legal Source or Authority: Banking Act (Cap. 19), MAS Notice 757 to Banks, Securities Industry Act (Cap. 289), MAS Notice 1201 to Securities Dealers, Finance Companies Act (Cap. 108), MAS Notice 816 to Finance Companies, Insurance Act (Cap. 142), MAS Notice 109 to Insurers, Monetary Authority of Singapore Act (Cap. 186), MAS Notice 1105 to Merchant Banks

    (c) Relevant Obligation: National Treatment (Article 73)

    (d) Description: (i) Where amounts exceed S$5 million per entity, [Note 1] banks [Note 2] may extend S$ credit facilities to non-residents for any purpose in Singapore or overseas, subject to the following conditions:

Note 1: For financial institutions seeking to obtain S$ credit facilities, each subsidiary is considered a separate entity while the head office and all overseas branches are collectively regarded as one entity.

Note 2: The restrictions in paragraph 4 of this Annex describe the measures in MAS Notice 757 to Banks. Similar measures are set out in MAS Notice 1201 to Securities Dealers, MAS Notice 816 to Finance Companies, MAS Notice 109 to Insurers, and MAS Notice 1105 to Merchant Banks.

(A)   for S$ investments in financial assets and real estate, banks are required to ensure that the S$ credit facilities are withdrawn when the investments, or part thereof, are in any way converted into S$ cash proceeds;

(B)   where the S$ proceeds are to be used offshore, the proceeds should be swapped into foreign currency upon draw-down. In this instance, banks are not allowed to convert the S$ proceeds into foreign currency via the spot or forward market. For S$ equity listings and bond issues by non-residents wishing to tap S$ markets to finance their activities offshore, non-residents are required to swap or convert the S$ proceeds into foreign currency for use offshore;

(Notification is required for bond issues by residents as well as non-residents.)

(ii)   where the bond issuer is an unrated foreign entity, banks may place or sell the S$ bonds to sophisticated investors [Note] only;

Note: "Sophisticated investors" is as defined in the Companies Act (Cap. 50).

(iii)   banks should not extend S$ credit facilities to non-residents for speculative activities in the S$ currency market;

(iv)   banks may lend in any amount S$-denominated securities to non-residents as long as it is fully collateralised with S$ cash or other S$ assets upon the extension of the S$-denominated securities loan;

(v)   banks may transact with non-residents S$ currency options as long as there is a requirement to hedge the S$ exchange rate risks arising from trade with, or economic and financial activities in, Singapore. This is subject to the following conditions:

(A)   the S$ option should have cashflows matching the S$/foreign currency flows if the option is exercised;

(B)   the S$ option offered must not be combined with a spot or any other transaction to constitute a S$ credit facility that would not be permitted under MAS Notice 757;

(C)   there must be documentary evidence of the non-resident's need to hedge its trade with, or its economic and financial activities in, Singapore.

(The above limitation shall not be construed as causing a delay in transfers as defined in Article 80.)

5.   (a)   Matter: Privatisation

    (b)   Legal Source or Authority: N/A

    (c)   Relevant Obligation: National Treatment (Article 73), Prohibition of Performance Requirements (Article 75)

    (d)   Description: National treatment and prohibition of performance requirements shall not apply to the privatisation or divestment of assets owned by the Government.

Sectoral Exceptions

6.   (a)   Sector: Investments in Services

    (b)   Legal Source or Authority: N/A

    (c)   Relevant Obligation: National Treatment (Article 73), Prohibition of Performance Requirements (Article 75)

    (d)   Description:

(i)   National treatment and prohibition of performance requirements shall not apply to services sectors not scheduled in Chapter 7.

Where a service sector is scheduled in Chapter 7, the provisions, terms, limitations, conditions and qualifications in Chapter 7 (including market access measures) shall apply to investments in that service sector under Chapter 8.

      (ii)   For the avoidance of doubt, the scheduled services in the telecommunications and financial sectors shall also be interpreted in accordance with Annexes IVA and IVB.

7.   (a)   Sector: Printing and Publishing Sector

     (b)   Legal Source or Authority: Newspaper and Printing Presses Act (Cap. 206), Ministry of Information, Communications and the Arts

     (c)   Relevant Obligation: National Treatment (Article 73), Prohibition of Performance Requirements (Article 75)

     (d)   Description: National treatment and prohibition of performance requirements shall not apply to the printing and publishing sector.

8.   (a)   Sector: Arms and Explosives Sector

     (b)   Legal Source or Authority: Arms and Explosives Act (Cap. 13)

     (c)   Relevant Obligation: National Treatment (Article 73), Prohibition of Performance Requirements (Article 75)

     (d)   Description: National treatment and prohibition of performance requirements shall not apply to the arms and explosives sector.

9.   (a)   Sector: Manufacturing Sector

     (b)   Legal Source or Authority: Control of Manufacture Act (Cap. 57)

     (c)   Relevant Obligation: National Treatment (Article 73), Prohibition of Performance Requirements (Article 75)

     (d)   Description: Statutory licensing requirements and conditions that are inconsistent with Article 73 or sub-paragraphs (f) to (i) of paragraph 1 of Article 75 may be imposed in connection with the manufacture of the following:

          (i)   firecrackers;
          (ii)   drawn steel products;
          (iii)   pig iron and sponge iron;
          (iv)   rolled steel products;
          (v)   steel ingots, billets, blooms and slabs;
          (vi)   beer and stout;
          (vii)   CD, CD-ROM, VCD;
          (viii)   DVD, DVD-ROM;

      (ix)   chewing gum, bubble gum, dental chewing gum or any like substance;

      (x)   cigarettes;

      (xi)   matches;

      (xii)   cigars;

      (xiii)   refrigerators;

      (xiv)   air-conditioners.

ANNEX VC

INVESTOR-TO-STATE DISPUTE SETTLEMENT
SPECIAL ARBITRATION PROCEDURE

1.   Any request to establish an arbitral tribunal pursuant to this Annex shall identify:

    (a)   the name and address of the investor concerned;

    (b)   the legal basis of the complaint including the provisions of Chapter 8 alleged to have been breached; and

    (c)   the factual basis for the complaint.

2.   The investor and the Party shall, within 30 days after the date of receipt of the request for the establishment of an arbitral tribunal, appoint one arbitrator each. If the Party fails to so appoint an arbitrator, the legal expert designated by that Party pursuant to paragraph 4 of Article 140 shall be appointed as an arbitrator. If the investor fails to so appoint an arbitrator, the legal expert designated by the Party of which the investor is a national pursuant to paragraph 4 of Article 140 shall be appointed as an arbitrator.

3.   The investor and the Party shall agree on and designate a third arbitrator, who shall chair the arbitral tribunal. If they fail to agree on the third arbitrator, they shall separately prepare and exchange a list of five persons hom they can accept as the third arbitrator. The third arbitrator shall be chosen in the following manner:

    (a)   if only one name is common to both lists, that person, if available, will be chosen as the third arbitrator;

    (b)   if more than one name appears on both lists, the investor and the Party shall consult for the purpose of agreeing on the third arbitrator from such names;

    (c)   if they are not able to reach agreement in accordance with sub-paragraph (b) above or if there is no name common to both lists, or the arbitrator agreed upon or chosen is not available and the investor and the Party cannot decide on a replacement for the arbitrator that is not available, then the two arbitrators appointed pursuant to paragraph 2 above shall agree on the third arbitrator; and

(d)   if the arbitrators are not able to reach agreement on the third arbitrator, the third arbitrator shall be chosen by random drawing in accordance with the procedure set out in the Appendix to this Annex.

4.   The third arbitrator shall be appointed within 40 days after the date of appointment of the second arbitrator.

5.   The third arbitrator shall not, unless the investor and the Party agree otherwise, be of the same nationality as the investor, nor be a national of the Party, nor have his or her usual place of residence in the territory of either of the Parties, nor be employed by either the investor or the Party, nor have dealt with the investment dispute in any capacity.

6.   The arbitral tribunal should be composed of arbitrators with relevant technical or legal expertise.

APPENDIX TO ANNEX VC

PROCEDURE FOR SELECTION OF THIRD ARBITRATOR FOR SPECIAL ARBITRATION PROCEDURE FOR INVESTOR-TO-STATE DISPUTE SETTLEMENT

The following procedure applies for the random drawing for a third arbitrator, as provided for in Annex VC pertaining to Investor-to-State Dispute Settlement (hereinafter referred to in this Appendix as "Annex VC"):

(a)   for the purposes of this Appendix, the investor that is requesting the establishment of the arbitral tribunal pursuant to Article 82 is hereinafter referred to as the "investor" and the Party to the investment dispute is hereinafter referred to as the "Party";

(b)   unless the investor and the Party agree otherwise, the drawing takes place in the territory of the Party, in the presence of representatives of both the investor and the Party;

(c)   the Party prepares a container with ten sealed envelopes, each of which has, inside it, the name of one of the persons listed on the lists ofthe investor and the Party, prepared pursuant to paragraph 3 of Annex VC, such that there is exactly one envelope corresponding to each of these persons;

(d)   a representative of the investor shall remove, from the container, one envelope, randomly and without being able to discern the identity of the person to whom the envelope corresponds until after the envelope is unsealed and opened;

(e)   the person to whom that envelope corresponds shall be the third arbitrator for the purposes of Annex VC; and

(f)   after the drawing, the container, and the envelopes remaining therein, shall be made available for verification by representatives of the investor in the presence of representatives of the Party.

ANNEX VI

SPECIFIC COMMITMENTS OF JAPAN
FOR THE MOVEMENT OF NATURAL PERSONS

PART A

There may be limitations on the treatment accorded under this Part to natural persons who are permanent residents of Singapore, where Japan adopts or maintains measures pursuant to its domestic laws and regulations whose implementation would be prejudiced if the treatment accorded to natural persons who are permanent residents of Singapore is equivalent to the treatment accorded to natural persons who are nationals of Singapore.

Such measures include those taken in accordance with the provisions of the Immigration Control and Refugee Recognition Act (Cabinet Order No. 319, 1951).

A.   Short-term business visitors

Entry and temporary stay will be granted to a natural person of Singapore who stays in Japan for a period not exceeding 90 days without acquiring remuneration from within Japan and without engaging in making direct sales to the general public or in supplying services himself, for the purposes of participating in business contacts including negotiations for the sale of goods or services, or other similar activities including those to prepare for establishing commercial presence in Japan.

B.   Intra-corporate transferees

1.   Entry and temporary stay will be granted to a natural person of Singapore who has been employed by a juridical person of Singapore that supplies services in Japan or by an enterprise of Singapore that invests in Japan for a period not less than one year immediately preceding the date of his application for the entry and temporary stay in Japan, and who is being transferred to a branch office, a juridical person or an enterprise constituted or registered in Japan owned or controlled by the aforementioned juridical person or enterprise of Singapore, provided that he will be engaged in one of the following activities:

(a)   activities to direct a branch office as its head;

(b)   activities to direct a juridical person or an enterprise as its board member or auditor;

(c)   activities to direct one or more departments of a juridical person or an enterprise;

(d)   activities which require technology and/or knowledge at an advanced level pertinent to physical sciences, engineering or other natural sciences, including information and communications technology; or (e) activities which require knowledge at an advanced level pertinent to jurisprudence, economics, business management, accounting or other human sciences.

Activities which require technology or knowledge at an advanced level pertinent to natural or human sciences referred to in sub-paragraphs (d) and (e) above mean activities in which the natural person may not be able to engage without the application of specialised technology or knowledge of natural or human sciences acquired by him, in principle, by completing college education (i.e. bachelor's degree) or higher education.

2.   Entry and temporary stay will be granted to a natural person of Singapore who has been employed by a juridical person of Singapore or has been a partner in it for a period not less than one year immediately preceding the date of his application for the entry and temporary stay in Japan, and who is being transferred to Japan and will return to the aforementioned juridical person of Singapore, provided that he will be engaged in one of the following activities of professional services which may be engaged only as a natural person and not as an employee:

(a)   legal services supplied by a lawyer qualified as "Bengoshi" under Japanese law;

(b)   consultancy on law of jurisdiction where the service supplier is a qualified lawyer;

(c)   legal services supplied by a patent attorney qualified as "Benrishi" under Japanese law;

(d)   legal services supplied by a maritime procedure agent qualified as "Kaijidairishi" under Japanese law;

(e)   accounting, auditing and bookkeeping services supplied by an accountant qualified as "Koninkaikeishi" under Japanese law; or

(f)   taxation services supplied by a tax accountant qualified as "Zeirishi" under Japanese law.

PART B

There may be limitations on the treatment accorded to natural persons who are permanent residents of Singapore, where Japan adopts or maintains measures pursuant to its domestic laws and regulations whose implementation would be prejudiced if the treatment accorded to natural persons who are permanent residents of Singapore is equivalent to the treatment accorded to natural persons who are nationals of Singapore.

Such measures include those taken in accordance with the provisions of the Immigration Control and Refugee Recognition Act (Cabinet Order No. 319, 1951).

A.   Investors

Entry and temporary stay will be granted to a natural person of Singapore who is engaged in the activities to commence the operation of business in Japan, to invest in business in Japan and to operate or manage that business, excluding the activities to engage in the operation or management of business which are required to be carried out by "Gaikokuhojimubengoshi", "Gaikokukoninkaikeishi" or those with other legal qualifications. Entry and temporary stay may be granted as long as the person concerned continues to meet the criteria and conditions stipulated at the time of his entry into Japan.

B.   Natural persons who engage in work on the basis of a personal contract with public or private organisations in the territory of Japan

Entry and temporary stay will be granted to a natural person of Singapore who engages in work which requires technology and/or knowledge pertinent to engineering on the basis of a personal contract with public or private organisations in the territory of Japan. Entry and temporary stay may be granted as long as such person concerned continues to meet the criteria and conditions stipulated at the time of his entry into Japan.

**SPECIFIC COMMITMENTS OF SINGAPORE
FOR THE MOVEMENT OF NATURAL PERSONS**

Definitions

For the purposes of Singapore's specific commitments:

(a)   the term "managers" means natural persons within an organisation who primarily direct the organisation or a department or sub-division of the organisation, supervise and control the work of other supervisory, professional or managerial employees, have the authority to hire and fire or take other personnel actions such as promotion or leave authorisation, and exercise discretionary authority over day-to-day operations. "Managers" does not include first line supervisors, unless the employees supervised are professionals, nor does it include employees who primarily perform tasks necessary for the provision of the service or operation of an investment;

(b)   the term "executives" means natural persons within an organisation who primarily direct the management of the organisation, exercise wide latitude in decision-making, and receive only general supervision or direction from higher level executives, the board of directors, or stockholders of the business. Executives would not directly perform tasks related to the actual provision of the service or the operation of an investment; and

(c)   the term "specialists" means natural persons within an organisation who possess knowledge at an advanced level of expertise and who possess proprietary knowledge of the organisation's service, research equipment, techniques, or management. "Specialists" may include but is not limited to members of licenced professions.

PART A

A.   Short-term business visitors

1.   Business visitors will be granted an initial stay of up to one month upon arrival. The stay may be extended up to a maximum of three months upon application.

2.   "Business visitors" means natural persons of Japan who seek temporary entry to Singapore to:

> (a)   negotiate the sale of services or goods where such negotiations do not involve direct sales to the general public;

(b)   establish an investment; or

(c)   conduct or participate in business-related conferences, seminars or workshops; provided that such persons do not acquire remuneration from within Singapore and are not seeking employment or residence in Singapore.

B.   Intra-corporate transferees

1.   Entry for intra-corporate transferees is limited to a two year period that may be extended for periods of up to three additional years each time for a total term not exceeding eight years. Further extensions may be possible.

2.   "Intra-corporate transferees" refers to natural persons of Japan who are managers, executives or specialists, who are employees of juridical persons of Japan that supply services in Singapore and enterprises of Japan that invest in Singapore through a branch, subsidiary, or affiliate established in Singapore and who have been in the prior employ of their firms in Japan for a period of not less than one year immediately preceding the date of their application for admission.

PART B

A.   Investors

1.   Entry for investors is limited to a two year period that may be extended for periods of up to three additional years each time for a total term not exceeding eight years. Further extensions may be possible.

2.   "Investor" refers to a natural person of Japan who establishes an enterprise in Singapore, to which the person has committed a substantial amount of capital, and who is a manager or an executive in the enterprise.

B.   Natural persons who engage in work on the basis of a personal contract with public or private organisations in the territory of Singapore

1.   Entry for natural persons with a personal contract with public or private organisations in the territory of Singapore who are employed as engineers is limited to a two year period that may be extended for periods of up to three additional years each time for a total term not exceeding eight years. Further extensions may be possible.

2.   "Engineers" refers to natural persons of Japan who possess acceptable educational qualifications, experience and any other conditions as required under the domestic laws and regulations of Singapore to provide engineering services in Singapore.

ANNEX VIIA

GOODS AND SERVICES

Goods and services listed in each Party's Appendix I to the GPA are to be procured in accordance with the provisions of Chapter 11 with the exception of the following services of the Universal List of Services, as contained in document MTN. GNS/W/120:
(Provisional Central Product Classification (CPC), 1991)

- 51 Construction work
- 867 Architectural, engineering and other technical services.

ANNEX VIIB

ENTITIES

Entities listed in Annexes 1 and 3 of each Party's Appendix I to the GPA are to procure goods and services in accordance with the provisions of Chapter 11 with the exception of those entities which have been privatised.

*

TRATADO DE LIBRE COMERCIO ENTRE CENTROAMÉRICA Y PANAMÁ *
[excerpts]

The Free Trade Agreement between the Central America and Panama was signed in January 2002. The market access negotiations are being held bilaterally between Panama and each Central American country. El Salvador and Panama already signed the protocol to the Agreement.

CUARTA PARTE

INVERSIÓN, SERVICIOS Y ASUNTOS RELACIONADOS

CAPÍTULO 10

Sección A – Inversión

Artículo 10.01 Ámbito de aplicación

1.   Este Capítulo se aplica a las medidas que adopte o mantenga una Parte relativas a:

   a)   los inversionistas de la otra Parte en todo lo relacionado con su inversión;

   b)   las inversiones de inversionistas de la otra Parte realizadas en territorio de la Parte;

   c)   todas las inversiones de los inversionistas de una Parte en el territorio de la otra Parte en lo relativo al Artículo 10.07.

2.   Este Capítulo no se aplica a las medidas que adopte o mantenga una Parte relativas a:

   a)   los servicios financieros;

   b)   las medidas que adopte una Parte para restringir la participación de las inversiones de inversionistas de la otra Parte en su territorio por razones de orden público o de seguridad nacional;

   c)   las actividades económicas reservadas a cada Parte, de conformidad con su legislación vigente a la fecha de la firma de este Tratado, las cuales se listarán en el Anexo III relativo a las actividades económicas reservadas a cada Parte;

   d)   los servicios o funciones gubernamentales tales como, la ejecución de las leyes, servicios de readaptación social, pensión o seguro de desempleo o servicios de

---

* *Source*: The Governments of the Central America countries and the Government of Panama (2002). "Tratado de Libre Comercio entre Centroamérica y Panamá ", available on the Internet (http://www.comex.go.cr). [Note added by the editor.]

seguridad social, bienestar social, educación pública, capacitación pública, salud y atención infantil o protección de la niñez;

e) las controversias o reclamaciones surgidas con anterioridad a la entrada en vigencia de este Tratado, o relacionadas con hechos acaecidos con anterioridad a su vigencia, incluso si sus efectos permanecen aún después de ésta.

3. Este Capítulo se aplica en todo el territorio de las Partes y en cualquier nivel de gobierno a pesar de las medidas incompatibles que pudieran existir en las legislaciones de esos niveles de gobierno.

4. No obstante lo dispuesto en el párrafo 2(d), si un inversionista de una Parte, debidamente autorizado, presta servicios o lleva a cabo funciones tales como servicios de readaptación social, pensión o seguro de desempleo o servicios de seguridad social, bienestar social, educación pública, capacitación pública, salud y atención infantil o protección de la niñez, las inversiones de ese inversionista estarán protegidas por las disposiciones de este Capítulo.

5. Este Capítulo cubre tanto las inversiones existentes a la fecha de entrada en vigencia de este Tratado como a las inversiones hechas o adquiridas con posterioridad.

Artículo 10.02 Trato nacional

1. Cada Parte otorgará a los inversionistas de la otra Parte un trato no menos favorable que el que otorgue, en circunstancias similares, a sus propios inversionistas en lo referente al establecimiento, adquisición, expansión, administración, conducción, operación, venta u otra disposición de las inversiones.

2. Cada Parte otorgará a las inversiones de inversionistas de la otra Parte un trato no menos favorable que el que otorga, en circunstancias similares, a las inversiones de sus propios inversionistas en lo referente al establecimiento, adquisición, expansión, administración, conducción, operación, venta u otra disposición de las inversiones.

Artículo 10.03 Trato de nación más favorecida

1. Cada Parte otorgará a los inversionistas de la otra Parte un trato no menos favorable que el que otorgue, en circunstancias similares, a los inversionistas de cualquier otra Parte o de un país no Parte, en lo referente al establecimiento, adquisición, expansión, administración, conducción, operación, venta u otra disposición de inversiones.

2. Cada Parte otorgará a las inversiones de inversionistas de la otra Parte un trato no menos favorable que el que otorgue, en circunstancias similares, a las inversiones de inversionistas de cualquier otra Parte o de un país no Parte, en lo referente al establecimiento, adquisición, expansión, administración, conducción, operación, venta u otra disposición de inversiones.

Artículo 10.04 Nivel de trato

Cada Parte otorgará a los inversionistas de la otra Parte y a las inversiones de los inversionistas de la otra Parte el mejor de los tratos requeridos por los Artículos 10.02 y 10.03.

Artículo 10.05 Trato en caso de pérdidas

Cada Parte otorgará a los inversionistas de la otra Parte, respecto de las inversiones que sufran pérdidas en su territorio debido a conflictos armados o contiendas civiles, un trato no discriminatorio respecto de cualquier medida que adopte o mantenga en relación con esas pérdidas.

Artículo 10.06 Nivel mínimo de trato

Una Parte otorgará a las inversiones de los inversionistas de la otra Parte un trato acorde con el Derecho Internacional, incluido un trato justo y equitativo, así como protección y seguridad plenas.

Artículo 10.07 Requisitos de desempeño

1.   Ninguna de las Partes podrá imponer ni hacer cumplir cualquiera de los siguientes requisitos o hacer cumplir ningún compromiso u obligación, en lo referente al establecimiento, adquisición, expansión, administración, conducción u operación de una inversión de un inversionista de una Parte en su territorio para:

   a)   exportar un determinado nivel o porcentaje de mercancías o servicios;

   b)   alcanzar un determinado grado o porcentaje de contenido nacional;

   c)   adquirir o utilizar u otorgar preferencia a mercancías producidas o a servicios prestados en su territorio, o adquirir mercancías o servicios de personas en su territorio;

   d)   relacionar en cualquier forma el volumen o valor de las importaciones con el volumen o valor de las exportaciones, o con el monto de las entradas de divisas asociadas con dicha inversión; este párrafo no se aplica a ningún otro requisito distinto a los señalados en el mismo.

2.   Ninguna de las Partes podrá condicionar la recepción de una ventaja o que se continúe recibiendo la misma, en relación con una inversión en su territorio por parte de un inversionista de una Parte, al cumplimiento de cualquiera de los siguientes requisitos:

   a)   alcanzar un determinado grado o porcentaje de contenido nacional;

   b)   adquirir, utilizar u otorgar preferencia a mercancías producidas en su territorio, o adquirir mercancías de productores en su territorio; o

   c)   relacionar, en cualquier forma, el volumen o valor de las importaciones con el volumen o valor de las exportaciones, o con el monto de las entradas de divisas asociadas con dicha inversión;

este párrafo no se aplica a ningún otro requisito distinto a los señalados en el mismo.

3.   Las disposiciones contenidas en:

a)   el párrafo 1(a), (b) y (c) y el párrafo 2(a) y (b) no se aplican en lo relativo a los requisitos para calificación de las mercancías y servicios con respecto a programas de promoción a las exportaciones y de ayuda externa;

b)   el párrafo 1(b) y (c) y el párrafo 2(a) y (b) no se aplican a las compras realizadas por una Parte o por una empresa del Estado;

c)   el párrafo 2(a) y (b) no se aplican a los requisitos impuestos por una Parte importadora relacionados con el contenido necesario de las mercancías para calificar respecto de aranceles o cuotas preferenciales.

4.   Nada de lo dispuesto en el párrafo 2 se interpretará como impedimento para que una Parte condicione la recepción de una ventaja o la continuación de su recepción, en relación con una inversión en su territorio por parte de un inversionista de una Parte, al cumplimiento de un requisito de que ubique la producción, preste un servicio, capacite o emplee trabajadores, construya o amplíe ciertas instalaciones, o lleve a cabo investigación y desarrollo, en su territorio.

5.   Siempre que dichas medidas no se apliquen de manera arbitraria o injustificada, o no constituyan una restricción encubierta al comercio o inversión internacionales, nada de lo dispuesto en los párrafos 1(b) ó (c) ó 2(a) ó (b) se interpretará en el sentido de impedir a una Parte adoptar o mantener medidas, incluidas las de naturaleza ambiental, necesarias para:

a)   asegurar el cumplimiento de leyes y reglamentaciones que no sean incompatibles con las disposiciones de este Tratado;

b)   proteger la vida o salud humana, animal o vegetal; o

c)   la preservación de recursos naturales no renovables, vivos o no.

6.   En caso de que, a juicio de una Parte, la imposición por la otra Parte de alguno de los requisitos señalados a continuación afecte negativamente el flujo comercial o constituya una barrera significativa a la inversión de un inversionista de la Parte, el asunto será considerado por la Comisión:

a)   restringir las ventas en su territorio de las mercancías que esa inversión produzca, relacionando de cualquier manera esas ventas al volumen o valor de sus exportaciones o a ganancias en divisas que generen;

b)   transferir a una persona en su territorio, tecnología, proceso productivo u otro conocimiento reservado, salvo cuando el requisito se imponga por un tribunal judicial o administrativo o autoridad competente para reparar una supuesta violación a la legislación en materia de competencia o para actuar de una manera que no sea incompatible con otras disposiciones de este Tratado; o

c)   actuar como el proveedor exclusivo de las mercancías que produzca para un mercado específico, regional o mundial.

7.   La medida que exija que una inversión emplee una tecnología para cumplir con requisitos de salud, seguridad o medio ambiente de aplicación general, no se considerará incompatible con

el párrafo 6(b). Para brindar mayor certeza, los Artículos 10.02 y 10.03 se aplican a la citada medida.

8.   Si la Comisión encontrare que, en efecto, el requisito en cuestión afecta negativamente el flujo comercial o constituye una barrera significativa a la inversión de un inversionista de la otra Parte, recomendará las disposiciones necesarias para suprimir la práctica de que se trate. Las Partes considerarán estas disposiciones como incorporadas a este Tratado.

Artículo 10.08 Altos ejecutivos y consejos de administración o juntas directivas

1.   Ninguna de las Partes podrá exigir que una empresa de esa Parte, que sea una inversión de un inversionista de la otra Parte, designe a individuos de alguna nacionalidad en particular para ocupar puestos de alta dirección en esa empresa.

2.   Una Parte podrá exigir que la mayoría de los miembros de los órganos de administración o juntas directivas de una empresa de esa Parte, que sea una inversión de un inversionista de la otra Parte, sean de una nacionalidad en particular, siempre que el requisito no menoscabe materialmente la capacidad del inversionista para ejercer el control de su inversión.

Artículo 10.09 Reservas y excepciones

1.   Los Artículos 10.02, 10.03, 10.07 y 10.08 no se aplican a:

   a)   cualquier medida disconforme existente que sea mantenida por:

   i)   una Parte a nivel nacional, como se estipula en su lista del Anexo I ó Ill; o

   ii)   un gobierno local o municipal;

   b)   la continuación o pronta renovación de cualquier medida disconforme a que se refiere el literal (a); ni

   c)   la modificación de cualquier medida disconforme a que se refiere el literal (a) siempre que dicha modificación no disminuya el grado de conformidad de la medida, tal y como estaba en vigencia antes de la modificación con los Artículos 10.02, 10.03, 10.07 y 10.08.

2.   Los Artículos 10.02, 10.03, 10.07 y 10.08 no se aplicarán a cualquier medida que una Parte adopte o mantenga, en relación con los sectores, subsectores o actividades, tal como se indica en su lista del Anexo Il.

3.   Ninguna de las Partes podrá exigir, de conformidad con cualquier medida adoptada después de la fecha de entrada en vigencia de este Tratado y comprendida en su lista del Anexo II, a un inversionista de la otra Parte, por razón de su nacionalidad, que venda o disponga de alguna otra manera de una inversión existente al momento en que la medida cobre vigencia.

4.   El Artículo 10.03 no se aplica al trato otorgado por una de las Partes de conformidad con los tratados, o con respecto a los sectores, estipulados en su lista del Anexo IV.

5.   Los Artículos 10.02, 10.03 y 10.08 no se aplican a:

a)   las compras realizadas por una Parte o por una empresa del Estado; o

b)   los subsidios o donaciones o aportaciones, incluyendo los préstamos, garantías y seguros respaldados por el gobierno, otorgados por una Parte o por una empresa del Estado.

Artículo 10.10 Transferencias

1.   Cada Parte permitirá que todas las transferencias relacionadas con la inversión de un inversionista de la otra Parte en el territorio de la Parte, se hagan libremente y sin demora. Dichas transferencias incluyen:

a)   utilidades, dividendos, intereses, ganancias de capital, pagos por regalías, gastos por administración, asistencia técnica y otros cargos, ganancias en especie y otros montos derivados de la inversión;

b)   productos derivados de la venta o liquidación, total o parcial, de la inversión;

c)   pagos realizados conforme a un contrato del que sea parte un inversionista o su inversión, incluidos pagos efectuados conforme a un convenio de préstamo;

d)   pagos efectuados de conformidad con el Artículo 10.11; y

e)   pagos que provengan de la aplicación de las disposiciones relativas al mecanismo de solución de controversias contenido en la Sección B de este Capítulo.

2.   Cada Parte permitirá que las transferencias se realicen en divisa de libre convertibilidad al tipo de cambio vigente de mercado en la fecha de la transferencia.

3.   Ninguna de las Partes podrá exigir a sus inversionistas que efectúen transferencias de sus ingresos, ganancias, o utilidades u otros montos derivados de, o atribuibles a, inversiones llevadas a cabo en territorio de la otra Parte, ni los sancionará en caso de que no realicen la transferencia.

4.   No obstante lo dispuesto en los párrafos 1 y 2, una Parte podrá establecer los mecanismos para impedir la realización de una transferencia, por medio de la aplicación equitativa, no discriminatoria de sus leyes en los siguientes casos:

a)   quiebra, insolvencia o protección de los derechos de los acreedores;

b)   infracciones penales o resoluciones administrativas en firme;

c)   incumplimiento del requisito de presentar informes de transferencias de divisas u otros instrumentos monetarios;

d)   aseguramiento del cumplimiento de sentencias y laudos dictados en procedimientos contenciosos; o

e)   relativas a asegurar el cumplimiento de las leyes y reglamentos para la emisión, comercio y operaciones de valores.

5.   El párrafo 3 no se interpretará como un impedimento para que una Parte, a través de la aplicación de sus leyes de manera equitativa, no discriminatoria, imponga cualquier medida relacionada con el párrafo 4 del (a) al (e).

Artículo 10.11 Expropiación e indemnización

1.   Ninguna de las Partes podrá nacionalizar ni expropiar, directa o indirectamente, una inversión de un inversionista de la otra Parte en su territorio, ni adoptar ninguna medida equivalente a la expropiación o nacionalización de esa inversión ("expropiación"), salvo que sea:

a)   por causa de utilidad pública u orden público e interés social, conforme a lo dispuesto en el Anexo 10.11(1);

b)   sobre bases no discriminatorias;

c)   con apego a los principios de legalidad y del debido proceso y al Artículo 10.06; y

d)   mediante indemnización conforme a las disposiciones de este Artículo.

2.   La indemnización será equivalente al valor justo de mercado que tenga la inversión expropiada inmediatamente antes de que la medida expropiatoria se haya llevado a cabo (fecha de expropiación), y no reflejará ningún cambio en el valor debido a que la intención de expropiar se conoció con antelación a la fecha de expropiación. Los criterios de valuación podrán incluir el valor corriente, el valor del activo, incluyendo el valor fiscal declarado de bienes tangibles, así como otros criterios que resulten apropiados para determinar el valor justo de mercado.

3.   El pago de la indemnización se hará sin demora y será completamente liquidable.

4.   Sin perjuicio de lo establecido en el párrafo 5, la cantidad pagada por concepto de indemnización no podrá ser inferior a la cantidad equivalente que, de acuerdo al tipo de cambio vigente en la fecha de determinación del justo valor de mercado, se hubiera pagado en dicha fecha al inversionista expropiado en una moneda de libre convertibilidad en el mercado financiero internacional. La indemnización incluirá el pago de intereses calculados desde el día de la desposesión de la inversión expropiada hasta el día de pago, los que serán calculados sobre la base de una tasa pasiva o de captación promedio para dicha moneda del sistema bancario nacional de la Parte donde se efectúa la expropiación.

5.   En caso de que la indemnización sea pagada en una moneda de libre convertibilidad, la indemnización incluirá intereses calculados desde el día de la desposesión de la inversión expropiada hasta el día de pago, los que serán calculados sobre la base de una tasa pasiva o de captación promedio para dicha moneda del sistema bancario nacional de la Parte donde se efectúa la expropiación.

6.   Una vez pagada, la indemnización podrá transferirse libremente de conformidad con el Artículo 10.10.

7.   Este Artículo no se aplica a la expedición de licencias obligatorias otorgadas en relación con derechos de propiedad intelectual, o a la revocación, limitación o creación de derechos de propiedad intelectual, en la medida que dicha expedición, revocación, limitación o creación sea conforme con el ADPIC.

8.   Para los efectos de este Artículo y para mayor certeza, no se considerará que una medida no discriminatoria de aplicación general es una medida equivalente a la expropiación de un valor de deuda o un préstamo cubiertos por este Capítulo, sólo porque dicha medida imponga costos a un deudor cuyo resultado sea la falta de pago de la deuda.

Artículo 10.12 Formalidades especiales y requisitos de información

1.   Ninguna disposición del Artículo 10.02 se interpretará en el sentido de impedir a una Parte adoptar o mantener una medida que prescriba formalidades especiales conexas al establecimiento de inversiones por inversionistas de la otra Parte, tales como que las inversiones se constituyan conforme a las leyes y reglamentos de la Parte, siempre que dichas formalidades no menoscaben significativamente la protección otorgada por una Parte de conformidad con este Capítulo.

2.   No obstante lo dispuesto en los Artículos 10.02 y 10.03, una Parte podrá exigir de un inversionista de la otra Parte o de su inversión, en su territorio, que proporcione información rutinaria referente a esa inversión, exclusivamente con fines de información o estadística. La Parte protegerá de cualquier divulgación la información de negocios que sea confidencial, que pudiera afectar negativamente la situación competitiva del inversionista o de la inversión.

Artículo 10.13 Relación con otros Capítulos

1.   En caso de incompatibilidad entre una disposición de este Capítulo y la disposición de otro, prevalecerá la de este último en la medida de la incompatibilidad.

2.   Si una Parte requiere a un prestador de servicios de la otra Parte que deposite una fianza u otra forma de garantía financiera como condición para prestar un servicio en su territorio, ello, por sí mismo no hace aplicable este Capítulo a la prestación transfronteriza de ese servicio. Este Capítulo se aplica al trato que otorgue esa Parte a la fianza depositada o garantía financiera.

Artículo 10.14 Denegación de beneficios

Previa notificación y consulta, hechas de acuerdo a lo prescrito en los Artículos 18.04 (Suministro de información) y 20.06 (Consultas), una Parte podrá denegar los beneficios de este Capítulo a un inversionista de la otra Parte que sea una empresa de dicha Parte y a las inversiones de tales inversionistas, si inversionistas de un país no Parte son propietarios o controlan la empresa en los términos indicados en la definición de "inversión de un inversionista de una Parte" del Artículo 10.40 y ésta no tiene actividades comerciales sustanciales en el territorio de la Parte conforme a cuya ley está constituida u organizada.

Artículo 10.15 Medidas relativas al medio ambiente

1.   Ninguna disposición del presente Capítulo se interpretará como impedimento para que una Parte adopte, mantenga o ponga en ejecución cualquier medida, consistente con este Capítulo, que considere apropiada para asegurar que las actividades de inversión en su territorio observen la legislación ecológica o medio ambiental en esa Parte.

2.   Las Partes reconocen que es inadecuado alentar la inversión por medio de un relajamiento de las medidas internas aplicables a la salud o la seguridad o relativas a la ecología o el medio ambiente. En consecuencia, ninguna Parte eliminará o se comprometerá a eximir de la

aplicación de esas medidas a la inversión de un inversionista, como medio para inducir el establecimiento, la adquisición, la expansión o conservación de la inversión de un inversionista en su territorio. Si una Parte estima que la otra Parte ha alentado una inversión de tal manera, podrá solicitar consultas con esa otra Parte.

Sección B – Solución de controversias entre una Parte y un inversionista de la otra Parte

Artículo 10.16 Objetivo

Sin perjuicio de los derechos y obligaciones de las Partes establecidos en el Capítulo 20 (Solución de Controversias), esta Sección establece un mecanismo para la solución de controversias en materia de inversión que se susciten como consecuencia de la violación de una obligación establecida en la Sección A de este Capítulo, y asegura, tanto el trato igual entre inversionistas de las Partes de acuerdo con el principio de reciprocidad, como el debido ejercicio de la garantía de audiencia y defensa dentro de un debido proceso legal ante un tribunal arbitral imparcial.

Artículo 10.17 Reclamación de un inversionista de una Parte, por cuenta propia

1.   De conformidad con esta Sección, un inversionista de una Parte podrá someter a arbitraje una reclamación cuyo fundamento sea que la otra Parte o una empresa controlada directa o indirectamente por esa Parte, ha violado una obligación establecida en este Capítulo, siempre y cuando el inversionista haya sufrido pérdidas o daños en virtud de esa violación o a consecuencia de ella.

2.   Un inversionista no podrá presentar una reclamación si han transcurrido más de tres (3) años a partir de la fecha en la cual tuvo conocimiento por primera vez o debió haber tenido conocimiento de la presunta violación, así como conocimiento de que sufrió pérdidas o daños.

Artículo 10.18 Reclamación de un inversionista de una Parte, en representación de una empresa

1.   Un inversionista de una Parte, en representación de una empresa de la otra Parte que sea una persona jurídica propiedad del inversionista o que esté bajo su control directo o indirecto, podrá someter a arbitraje, de conformidad con esta Sección, una reclamación cuyo fundamento sea que la otra Parte o una empresa controlada directa o indirectamente por esa Parte haya violado una obligación establecida en este Capítulo, siempre y cuando la empresa haya sufrido pérdidas o daños en virtud de esa violación o a consecuencia de ella.

2.   Un inversionista no podrá presentar una reclamación en representación de la empresa a la que se refiere el párrafo 1, si han transcurrido más de tres (3) años a partirde la fecha en la cual la empresa tuvo conocimiento por primera vez, o debió tener conocimiento de la presunta violación, así como conocimiento de que sufrió pérdidas o daños.

3.   Cuando un inversionista presente una reclamación de conformidad con este Artículo y, de manera paralela un inversionista que no tenga el control de una empresa, presente una reclamación en los términos del Artículo 10.17 como consecuencia de los mismos actos que dieron lugar a la presentación de una reclamación de acuerdo con este Artículo, o dos o más reclamaciones se sometan a arbitraje en los términos del Artículo 10.21, el Tribunal establecido

conforme al Artículo 10.27, examinará conjuntamente dichas reclamaciones, salvo que el Tribunal de acumulación determine que los intereses de una parte contendiente se verían perjudicados por ello.

4.   Una inversión no podrá presentar una reclamación a arbitraje conforme a esta Sección.

Artículo 10.19 Solución de una controversia mediante consulta y negociación

Las partes contendientes intentarán primero dirimir la controversia por vía de consulta o negociación.

Artículo 10.20 Notificación de la intención de someter la reclamación a arbitraje

El inversionista contendiente notificará por escrito a la Parte contendiente su intención de someter una reclamación a arbitraje al menos noventa (90) días antes de que se presente la reclamación, y la notificación señalará lo siguiente:

a)   el nombre y dirección del inversionista contendiente y cuando la reclamación se haya realizado conforme al Artículo 10.18, incluirá la denominación o razón social y el domicilio de la empresa;

b)   las disposiciones de este Capítulo presuntamente incumplidas y cualquier otra disposición aplicable;

c)   las cuestiones de hecho y de derecho en que se fundamente la reclamación; y

d)   la reparación que se solicita y el monto aproximado de los daños reclamados.

Artículo 10.21 Sometimiento de la reclamación al arbitraje

1.   Salvo lo dispuesto en el Anexo 10.21 y siempre que hayan transcurrido seis (6) meses desde que tuvieron lugar los actos que motivan la reclamación, un inversionista contendiente podrá someter la reclamación a arbitraje de acuerdo con:

   a)   el Convenio del CIADI, siempre que tanto la Parte contendiente como la Parte del inversionista, sean Estados parte del mismo;

   b)   las Reglas del Mecanismo Complementario del CIADI, cuando la Parte contendiente o la Parte del inversionista, pero no ambas, sea Parte del Convenio del CIADI; o

   c)   las Reglas de Arbitraje de la CNUDMI.

2.   Las reglas propias de cada uno de los procedimientos arbitrales establecidos en este Capítulo regirán el arbitraje, salvo en la medida de lo modificado en esta Sección.

Artículo 10.22 Condiciones previas al sometimiento de una reclamación al procedimiento arbitral

1.   El consentimiento de las partes contendientes al procedimiento de arbitraje conforme a este Capítulo se considerará como consentimiento a ese arbitraje con exclusión de cualquier otro mecanismo.

2.   Cada Parte podrá exigir el agotamiento previo de sus recursos administrativos como condición a su consentimiento al arbitraje conforme a este Capítulo. Sin embargo, si transcurridos seis (6) meses a partir del momento en que se interpusieron los recursos administrativos correspondientes, las autoridades administrativas no han emitido su resolución final, el inversionista podrá recurrir directamente al arbitraje, de conformidad con lo establecido en esta Sección.

3.   Un inversionista contendiente podrá someter una reclamación al procedimiento arbitral de conformidad con el Artículo 10.17, sólo si:

    a)   consiente someterse al arbitraje en los términos de los procedimientos establecidos en esta Sección; y

    b)   el inversionista y, cuando la reclamación se refiera a pérdida o daño de una participación en una empresa de la otra Parte que sea una persona jurídica propiedad del inversionista o que esté bajo su control directo o indirecto, la empresa renuncian a su derecho a iniciar o continuar cualquier procedimiento ante cualquier tribunal judicial conforme al derecho de cualquiera de las Partes u otros procedimientos de solución de controversias respecto a la medida de la Parte contendiente presuntamente violatoria de las disposiciones a las que se refiere el Artículo 10.17, salvo los procedimientos que no tengan por objeto el pago de daños, en los que se solicite la aplicación de medidas precautorias de carácter suspensivo, declaratorio o extraordinario, ante el tribunal administrativo o judicial, conforme a la legislación de la Parte contendiente.

    En consecuencia, una vez que el inversionista o la empresa hayan sometido la reclamación a un procedimiento arbitral de conformidad con esta Sección, la elección de dicho procedimiento será única y definitiva excluyendo la posibilidad de someter la reclamación ante el tribunal nacional competente de la parte contendiente o a otros procedimientos de solución de controversias, sin perjuicio de las excepciones señaladas anteriormente con respecto a medidas precautorias.

4.   Un inversionista contendiente podrá someter una reclamación al procedimiento arbitral de conformidad con el Artículo 10.18, sólo si tanto el inversionista como la empresa:

    a)   consienten en someterse al arbitraje en los términos de los procedimientos establecidos en esta Sección; y

    b)   renuncian a su derecho de iniciar o continuar cualquier procedimiento con respecto a la medida de la Parte contendiente que presuntamente sea una de las violaciones a las que se refiere el Artículo 10.18 ante cualquier tribunal judicial conforme al derecho de una Parte u otros procedimientos de solución de controversias, salvo los procedimientos que no tengan por objeto el pago de daños, en los que se solicite la aplicación de medidas precautorias de carácter suspensivo, declaratorio o extraordinario, ante el tribunal administrativo o judicial, conforme al derecho de la Parte contendiente.

En consecuencia, una vez que el inversionista o la empresa hayan sometido la reclamación a un procedimiento arbitral de conformidad con esta Sección, la elección de dicho procedimiento será única y definitiva excluyendo la posibilidad de someter la reclamación ante el tribunal nacional competente de la parte contendiente o a otros procedimientos de solución de controversias, sin perjuicio de las excepciones señaladas anteriormente con respecto a medidas precautorias.

5.   El consentimiento y la renuncia requeridos por este Artículo se manifestarán por escrito, se entregarán a la Parte contendiente y se incluirán en el sometimiento de la reclamación a arbitraje.

6.   Sólo en el caso que la Parte contendiente haya privado al inversionista contendiente del control de una empresa, no se requerirá la renuncia de la empresa conforme a los párrafos 3(b) y 4(b).

Artículo 10.23 Consentimiento al arbitraje

1.   Cada Parte consiente en someter reclamaciones a arbitraje con apego a los procedimientos y requisitos establecidos en esta Sección.

2.   El consentimiento a que se refiere el párrafo 1 y el sometimiento de una reclamación a arbitraje por parte de un inversionista contendiente implicará haber cumplido con los requisitos señalados en:

   a)   el Capítulo II del Convenio del CIADI (Jurisdicción del Centro) y las Reglas del Mecanismo Complementario que exigen el consentimiento por escrito de las Partes;

   b)   el Artículo II de la Convención de Nueva York, que exige un acuerdo por escrito; y

   c)   el Artículo I de la Convención Interamericana, que requiere un acuerdo.

Artículo 10.24 Número de árbitros y método de nombramiento

Con excepción de lo que se refiere al Tribunal establecido conforme al Artículo 10.27, y a menos que las partes contendientes acuerden algo distinto, el Tribunal estará integrado por tres (3) árbitros. Cada una de las partes contendientes nombrará a uno (1). El tercer árbitro, quien será el presidente del Tribunal, será designado por acuerdo de las partes contendientes.

Artículo 10.25 Integración del Tribunal en caso de que una parte contendiente no designe árbitro o las partes contendientes no logren un acuerdo en la designación del presidente del Tribunal

1.   En caso de que una parte contendiente no designe árbitro o no se logre un acuerdo en la designación del presidente del Tribunal, el Secretario General nombrará a los árbitros en los procedimientos de arbitraje, de conformidad con esta Sección.

2.   Cuando un Tribunal, que no sea el establecido de conformidad con el Artículo 10.27, no se integre en un plazo de noventa (90) días a partir de la fecha en que la reclamación se someta al arbitraje, el Secretario General, a petición de cualquiera de las partes contendientes y, en lo posible, previa consulta de las mismas, nombrará al árbitro o árbitros no designados todavía, pero no al presidente del Tribunal quien será designado conforme a lo dispuesto en el párrafo 3. En todo caso, la mayoría de los árbitros no podrá ser nacional de la Parte contendiente o nacional de la Parte del inversionista contendiente.

3.   El Secretario General designará al presidente del Tribunal de la lista de árbitros a la que se refiere el párrafo 4, asegurándose que el presidente del Tribunal no sea nacional de la Parte contendiente o nacional de la Parte del inversionista contendiente. En caso de que no se encuentre en la lista un árbitro disponible para presidir el Tribunal, el Secretario General designará, de la Lista de Árbitros del CIADI, al presidente del Tribunal, siempre que sea de nacionalidad distinta a la de la Parte contendiente o a la de la Parte del inversionista contendiente.

4.   A la fecha de entrada en vigencia de este Tratado, las Partes establecerán y mantendrán una lista de dieciocho (18) árbitros como posibles presidentes del Tribunal, ninguno de los cuales podrá ser nacional de una Parte, que reúnan los requisitos establecidos en el Convenio del CIADI y en las reglas contempladas en el Artículo 10.21 y que cuenten con experiencia en Derecho Internacional y en materia de inversión. Los miembros de la lista serán designados por mutuo acuerdo sin importar su nacionalidad por un plazo de dos (2) años, renovables si por consenso las Partes así lo acuerdan. En caso de muerte o renuncia de un miembro de la lista, las Partes de mutuo acuerdo designarán a otra persona que le reemplace en sus funciones para el resto del período para el que aquél fue nombrado.

Artículo 10.26 Consentimiento para la designación de árbitros

Para los propósitos del Artículo 39 del Convenio del CIADI y del Artículo 7 de la Parte C de las Reglas del Mecanismo Complementario, y sin perjuicio de objetar a un árbitro de conformidad con el Artículo 10.25(3) o sobre base distinta a la nacionalidad:

a)   la Parte contendiente acepta la designación de cada uno de los miembros de un Tribunal establecido de conformidad con el Convenio del CIADI o con las Reglas del Mecanismo Complementario;

b)   un inversionista contendiente a que se refiere el Artículo 10.17 podrá someter una reclamación a arbitraje o continuar el procedimiento conforme al Convenio del CIADI o a las Reglas del Mecanismo Complementario, únicamente a condición de que el inversionista contendiente manifieste su consentimiento por escrito sobre la designación de cada uno de los miembros del Tribunal;

c)   el inversionista contendiente a que se refiere el Artículo 10.18(1) podrá someter una reclamación a arbitraje o continuar el procedimiento conforme al Convenio del CIADI o a las Reglas del Mecanismo Complementario, únicamente a condición de que el inversionista contendiente y la empresa que representa manifiesten su consentimiento por escrito sobre la designación de cada uno de los miembros del Tribunal.

Artículo 10.27 Acumulación de procedimientos

1.   Un Tribunal de acumulación establecido conforme a este Artículo se instalará con apego a las Reglas de Arbitraje de la CNUDMI y procederá de conformidad con lo contemplado en dichas Reglas, salvo lo dispuesto en esta Sección.

2.   Cuando un Tribunal de acumulación establecido conforme a este Artículo determine que las reclamaciones sometidas a arbitraje de acuerdo con el Artículo 10.21 plantean una cuestión en común de hecho o de derecho, el Tribunal de acumulación, en interés de una resolución justa y eficiente, y habiendo escuchado a las partes contendientes, podrá ordenar que:

   a)   asuma jurisdicción, conozca y resuelva todas o parte de las reclamaciones, de manera conjunta; o

   b)   asuma jurisdicción, conozca y resuelva una o más de las reclamaciones sobre la base de que ello contribuirá a la resolución de las otras.

3.   Una parte contendiente que pretenda obtener una orden de acumulación en los términos del párrafo 2, solicitará al Secretario General que instale un Tribunal de acumulación y especificará en su solicitud:

   a)   el nombre de la Parte contendiente o de los inversionistas contendientes contra los cuales se pretenda obtener la orden de acumulación;

   b)   la naturaleza de la orden de acumulación solicitada; y

   c)   el fundamento en que se apoya la solicitud.

4.   La parte contendiente entregará copia de su solicitud a la Parte contendiente o a los inversionistas contendientes contra quienes se pretende obtener la orden de acumulación.

5.   En un plazo de sesenta (60) días a partir de la fecha de la recepción de la solicitud, el Secretario General instalará un Tribunal de acumulación integrado por tres (3) árbitros. El Secretario General nombrará al presidente del Tribunal de acumulación de la lista de árbitros a la que se refiere el Artículo 10.25(4). En caso que no se encuentre en la lista un (1) árbitro disponible para presidir el Tribunal de acumulación, el Secretario General designará, de la Lista de Árbitros del CIADI, al presidente del Tribunal de acumulación quien no será nacional de ninguna de las Partes. El Secretario General designará a los otros dos (2) integrantes del Tribunal de acumulación de la lista a la que se refiere el Artículo 10.25(4) y, cuando no estén disponibles en dicha lista, los seleccionará de la Lista de Árbitros del CIADI; de no haber disponibilidad de árbitros en esta Lista, el Secretario General hará discrecionalmente los nombramientos faltantes. Uno (1) de los miembros será nacional de la Parte contendiente y el otro miembro del Tribunal de acumulación será nacional de la Parte de los inversionistas contendientes.

6.   Cuando se haya establecido un Tribunal de acumulación conforme a este Artículo, el inversionista contendiente que haya sometido una reclamación a arbitraje conforme al Artículo 10.17 ó 10.18 y no haya sido mencionado en la solicitud de acumulación hecha de acuerdo con el párrafo 3, podrá solicitar por escrito al Tribunal de acumulación que se le incluya en una solicitud de acumulación de acuerdo con el párrafo 2, y especificará en dicha solicitud:

a)   el nombre y dirección del inversionista contendiente y en su caso la denominación o razón social y el domicilio de la empresa;

b)   la naturaleza de la orden de acumulación solicitada; y

c)   los fundamentos en que se apoya la solicitud.

7.   Un inversionista contendiente al que se refiere el párrafo 6, entregará copia de su solicitud a las partes contendientes señaladas en una solicitud hecha conforme al párrafo 3.

8.   Un Tribunal establecido conforme al Artículo 10.21 no tendrá jurisdicción para resolver una reclamación, o parte de ella, respecto de la cual haya asumido jurisdicción un Tribunal de acumulación establecido conforme a este Artículo.

9.   A solicitud de una parte contendiente, un Tribunal de acumulación establecido de conformidad con este Artículo podrá, en espera de su decisión conforme al párrafo 2, disponer que los procedimientos de un Tribunal establecido de acuerdo al Artículo 10.21 se aplacen a menos que ese último Tribunal haya suspendido sus procedimientos hasta tanto se resuelva sobre la procedencia de la acumulación.

10.   Una Parte contendiente entregará al Secretariado en un plazo de quince (15) días a partir de la fecha en que se reciba por la Parte contendiente, una copia de:

a)   una solicitud de arbitraje hecha conforme al párrafo 1 del Artículo 36 del Convenio del CIADI;

b)   una notificación de arbitraje en los términos del Artículo 2 de la Parte C de las Reglas del Mecanismo Complementario del CIADI; o

c)   una notificación de arbitraje en los términos previstos por las Reglas de Arbitraje de la CNUDMI.

11.   Una Parte contendiente entregará al Secretariado copia de la solicitud formulada en los términos del párrafo 3:

a)   en un plazo de quince (15) días a partir de la recepción de la solicitud en el caso de una petición hecha por el inversionista contendiente;

b)   en un plazo de quince (15) días a partir de la fecha en que la solicitud fue hecha en el caso de una petición hecha por la Parte contendiente.

12.   Una Parte contendiente entregará al Secretariado, copia de una solicitud formulada en los términos del párrafo 6 en un plazo de quince (15) días a partir de la fecha de recepción de la solicitud.

13.   El Secretariado conservará un registro público de los documentos a los que se refieren los párrafos 10, 11 y 1 2.

Artículo 10.28 Notificación

La Parte contendiente entregará a la otra Parte:

a)   notificación escrita de una reclamación que se haya sometido a arbitraje a más tardar treinta (30) días después de la fecha de sometimiento de la reclamación a arbitraje; y

b)   copias de todos los escritos de alegatos presentados en el procedimiento arbitral.

Artículo 10.29 Participación de una Parte

Previa notificación escrita a las partes contendientes, una Parte podrá plantear a un Tribunal establecido conforme a esta Sección sus puntos de vista sobre una cuestión de interpretación de este Tratado.

Artículo 10.30 Documentación

1.   Una Parte tendrá, a su costa, derecho a recibir de la Parte contendiente una copia de:

a)   las pruebas ofrecidas a cualquier Tribunal establecido conforme a esta Sección; y

b)   los argumentos escritos presentados por las partes contendientes.

2.   Una Parte que reciba información conforme a lo dispuesto en el párrafo 1, dará tratamiento confidencial a la información como si fuera una Parte contendiente.

Artículo 10.31 Sede del procedimiento arbitral

Salvo que las partes contendientes acuerden algo distinto, un Tribunal establecido conforme a esta Sección llevará a cabo el procedimiento arbitral en territorio de una Parte que sea parte de la Convención de Nueva York, el cual será elegido de conformidad con:

a)   las Reglas del Mecanismo Complementario del CIADI, si el arbitraje se rige por esas Reglas o por el Convenio del CIADI; o

b)   las Reglas de Arbitraje de la CNUDMI, si el arbitraje se rige por esas Reglas.

Artículo 10.32 Derecho aplicable

1.   Un Tribunal establecido conforme a esta Sección decidirá las controversias que se sometan a su consideración de conformidad con este Tratado y con las reglas aplicables del Derecho Internacional.

2.   La interpretación que formule la Comisión sobre una disposición de este Tratado será obligatoria para un Tribunal establecido de conformidad con esta Sección.

Artículo 10.33 Interpretación de los Anexos

1.   Cuando una Parte alegue como defensa que una medida presuntamente violatoria cae en el ámbito de una reserva o excepción consignada en cualquiera de los Anexos a petición de la

Parte contendiente, cualquier Tribunal establecido de conformidad con esta Sección solicitará a la Comisión una interpretación sobre ese asunto. La Comisión, en un plazo de sesenta (60) días a partir de la entrega de la solicitud, presentará por escrito al Tribunal su interpretación.

2.   En seguimiento al Artículo 10.32(2), la interpretación de la Comisión sometida conforme al párrafo 1 será obligatoria para cualquier Tribunal establecido de conformidad con esta Sección. Si la Comisión no somete una interpretación dentro de un plazo de sesenta (60) días, el Tribunal decidirá sobre el asunto.

Artículo 10.34 Dictámenes de expertos

Sin perjuicio de la designación de otro tipo de expertos cuando lo autoricen las reglas de arbitraje aplicables, el Tribunal, a petición de una parte contendiente, o por iniciativa propia, podrá designar uno o más expertos para dictaminar por escrito cualquier cuestión relacionada con la controversia.

Artículo 10.35 Medidas provisionales de protección

Un Tribunal establecido conforme a esta Sección podrá solicitar a los tribunales nacionales, o dictar a las partes contendientes, medidas provisionales de protección para preservar los derechos de la parte contendiente o para asegurar que la competencia o jurisdicción del Tribunal surta plenos efectos. Ese Tribunal no podrá ordenar el secuestro o embargo, o el acatamiento a, o la suspensión de la aplicación de la medida presuntamente violada a la que se refiere el Artículo 10.17 ó 10.18.

Artículo 10.36 Laudo definitivo

1.   Cuando un Tribunal establecido de conformidad con esta Sección dicte un laudo definitivo desfavorable a una Parte, dicho Tribunal sólo podrá resolver sobre:

   a)   daños pecuniarios y los intereses que procedan; o

   b)   la restitución de la propiedad, en cuyo caso el laudo dispondrá que la Parte contendiente podrá pagar daños pecuniarios, más los intereses que procedan, en lugar de la restitución.

Un Tribunal podrá también otorgar el pago de costas de acuerdo con las reglas de arbitraje aplicables.

2.   De conformidad con el párrafo 1, cuando la reclamación se haga conforme al Artículo 10.18(1):

   a)   el laudo que prevea la restitución de la propiedad, dispondrá que la restitución se otorgue a la empresa;

   b)   el laudo que conceda daños pecuniarios e intereses que procedan, dispondrá que la suma de dinero se pague a la empresa.

3.   Para efectos de los párrafos 1 y 2, los daños se determinarán en la moneda en que se haya realizado la inversión.

4.   El laudo se dictará sin perjuicio de los derechos que un tercero con interés jurídico tenga sobre la reparación de los daños que haya sufrido, conforme a la legislación aplicable.

Artículo 10.37 Definitividad y ejecución del laudo

1.   El laudo dictado por cualquier Tribunal establecido conforme a esta Sección será obligatorio sólo para las partes contendientes y únicamente respecto del caso concreto.

2.   Conforme a lo dispuesto en el párrafo 3 y al procedimiento de revisión, aclaración o anulación aplicable a un laudo previstos bajo el mecanismo aplicable que sea procedente a juicio del Secretario General, una parte contendiente acatará y cumplirá con un laudo sin demora.

3.   Una parte contendiente podrá solicitar la ejecución de un laudo definitivo en tanto:

    a)   en el caso de un laudo definitivo dictado conforme al Convenio del CIADI:

        i)   hayan transcurrido ciento veinte (120) días desde la fecha en que se dictó el laudo y sin que ninguna parte contendiente haya solicitado la revisión o anulación del mismo; o

        ii)   hayan concluido los procedimientos de aclaración, revisión o anulación; y

    b)   en el caso de un laudo definitivo conforme a las Reglas del Mecanismo Complementario del CIADI o las Reglas de Arbitraje de la CNUDMI:

        i)   hayan transcurrido tres (3) meses desde la fecha en que se dictó el laudo y sin que ninguna parte contendiente haya iniciado un procedimiento para revisarlo, revocarlo o anularlo; o

        ii)   un tribunal de la Parte contendiente haya desechado o admitido una solicitud de reconsideración, revocación o anulación del laudo que una de las partes contendientes haya presentado y esta resolución no pueda recurrirse.

4.   Cada Parte dispondrá la debida ejecución de un laudo en su territorio.

5.   Cuando una Parte contendiente incumpla o no acate un laudo definitivo, la Comisión, a la entrega de una solicitud de una Parte cuyo inversionista fue parte en el procedimiento de arbitraje, integrará un grupo arbitral conforme al Artículo 20.08 (Solicitud de integración del grupo arbitral). La Parte solicitante podrá invocar dichos procedimientos para obtener:

    a)   una determinación en el sentido de que el incumplimiento o desacato de los términos del laudo definitivo es contrario a las obligaciones de este Tratado; y

    b)   una recomendación en el sentido de que la Parte cumpla y acate el laudo definitivo.

6.   El inversionista contendiente podrá recurrir a la ejecución de un laudo arbitral conforme al Convenio del CIADI, la Convención de Nueva York o la Convención Interamericana,

independientemente de que se hayan iniciado o no los procedimientos contemplados en el párrafo 5.

7.   Para los efectos del Artículo 1 de la Convención de Nueva York y del Artículo 1 de la Convención Interamericana, se considerará que la reclamación que se somete a arbitraje conforme a esta Sección, surge de una relación u operación comercial.

Artículo 10.38 Disposiciones generales

Momento en que la reclamación se considera sometida al procedimiento arbitral

1.   Una reclamación se considera sometida a arbitraje en los términos de esta Sección cuando:

a)   la solicitud para un arbitraje conforme al párrafo 1 del Artículo 36 del Convenio del CIADI ha sido recibida por el Secretario General;

b)   la notificación de arbitraje de conformidad con el Artículo 2 de la Parte C de las Reglas del Mecanismo Complementario del CIADI ha sido recibida por el Secretario General; o

c)   la notificación de arbitraje contemplada en las Reglas de Arbitraje de la CNUDMI ha sido recibida por la Parte contendiente.

Entrega de la notificación y otros documentos

2.   La entrega de la notificación y otros documentos a una Parte se hará en el lugar designado por ella en el Anexo 10.38(2).

Pagos conforme a contratos de seguro o garantía

3.   En un procedimiento arbitral conforme a lo previsto en esta Sección, una Parte no aducirá como defensa, contrademanda, derecho de compensación, u otros, que el inversionista contendiente ha recibido o recibirá, de acuerdo a un contrato de seguro o garantía, indemnización u otra compensación por todos o por parte de los presuntos daños cuya restitución solicita.

Publicación de un laudo

4.   Los laudos se publicarán únicamente en el caso de que exista acuerdo por escrito entre las partes contendientes.

Artículo 10.39 Exclusiones

Las disposiciones de solución de controversias de esta Sección o las del Capítulo 20 (Solución de Controversias) no se aplicarán a los supuestos contenidos en el Anexo 10.39.

Sección C – Definiciones

Artículo 10.40 Definiciones

Para efectos de este Capítulo, se entenderá por:

CIADI: el Centro Internacional de Arreglo de Diferencias Relativas a Inversiones;
Convención de Nueva York: la Convención de Naciones Unidas sobre el Reconocimiento y Ejecución de las Sentencias Arbitrales Extranjeras, celebrada en Nueva York el 10 de junio de 1958;

Convención Interamericana: la Convención Interamericana sobre Arbitraje Comercial Internacional, celebrada en Panamá el 30 de enero de 1975;

Convenio del CIADI: el Convenio sobre Arreglo de Diferencias Relativas a Inversiones entre Estados y Nacionales de otros Estados, celebrado en Washington el 18 de marzo de 1965;

empresa: "empresa" tal como se define en el Capítulo 2 (Definiciones Generales);

empresa de una Parte: una empresa constituida u organizada de conformidad con la ley de una Parte; y una sucursal ubicada en territorio de una Parte y que desempeñe actividades comerciales en el mismo;

inversión: toda clase de bienes o derechos de cualquier naturaleza, adquiridos o utilizados con el propósito de obtener un beneficio económico u otros fines empresariales, adquiridos con recursos transferidos o reinvertidos por un inversionista, y comprenderá:

a)	una empresa, acciones de una empresa, participaciones en el capital social de una empresa, que le permitan al propietario participar en los ingresos o en las utilidades de la misma. Instrumentos de deuda de una empresa y préstamos a una empresa cuando:

	i)	la empresa es una filial del inversionista, o

	ii)	la fecha de vencimiento original del instrumento de deuda o el préstamo sea por lo menos de tres (3) años;

b)	una participación en una empresa que otorgue derecho al propietario para participar del haber social de esa empresa en una liquidación, siempre que éste no derive de un instrumento de deuda o un préstamo excluidos conforme al literal (a);

c)	bienes raíces u otra propiedad, tangibles o intangibles, incluidos los derechos en el ámbito de la propiedad intelectual, así como cualquier otro derecho real (tales como hipotecas, derechos de prenda, usufructo y derechos similares) adquiridos con la expectativa de, o utilizados con el propósito de, obtener un beneficio económico o para otros fines empresariales; y

d)	la participación o beneficio que resulte de destinar capital u otros recursos comprometidos para el desarrollo de una actividad económica en territorio de una Parte, entre otros, conforme a:

i)   contratos que involucran la presencia de la propiedad de un inversionista en territorio de la Parte, incluidos, las concesiones, los contratos de construcción y de llave en mano; o

ii)   contratos donde la remuneración depende sustancialmente de la producción, ingresos o ganancias de una empresa;

pero inversión no significa,

- una obligación de pago de, ni el otorgamiento de un crédito a, el Estado o una empresa del Estado;

- reclamaciones pecuniarias derivadas exclusivamente de:

i)   contratos comerciales para la venta de bienes o servicios por un nacional o empresa en territorio de una Parte a una empresa en territorio de la otra Parte; o

ii)   el otorgamiento de crédito en relación con una transacción comercial, cuya fecha de vencimiento sea menor a tres (3) años, como el financiamiento al comercio; salvo un préstamo cubierto por las disposiciones de un préstamo a una empresa según se establece en el literal (a); o

- cualquier otra reclamación pecuniaria que no conlleve los tipos de interés dispuestos en los literales del (a) al (d);

inversionista contendiente: un inversionista que formula una reclamación en los términos de la Sección B de este Capítulo;

inversión de un inversionista de una Parte: la inversión propiedad o bajo control directo o indirecto de un inversionista de dicha Parte.

En caso de una empresa, una inversión es propiedad de un inversionista de una Parte si ese inversionista tiene la titularidad de más del cincuenta por ciento (50%) de su capital social.

Una inversión está bajo el control de un inversionista de una Parte si ese inversionista tiene la facultad de:

i)   designar a la mayoría de sus directores; o

ii)   dirigir legalmente de otro modo sus operaciones;

inversionista de una Parte: una Parte o una empresa de la misma, o un nacional o empresa de dicha Parte, que pretende realizar o, en su caso, realice o haya realizado una inversión en territorio de la otra Parte. La intención de pretender realizar una inversión podrá manifestarse, entre otras formas, mediante actos jurídicos tendientes a materializar la inversión, o estando en vías de comprometer los recursos necesarios para realizarla;

Parte contendiente: la Parte contra la cual se hace una reclamación en los términos de la Sección B de este Capítulo;

parte contendiente: el inversionista contendiente o la Parte contendiente;

partes contendientes: el inversionista contendiente y la Parte contendiente;

reclamación: la demanda hecha por el inversionista contendiente contra una Parte en los términos de la Sección B de este Capítulo;

Reglas de Arbitraje de la CNUDMI: las Reglas de Arbitraje de la Comisión de las Naciones Unidas sobre Derecho Mercantil Internacional (CNUDMI), aprobadas por la Asamblea General de las Naciones Unidas el 15 de diciembre de 1976;

Secretario General: el Secretario General del CIADI;

transferencias: transferencias y pagos internacionales;

Tribunal: un tribunal arbitral establecido conforme al Artículo 10.21; y

Tribunal de acumulación: un tribunal arbitral establecido conforme al Artículo 10.27.

ANEXO 10.38(2)

ENTREGA DE NOTIFICACIONES Y OTROS DOCUMENTOS

1.   Para efectos del Artículo 10.38(2), el lugar para la entrega de notificaciones y otros documentos será:

a)   para el caso de Costa Rica: Dirección General de Comercio Exterior, o su sucesora Centro de Comercio Exterior Paseo Colón San José, Costa Rica

b)   para el caso de El Salvador: Dirección de Política Comercial del Ministerio de Economía, o su sucesora Alameda Juan Pablo II, Calle Guadalupe, Edificio C-2, Planta 3 Centro de Gobierno San Salvador, El Salvador

c)   para el caso de Guatemala: Ministerio de Economía, o su sucesor 8ª. Avenida 10-43 zona 1 Guatemala, Guatemala

d)   para el caso de Honduras: Secretaría de Estado en los Despachos de Industria y Comercio Dirección General de Administración de Tratados, o su sucesora Calle Peatonal, Antiguo local de Lloyds Bank, Segundo Piso Tegucigalpa, Honduras

d)   para el caso de Nicaragua: Dirección General de Comercio Exterior, o su sucesora Ministerio de Fomento Industria y Comercio Km. 6 Carretera a Masaya Managua, Nicaragua

f)   para el caso de Panamá: Ministerio de Comercio e Industrias Viceministerio de Comercio Exterior, o su sucesor Dirección Nacional de Negociaciones Comerciales Internacionales, Vía Ricardo J. Alfaro, Plaza Edison, Piso #3, Panamá, República de Panamá

2.   Las Partes comunicarán cualquier cambio del lugar designado para la entrega de notificaciones y otros documentos.

CAPITULO 12

SERVICIOS FINANCIEROS

Artículo 12.01 Definiciones

Para efectos de este Capítulo, se entenderá por:

autoridades reguladoras: cualquier entidad gubernamental que ejerza autoridad de supervisión sobre prestadores de servicios financieros o instituciones financieras;

entidad pública: un banco central o autoridad monetaria de una Parte, o cualquier institución financiera de naturaleza pública, propiedad de una Parte o que esté bajo su control, cuando no esté ejerciendo funciones comerciales;

empresa: "empresa" tal como se define en el Capítulo 2 (Definiciones Generales);

institución financiera: cualquier empresa o intermediario financiero que esté autorizado para hacer negocios de prestar servicios financieros y esté regulado o supervisado como una institución financiera conforme a la legislación de la Parte en cuyo territorio se encuentre establecida;

institución financiera de la otra Parte: una institución financiera, incluso una sucursal de la misma, constituida de acuerdo con la legislación vigente, ubicada en territorio de una Parte que sea propiedad o esté controlada por personas de la otra Parte;

inversión: toda clase de bienes o derechos de cualquier naturaleza, adquiridos o utilizados con el propósito de obtener un beneficio económico u otros fines empresariales, adquiridos con recursos transferidos o reinvertidos por un inversionista, y comprenderá:

a)   una empresa, acciones de una empresa; participaciones en el capital social de una empresa, que le permitan al propietario participar en los ingresos o en las utilidades de la misma. Instrumentos de deuda de una empresa y préstamos a una empresa cuando:

i)   la empresa es una filial del inversionista; o

ii)   la fecha de vencimiento original del instrumento de deuda o el préstamo sea por lo menos de tres (3) años;

b)   una participación en una empresa que otorgue derecho al propietario para participar del haber social de esa empresa en una liquidación, siempre que éste no derive de un instrumento de deuda o un préstamo excluidos conforme al literal (a);

257

c) bienes raíces u otra propiedad, tangibles o intangibles, incluidos los derechos en el ámbito de la propiedad intelectual, así como cualquier otro derecho real (tales como hipotecas, derechos de prenda, usufructo y derechos similares) adquiridos con la expectativa de, o utilizados con el propósito de, obtener un beneficio económico o para otros fines empresariales;

d) la participación o beneficio que resulte de destinar capital u otros recursos comprometidos para el desarrollo de una actividad económica en territorio de una Parte, entre otros, conforme a:

   i) contratos que involucran la presencia de la propiedad de un inversionista en territorio de la Parte, incluidos, las concesiones, los contratos de construcción y de llave en mano; o

   ii) contratos donde la remuneración depende sustancialmente de la producción, ingresos o ganancias de una empresa; y

e) un préstamo otorgado por un prestador de servicios financieros transfronterizos o un valor de deuda propiedad del mismo, excepto un préstamo a una institución financiera o un valor de deuda emitido por la misma;

pero inversión no significa,

- una obligación de pago de, ni el otorgamiento de un crédito a, el Estado o una empresa del Estado;

- reclamaciones pecuniarias derivadas exclusivamente de:

   i) contratos comerciales para la venta de bienes o servicios por un nacional o empresa en territorio de una Parte a una empresa en territorio de la otra Parte; o

   ii) el otorgamiento de crédito en relación con una transacción comercial, cuya fecha de vencimiento sea menor a tres (3) años, como el financiamiento al comercio; salvo un préstamo cubierto por las disposiciones del literal (a);

- cualquier otra reclamación pecuniaria que no conlleve los tipos de interés dispuestos en los literales del (a) al (e);

- un préstamo otorgado a una institución financiera o un valor de deuda propiedad de una institución financiera, salvo que se trate de un préstamo a una institución financiera que sea tratado como capital para efectos regulatorios, por cualquier Parte en cuyo territorio esté ubicada la institución financiera;

inversión de un inversionista de una Parte: la inversión propiedad o bajo control directo o indirecto de un inversionista de dicha Parte.

En caso de una empresa, una inversión es propiedad de un inversionista de una Parte si ese inversionista tiene la titularidad de más del cincuenta por ciento (50%) de su capital social.

Una inversión está bajo el control de un inversionista de una Parte si ese inversionista tiene la facultad de:

i)   designar a la mayoría de sus directores; o

ii)   dirigir legalmente de otro modo sus operaciones;

inversionista de una Parte: una Parte o una empresa de la misma, o un nacional o empresa de dicha Parte, que pretende realizar o, en su caso, realice o haya realizado una inversión en territorio de la otra Parte. La intención de pretender realizar una inversión podrá manifestarse, entre otras formas, mediante actos jurídicos tendientes a materializar la inversión, o estando en vías de comprometer los recursos necesarios para realizarla;

inversionista contendiente: un inversionista que someta a arbitraje una reclamación en los términos del Artículo 12.19 y de la Sección B del Capítulo 10 (Inversión);

nuevo servicio financiero: un servicio financiero no prestado en territorio de una Parte que sea prestado en territorio de la otra Parte, incluyendo cualquier forma nueva de distribución de un servicio financiero o de venta de un producto financiero que no sea vendido en el territorio de la Parte;

organismos autoregulados: una entidad no gubernamental, incluso una bolsa o mercado de valores o de futuros, central de valores, cámara de compensación o cualquier otra asociación u organización que ejerza una autoridad, propia o delegada, de regulación o de supervisión;

prestación transfronteriza de servicios financieros o comercio transfronterizo de servicios financieros:

la prestación de un servicio financiero:

a)   del territorio de una Parte al territorio de la otra Parte;

b)   en el territorio de una Parte a un consumidor de servicios de la otra Parte; o

c)   por un prestador de servicios de una Parte mediante la presencia de personas físicas de una Parte en territorio de la otra Parte;

prestador de servicios financieros de una Parte: una persona de una Parte que se dedica al negocio de prestar algún servicio financiero en territorio de la Parte;

prestador de servicios financieros transfronterizos de una Parte: una persona autorizada de una Parte que se dedica al negocio de prestar servicios financieros en su territorio y que pretenda realizar o realice la prestación transfronteriza de servicios financieros; y

servicio financiero: un servicio de naturaleza financiera inclusive banca, seguros, reaseguros, y cualquier servicio conexo o auxiliar a un servicio de naturaleza financiera.

Artículo 12.02 Ámbito de aplicación

1.   Este Capítulo se aplica a las medidas que adopte o mantenga una Parte relativas a:

a)   instituciones financieras de la otra Parte;

b)   inversionistas de una Parte e inversiones de esos inversionistas en instituciones financieras en territorio de la otra Parte; y

c)   el comercio transfronterizo de servicios financieros.

2.   Ninguna disposición del presente Capítulo se interpretará en el sentido de impedir a una Parte, o a sus entidades públicas, que conduzcan o presten en forma exclusiva en su territorio:

a)   las actividades realizadas por las autoridades monetarias o por cualquier otra institución pública, dirigidas a la consecución de políticas monetarias o cambiarias;

b)   las actividades y servicios que formen parte de planes públicos de retiro o de sistemas obligatorios de seguridad social; o

c)   otras actividades o servicios por cuenta de la Parte, con su garantía, o que usen los recursos financieros de la misma o de sus entidades públicas.

3.   Las disposiciones de este Capítulo prevalecerán sobre las de otros, salvo en los casos en que se haga remisión expresa a esos Capítulos.

4.   El Artículo 10.11 (Expropiación e indemnización) forma parte integrante de este Capítulo.

Artículo 12.03 Organismos autoregulados.

Cuando una Parte requiera que una institución financiera o un prestador de servicios financieros transfronterizos de la otra Parte sea miembro, participe, o tenga acceso a un organismo autoregulado para ofrecer un servicio financiero en su territorio o hacia éste, la Parte hará todo lo que esté a su alcance para que ese organismo cumpla con las obligaciones de este Capítulo.

Artículo 12.04 Derecho de establecimiento

1.   Las Partes reconocen el principio que a los inversionistas de una Parte, se les debe permitir establecer una institución financiera en el territorio de la otra Parte, mediante cualesquiera de las modalidades de establecimiento y de operación que la legislación de esta Parte permita.

2.   Cada Parte podrá imponer, en el momento del establecimiento de una institución financiera, términos y condiciones que sean compatibles con el Artículo 12.06.

Artículo 12.05 Comercio transfronterizo

1.   Ninguna Parte incrementará el grado de disconformidad de sus medidas relativas al comercio transfronterizo de servicios financieros, en relación con las disposiciones de este Tratado, que realicen los prestadores de servicios financieros transfronterizos de la otra Parte, después de la entrada en vigencia de este Tratado, excepto lo dispuesto en la Sección B de la lista de la Parte del Anexo VI.

2.   Cada Parte permitirá a personas ubicadas en su territorio y a sus nacionales, donde quiera que se encuentren, adquirir servicios financieros de prestadores de servicios financieros transfronterizos de la otra Parte ubicados en territorio de esa otra Parte. Esto no obliga a una Parte a permitir que estos prestadores de servicios financieros transfronterizos hagan negocios o se anuncien en su territorio. Las Partespodrán definir lo que es "anunciarse" y "hacer negocios" para efectos de esta obligación.

3.   Sin perjuicio de otros medios de regulación prudencial al comercio transfronterizo de servicios financieros, la Parte podrá exigir el registro de prestadores de servicios financieros transfronterizos de la otra Parte y de instrumentos financieros.

Artículo 12.06 Trato nacional

1.   Cada Parte otorgará a los inversionistas de la otra Parte un trato no menos favorable que el que otorga a sus propios inversionistas respecto al establecimiento, adquisición, expansión, administración, conducción, operación, venta, así como otras formas de enajenación de instituciones financieras similares e inversiones en instituciones financieras similares en su territorio.

2.   Cada Parte otorgará a las instituciones financieras de la otra Parte y a las inversiones de los inversionistas de la otra Parte en instituciones financieras, un trato no menos favorable que el que otorga a sus propias instituciones financieras similares y a las inversiones de sus propios inversionistas en instituciones financieras similares respecto al establecimiento, adquisición, expansión, administración, conducción, operación, venta y otras formas de enajenación de instituciones financieras e inversiones.

3.   Conforme al Artículo 12.05, cuando una Parte permita la prestación transfronteriza de un servicio financiero, otorgará a prestadores de servicios financieros transfronterizos de la otra Parte, un trato no menos favorable que el que otorga a sus propios prestadores de servicios financieros similares, respecto a la prestación de ese servicio.

4.   El trato que una Parte otorgue a instituciones financieras similares y a prestadores de servicios financieros transfronterizos similares de la otra Parte, ya sea idéntico o diferente al otorgado a sus propias instituciones o prestadores de servicios similares, es congruente con los párrafos 1 al 3, si ofrece igualdad en las oportunidades para competir.

5.   El tratamiento de una Parte no ofrece igualdad en las oportunidades para competir si sitúa en una posición desventajosa a las instituciones financieras similares y a los prestadores de servicios financieros transfronterizos similares de la otra Parte en su capacidad de prestar servicios financieros, comparada con la capacidad de las propias instituciones financieras similares y prestadores de servicios similares de la Parte para prestar esos servicios.

Artículo 12.07 Trato de nación más favorecida

Cada Parte otorgará a los inversionistas de la otra Parte, a las instituciones financieras de la otra Parte, a las inversiones de los inversionistas en instituciones financieras y a los prestadores de servicios financieros transfronterizos de la otra Parte, un trato no menos favorable que el otorgado a los inversionistas, a las instituciones financieras similares, a las inversiones de los inversionistas en instituciones financieras similares y a los prestadores de servicios financieros transfronterizos similares de la otra Parte o de un país no Parte.

Artículo 12.08 Reconocimiento y armonización

1.   Al aplicar las medidas comprendidas en este Capítulo, una Parte podrá reconocer las medidas prudenciales de la otra Parte o de un país no Parte. Ese reconocimiento podrá ser:

   a)   otorgado unilateralmente;

   b)   alcanzado a través de la armonización u otros medios; o

   c)   con base en un acuerdo o arreglo con la otra Parte o con el país no Parte.

2.   La Parte que otorgue el reconocimiento de medidas prudenciales de conformidad con el párrafo 1, brindará oportunidades apropiadas a la otra Parte para demostrar que existen circunstancias por las cuales hay o habrá regulaciones equivalentes, supervisión y puesta en práctica de la regulación y, de ser conveniente, procedimientos para compartir información entre las Partes.

3.   Cuando una Parte otorgue reconocimiento a las medidas prudenciales de conformidad con el párrafo 1(c) y las circunstancias dispuestas en el párrafo 2 existan, esa Parte brindará oportunidades adecuadas a la otra Parte para negociar la adhesión al acuerdo o arreglo, o para negociar un acuerdo o arreglo similar.

4.   Ninguna disposición del presente Artículo se debe interpretar como la implementación de un mecanismo obligatorio de revisión del sistema financiero o de las medidas prudenciales de una Parte por la otra Parte.

Artículo 12.09 Excepciones

1.   Ninguna disposición del presente Capítulo, se interpretará como impedimento para que una Parte adopte o mantenga medidas prudenciales, tales como:

   a)   proteger a administradores de fondos, inversionistas, depositantes, participantes en el mercado financiero, tenedores o beneficiarios de pólizas, o personas acreedoras de obligaciones fiduciarias a cargo de una institución financiera o de un prestador de servicios financieros transfronterizos;

   b)   mantener la seguridad, solidez, integridad o responsabilidad financiera de instituciones financieras o de prestadores de servicios financieros transfronterizos; y

   c)   asegurar la integridad y estabilidad del sistema financiero de una Parte.

2.   Ninguna disposición del presente Capítulo se aplica a medidas no discriminatorias de aplicación general adoptadas por una entidad pública en la conducción de políticas monetarias o de políticas de crédito conexas, o bien de políticas cambiarias. Este párrafo no afectará las obligaciones de cualquiera de las Partes derivadas de requisitos de desempeño en inversión respecto a las medidas cubiertas por el Capítulo 10 (Inversión) o del Artículo 12.17.

3.   El Artículo 12.06, no se aplicará al otorgamiento de derechos de exclusividad que haga una Parte a una institución financiera, para prestar uno de los servicios financieros a que se refiere el párrafo 2(b) del Artículo 12.02.

4.   No obstante lo dispuesto en los párrafos del 1 al 3 del Artículo 12.17, una Parte podrá evitar o limitar las transferencias de una institución financiera o de un prestador de servicios financieros transfronterizos, o en beneficio de una filial o una persona relacionada con esa institución o con ese prestador de servicios, por medio de la aplicación justa y no discriminatoria de medidas relacionadas con el mantenimiento de la seguridad, solidez, integridad o responsabilidad financiera de instituciones financieras o de prestadores de servicios financieros transfronterizos. Lo establecido en este párrafo se aplicará sin perjuicio de cualquier otra disposición de este Tratado que permita a una Parte restringir transferencias.

Artículo 12.10 Transparencia

1.   Además de lo dispuesto en el Artículo 18.03 (Publicación), cada Parte se asegurará que cualquier medida que adopte sobre asuntos relacionados con este Capítulo se publique oficialmente o se dé a conocer con oportunidad a los destinatarios de la misma por algún otro medio escrito.

2.   Las autoridades reguladoras de cada Parte pondrán a disposición de los interesados toda información relativa a los requisitos para llenar y presentar una solicitud para la prestación de servicios financieros.

3.   A petición del solicitante, la autoridad reguladora le informará sobre la situación de su solicitud. Cuando esa autoridad requiera del solicitante información adicional, se lo notificará sin demora injustificada.

4.   Cada una de las autoridades reguladoras dictará en un plazo no mayor de ciento veinte (120) días, una resolución administrativa respecto a una solicitud completa relacionada con la prestación de un servicio financiero, presentada por un inversionista en una institución financiera, por una institución financiera o por un prestador de servicios financieros transfronterizos de la otra Parte. La autoridad notificará al interesado, sin demora, la resolución. No se considerará completa la solicitud hasta que se celebren todas las audiencias pertinentes y se reciba toda la información necesaria. Cuando no sea viable dictar una resolución en el plazo de ciento veinte (120) días, la autoridad reguladora lo comunicará al interesado sin demora injustificada y posteriormente procurará emitir la resolución en un plazo de sesenta (60) días.

5.   Ninguna disposición de este Capítulo obliga a una Parte a divulgar ni a permitir acceso a:

a)   información relativa a los asuntos financieros y cuentas de clientes individuales de instituciones financieras o de prestadores de servicios financieros transfronterizos; ni.

b)   cualquier información confidencial cuya divulgación pudiera dificultar la aplicación de la ley, o, de algún otro modo, ser contraria al interés público o dañar intereses comerciales legítimos de empresas determinadas.

Artículo 12.11 Comité de Servicios Financieros

1.   Las Partes establecen el Comité de Servicios Financieros cuya composición se señala en el Anexo

2.   El Comité conocerá los asuntos relativos a este Capítulo y, sin perjuicio de lo dispuesto en el Artículo 19.05(2) (Comités), tendrá las siguientes funciones:

   a)   supervisar la aplicación de este Capítulo y su desarrollo posterior;

   b)   considerar aspectos relativos a servicios financieros que le sean presentados por una Parte;

   c)   participar en los procedimientos de solución de controversias de conformidad con los Artículos 12.18 y 12.19; y

   d)   facilitar el intercambio de información entre autoridades de supervisión y cooperar en materia de asesoría sobre regulación prudencial, procurando la armonización de los marcos normativos de regulación así como de las otras políticas, cuando se considere conveniente.

3.   El Comité se reunirá cuando sea necesario o a petición de una de las Partes para evaluar la aplicación de este Capítulo.

Artículo 12.12 Consultas

1.   Sin perjuicio de lo establecido en el Artículo 20.06 (Consultas), cualquier Parte podrá solicitar consultas con la otra Parte, respecto a cualquier asunto relacionado con este Tratado que afecte los servicios financieros. La otra Parte considerará favorablemente esa solicitud. La Parte consultante dará a conocer al Comité los resultados de sus consultas, durante las reuniones que éste celebre.

2.   En las consultas previstas en este Artículo participarán funcionarios de las autoridades competentes señaladas en el Anexo 12.11.

3.   Una Parte podrá solicitar que las autoridades reguladoras de la otra Parte intervengan en las consultas realizadas de conformidad con este Artículo, para discutir las medidas de aplicación general de esa otra Parte que puedan afectar las operaciones de las instituciones financieras o de los prestadores de servicios financieros transfronterizos en el territorio de la Parte que solicitó la consulta.

4.   Ninguna disposición del presente Artículo será interpretado en el sentido de obligar a las autoridades reguladoras que intervengan en las consultas conforme al párrafo 3, a divulgar información o a actuar de manera que pudiera interferir en asuntos particulares en materia de regulación, supervisión, administración o aplicación de medidas.

5.   En los casos que, para efectos de supervisión, una Parte necesite información sobre una institución financiera en territorio de la otra Parte o sobre prestadores de servicios financieros transfronterizos en territorio de la otra Parte, la Parte podrá acudir a la autoridad reguladora responsable en territorio de esa otra Parte para solicitar la información.

Artículo 12.13 Nuevos servicios financieros y procesamiento de datos

1.   Cada Parte permitirá que, una institución financiera de la otra Parte preste cualquier nuevo servicio financiero de tipo similar a aquellos que esa Parte, conforme a su legislación, permita prestar a sus instituciones financieras. La Parte podrá decidir la modalidad institucional y jurídica a través de la cual se ofrezca ese servicio y podrá exigir autorización para la prestación del mismo. Cuando esa autorización se requiera, la resolución respectiva se dictará en un plazo razonable y solamente podrá ser denegada por razones prudenciales, siempre que éstas no sean contrarias a la legislación de la Parte, y a los Artículos 12.06 y 12.07.

2.   Cada Parte permitirá a las instituciones financieras de la otra Parte transferir, para su procesamiento, información hacia el interior o el exterior del territorio de la Parte, utilizando cualquiera de los medios autorizados en ella, cuando sea necesario para llevar a cabo las actividades ordinarias de negocios de esas instituciones.

3.   Cada Parte se compromete a respetar la confidencialidad de la información procesada dentro de su territorio que provenga de una institución financiera ubicada en la otra Parte.

Artículo 12.14 Altos ejecutivos y consejo de administración o juntas directivas

1.   Ninguna Parte podrá obligar a las instituciones financieras de la otra Parte a que contraten personal de una nacionalidad en particular, para ocupar puestos de alta dirección empresarial u otros cargos esenciales.

2.   Ninguna Parte podrá exigir que la junta directiva o el consejo de administración de una institución financiera de la otra Parte se integre por nacionales de la Parte, por residentes en su territorio o una combinación de ambos.

Artículo 12.15 Reservas y compromisos específicos

1.   Los Artículos del 12.04 al 12.07, 12.13 y 12.14 no se aplican a:

   a)   cualquier medida disconforme existente que sea mantenida por una de las Partes a nivel nacional, según lo indicado en la Sección A de su lista en el Anexo VI;

   b)   la continuación o pronta renovación de cualquier medida disconforme a que se refiere el literal (a); ni

   c)   la modificación de cualquier medida disconforme a que se refiere el literal (a) en tanto dicha modificación no reduzca la conformidad de la medida con los Artículos del 12.04 al 12.07, 12.13 y 12.14, tal como la propia medida estaba en vigencia inmediatamente antes de la modificación.

2.   Los Artículos del 12.04 al 12.07, 12.13 y 12.14 no se aplicarán a ninguna medida que una Parte adopte o mantenga de acuerdo con la Sección B de su lista del Anexo VI.

3.   La Sección C de la lista de cada una de las Partes en el Anexo VI podrá establecer ciertos compromisos específicos de esa Parte.

4.   Cuando una Parte haya establecido en los Capítulos 10 (Inversión) y 11 (Comercio Transfronterizo de Servicios), una reserva a cuestiones relativas a presencia local, trato nacional, trato de nación más favorecida, y altos ejecutivos y consejo de administración o juntas directivas, la reserva se entenderá hecha a los Artículos del 12.04 al 12.07, 12.13 y 12.14, según sea el caso, en el grado que la medida, sector, subsector o actividad especificados en la reserva estén cubiertos por este Capítulo.

Artículo 12.16 Denegación de beneficios

Una Parte podrá denegar, parcial o totalmente, los beneficios derivados de este Capítulo a un prestador de servicios financieros de la otra Parte o a un prestador de servicios financieros transfronterizos de la otra Parte, previa notificación y realización de consultas, de conformidad con los Artículos 12.10 y 12.12, cuando la Parte determine que el servicio está siendo prestado por una empresa que no realiza actividades comerciales sustanciales en territorio de esa otra Parte y que es propiedad de personas de un país no Parte o está bajo el control de las mismas.

Artículo 12.17 Transferencias

1.   Cada Parte permitirá que todas las transferencias relacionadas con la inversión en su territorio de un inversionista de la otra Parte, se hagan libremente y sin demora. Esas transferencias incluyen:

a)   ganancias, dividendos, intereses, ganancias de capital, pagos por regalías, gastos por administración, asistencia técnica y otros cargos, ganancias en especie y otros montos derivados de la inversión;

b)   productos derivados de la venta o liquidación, total o parcial, de la inversión;

c)   pagos realizados conforme a un contrato del que sea parte un inversionista o su inversión, incluidos pagos efectuados conforme a un convenio de préstamo;

d)   pagos efectuados de conformidad con el Artículo 10.11 (Expropiación e indemnización); y

e)   pagos que resulten de un procedimiento de solución de controversias entre una Parte y un inversionista de la otra Parte conforme a este Capítulo y a la Sección B del Capítulo 10 (Inversión).

2.   Cada Parte permitirá que las transferencias se realicen en divisa de libre convertibilidad, al tipo de cambio vigente de mercado en la fecha de la transferencia.

3.   Ninguna Parte podrá exigir a sus inversionistas que efectúen transferencias de sus ingresos, ganancias, o utilidades u otros montos derivados de inversiones llevadas a cabo en territorio de la otra Parte o atribuibles a las mismas ni los sancionará en caso que no realicen la transferencia.

4.   No obstante lo dispuesto en los párrafos 1 y 2, una Parte podrá establecer los mecanismos para impedir la realización de una transferencia, por medio de la aplicación equitativa, no discriminatoria de sus leyes en los siguientes casos:

a)   quiebra, insolvencia o protección de los derechos de los acreedores;

b)   infracciones penales o resoluciones administrativas en firme;

c)   incumplimiento del requisito de presentar informes de transferencias de divisas u otros instrumentos monetarios;

d)   aseguramiento del cumplimiento de sentencias y laudos dictados en procedimientos contenciosos; o

e)   relativas a asegurar el cumplimiento de las leyes y reglamentos para la emisión, comercio y operaciones de valores.

5.   El párrafo 3 no se interpretará como un impedimento para que una Parte, a través de la aplicación de su legislación de manera equitativa y no discriminatoria, imponga cualquier medida relacionada con los literales del párrafo 4.

Artículo 12.18 Solución de controversias entre las Partes

1.   En los términos en que lo modifica este Artículo, el Capítulo 20 (Solución de Controversias) se aplica a la solución de controversias que surjan entre las Partes respecto a este Capítulo.

2.   El Comité de Servicios Financieros integrará por consenso una lista de hasta dieciocho (18) individuos que incluya tres (3) individuos de cada Parte, que cuenten con las aptitudes y disposiciones necesarias para actuar como árbitros en controversias relacionadas con este Capítulo. Los integrantes de esta lista deberán, además de satisfacer los requisitos establecidos en el Capítulo 20 (Solución de Controversias), tener conocimientos especializados en materia financiera, amplia experiencia derivada del ejercicio de responsabilidades en el sector financiero o en su regulación.

3.   Para los fines de la constitución del grupo arbitral, se utilizará la lista a que se refiere el párrafo 2, excepto que las Partes contendientes acuerden que pueden formar parte del grupo arbitral individuos no incluidos en esa lista, siempre que cumplan con los requisitos establecidos en el párrafo 2. El presidente siempre será escogido de esa lista.

4.   En cualquier controversia en que el grupo arbitral haya encontrado que una medida es incompatible con las obligaciones de este Capítulo cuando proceda la suspensión de beneficios a que se refiere el Capítulo 20 (Solución de Controversias) y la medida afecte:

a)   sólo al sector de los servicios financieros, la Parte reclamante podrá suspender sólo beneficios en ese sector;

b)   al sector de servicios financieros y a cualquier otro sector, la Parte reclamante podrá suspender beneficios en el sector de los servicios financieros que tengan un efecto equivalente al efecto de esa medida en el sector de servicios financieros; o

c)   cualquier otro sector que no sea el de servicios financieros, la Parte reclamante no podrá suspender beneficios en el sector de los servicios financieros.

Artículo 12.19 Solución de controversia sobre inversión en materia de servicios financieros entre un inversionista de una Parte y una Parte

1. La Sección B del Capítulo 10 (Inversión) se incorpora a este Capítulo y es parte integrante del mismo.

2. Cuando un inversionista de la otra Parte, de conformidad con el Artículo 10.17 (Reclamación de un inversionista de una Parte, por cuenta propia) o 10.18 (Reclamación de un inversionista de una Parte, en representación de una empresa) y al amparo de la Sección B del Capítulo 10 (Inversión) someta a arbitraje una reclamación en contra de una Parte, y esa Parte contendiente invoque el Artículo 12.09 a solicitud de ella misma, el Tribunal remitirá por escrito el asunto al Comité para su decisión. El Tribunal no podrá proceder hasta que haya recibido una decisión según los términos de este Artículo.

3. En la remisión del asunto conforme al párrafo 1, el Comité decidirá si el Artículo 12.09 es una defensa válida contra la reclamación del inversionista y en qué grado lo es. El Comité transmitirá copia de su decisión al Tribunal y a la Comisión. Esa decisión será obligatoria para el Tribunal.

4. Cuando el Comité no haya tomado una decisión en un plazo de sesenta (60) días a partir de que reciba la remisión conforme al párrafo 1, la Parte contendiente o la Parte del inversionista contendiente podrán solicitar que se establezca un grupo arbitral de conformidad con el Artículo 20.08 (Solicitud de integración del grupo arbitral). El grupo arbitral estará constituido conforme al Artículo 12.18 y enviará al Comité y al Tribunal su determinación definitiva, que será obligatoria para el Tribunal.

5. Cuando no se haya solicitado la instalación de un grupo arbitral en los términos del párrafo 4 dentro de un lapso de diez (10) días a partir del vencimiento del plazo de sesenta (60) días a que se refiere ese párrafo, el Tribunal podrá proceder a resolver el caso.

ANEXO 12.11
COMITÉ DE SERVICIOS FINANCIEROS

1. El Comité de Servicios Financieros establecido en el Artículo 12.11 estará integrado:

   a) para el caso de Costa Rica, el Ministerio de Comercio Exterior, o su sucesor, en consulta con la autoridad competente que corresponda (Banco Central de Costa Rica, Superintendencia General de Entidades Financieras, Superintendencia de Pensiones y Superintendencia de Valores);

   b) para el caso de El Salvador, el Ministerio de Economía, Superintendencia del Sistema Financiero, Superintendencia de Valores, Superintendencia del Sistema de Pensiones y Banco Central de Reserva;

   c) para el caso de Guatemala, Ministerio de Economía, Banco de Guatemala y Superintendencia de Bancos;

d)   para el caso de Honduras, la Secretaría de Estado en los Despachos de Industria y Comercio, Banco Central de Honduras y Comisión Nacional de Bancos y Seguros;

e)   para el caso de Nicaragua, el Ministerio de Fomento Industria y Comercio; Banco Central de Nicaragua, Superintendencia de Bancos y de Otras Instituciones Financieras; y

f)   para el caso de Panamá, el Ministerio de Comercio e Industrias por conducto del Viceministerio de Comercio Exterior, o su sucesor, en consulta con la autoridad competente que corresponda (Superintendencia de Bancos, Superintendencia de Seguros y Reaseguros y Comisión Nacional de Valores).

2.   El representante principal de cada Parte será el que esa Parte designe para tal efecto.

*

PART THREE

PROTOTYPE INSTRUMENTS

AGREEMENT BETWEEN THE GOVERNMENT OF THE REPUBLIC OF SOUTH AFRICA AND THE GOVERNMENT OF _____ FOR THE RECIPROCAL PROMOTION AND PROTECTION OF INVESTMENTS*

Preamble

The Government of the Republic of South Africa and the Government of the Government of _____, (hereinafter jointly referred to as the "Parties", and separately as a "Party");

DESIRING to create favourable conditions for greater investment by investors of either Party in the territory of the other Party; and

RECOGNISING that the encouragement and reciprocal protection under international agreement of such investments will be conducive to the stimulation of individual business initiative and will increase prosperity in the territories of both Parties;

HEREBY AGREE as follows:

ARTICLE 1
Definitions

In this Agreement, unless the context indicates otherwise -

"investment" means every kind of asset and in particular, though not exclusively, includes:

(i) movable and immovable property as well as other rights such as mortgages, liens or pledges;

(ii) shares in and stock and debentures of a company and any other form of participation in a company;

(iii) claims to money, or to any performance under contract having an economic value;

(iv) intellectual property rights, in particular copyrights, patents, utility-model patents, registered designs, trade-marks, trade-names, trade and business secrets, technical processes, know-how, and goodwill;

(v) rights or permits conferred by law or under contract, including concessions to search for, cultivate, extract or exploit natural resources;

and any change in the form in which assets are invested does not affect their character as investments.

---

* *Source*: The Government of South Africa, Department of Trade and Industry. [Note added by the editor.]

"investor" means in respect to either Party:

    (i)   the "nationals" of a Party, being those natural persons deriving their status as nationals of a Party from the law of that Party; and

    (ii)   the "companies" of a Party, being any legal person, corporation, firm or association incorporated or constituted in accordance with the law of that Party;

"returns" means the amounts yielded by an investment and in particular, though not exclusively, includes profit, interest, capital gains, dividends, royalties and fees;

"territory" means the territory of a Party, including the territorial sea and any maritime area situated beyond the territorial sea of that Party, which has been or might in the future be designated under the national law of the Party concerned, in accordance with international law, as an area within which the Party may exercise sovereign rights and jurisdiction.

ARTICLE 2
Promotion of Investments

(1)   Each Party shall, subject to its general policy in the field of foreign investment, encourage investments in its territory by investors of the other Party, and, subject to its right to exercise powers conferred by the domestic law of its country, shall admit such investments.

(2)   Each Party shall grant, in accordance with the domestic law of its country, the necessary permits in connection with such investments and with the carrying out of licensing agreements and contracts for technical, commercial or administrative assistance.

(3)   In order to create favourable conditions for assessing the financial position and results of activities related to investments in the territory of a Party, that Party shall - notwithstanding its own requirements for bookkeeping and auditing - permit the investment to be subject also to bookkeeping and auditing according to standards which the investor is subjected to by his or its national requirements or according to internationally accepted standards (such as International Accountancy Standards (IAS) drawn up by the International Accountancy Standards Committee (IASA)). The results of such accountancy and audit shall be freely transferable to the investor.

ARTICLE 3
Treatment of Investments

(1)   Investments and returns of investors of either Party shall at all times be accorded fair and equitable treatment and shall enjoy full protection in the territory of the other Party. Neither Party shall in any way impair by unreasonable or discriminatory measures the management, maintenance, use, enjoyment or disposal of investments in its territory of investors of the other Party.

(2)   Each Party shall in its territory accord to investments and returns of investors of the other Party treatment not less favourable than that which it accords to investments and returns of its own investors or to investments and returns of investors of any third State.

(3)   Each Party shall in its territory accord to investors of the other Party treatment not less favourable than that which it accords to its own investors or to investors of any third State.

(4)   The provisions to paragraphs (2) and (3) shall not be construed so as to oblige one Party to extend to the investors of the other Party the benefit of any treatment, preference or privilege resulting from:

(a)   any existing or future customs union, free trade area, common market, any similar international agreement or any interim arrangement leading up to such customs union, free trade area, or common market to which either of the Parties is or may become a party, or

(b)   any international agreement or arrangement relating wholly or mainly to taxation or any domestic legislation relating wholly or mainly to taxation.

(c)   any law or other measure the purpose of which is to promote the achievement of equality in its territory, or designed to protect or advance persons, or categories of persons, disadvantaged by unfair discrimination in its territory.

(5)   If a Party accords special advantages to development finance institutions with foreign participation and established for the exclusive purpose of development assistance through mainly non-profit activities, that Party shall not be obliged to accord such advantages to development finance institutions or other investors of the other Party.

ARTICLE 4
Compensation for Losses

(1)   Investors of one Party whose investments in the territory of the other Party suffer losses owing to war or other armed conflict, revolution, a state of national emergency, revolt, insurrection or riot in the territory of the latter Party shall be accorded by the latter Party treatment, as regards restitution, indemnification, compensation or other settlement, not less favourable than that which the latter Party accords to its own investors or to investors of any third State.

(2)   Without derogating from the provisions of paragraph (1) of this Article, investors of one Party who in any of the situations referred to in that paragraph suffer losses in the territory of the other Party resulting from:

(a)   requisitioning of their property by the forces or authorities of the latter Party, or

(b)   destruction of their property by the forces or authorities of the latter Party, which was not caused in combat action or was not required by the necessity of the situation,

shall be accorded restitution or adequate compensation.

ARTICLE 5
Expropriation

(1)   Investments of investors of either Party shall not be nationalised, expropriated or subjected to measures having effects equivalent to nationalisation or expropriation (hereinafter referred to as "expropriation") in the territory of the other Party except for public purposes, under due process of law, on a non-discriminatory basis and against prompt, adequate and effective

compensation. Such compensation shall be at least equal to the market value of the investment expropriated immediately before the expropriation or before the impending expropriation became public knowledge, whichever is the earlier, shall include interest at a normal commercial rate until the date of payment, shall be made without delay, and be effectively realizable.

(2)   The investor affected by the expropriation shall have a right, under the domestic law of the country of the Party making the expropriation, to prompt review, by a court of law of other independent and impartial forum of that Party, of his or its case and of the valuation of his or its investment in accordance with the principles referred to in paragraph (1).

ARTICLE 6
Transfers of Investments and Returns

(1)   Each Party shall allow investors of the other Party the free transfer of payments relating to their investments and returns, including compensation paid pursuant to articles 4 and 5.

(2)   All transfers shall be effected without delay in any convertible currency at the market rate of exchange applicable on the date of transfer. In the absence of a market for foreign exchange, the rate to be used will be the most recent exchange rate applied to inward investments or the most recent exchange rate for conversion of currencies into Special Drawing Rights, whichever is the more favourable to the investor.

(3)   Transfers shall be done in accordance with the domestic laws of the country pertaining thereto. Such laws shall not, however, regarding either the requirements or the application thereof, impair or derogate from the free and undelayed transfer allowed in terms of paragraphs (1) and (2).

ARTICLE 7
Settlement of Disputes between
an Investor and a Party

(1)   Any legal dispute between an investor of one Party and the other Party relating to an investment of the former which has not been amicably settled shall, after a period of six months from written notification of a claim, be submitted to international arbitration if the investor concerned so wishes.

(2)   Where the dispute is referred to international arbitration, the investor and the Party concerned in the dispute may agree to refer the dispute either to:

   (a)   the International Centre for the Settlement of Investment Disputes (ICSID) established by the Convention on the Settlement of Investment Disputes between States and Nationals of other States, opened for signature at Washington DC on 18 March 1965, when each Party has become a party to said Convention.

   As long as this requirement is not met, each Party agrees that the dispute may be settled under the rules governing the Additional Facility for the Administration of Proceedings by the Secretariat of ICSID; or

   (b)   an international arbitrator or ad hoc arbitration tribunal to be established by agreement between the parties to the dispute.

(3)   If after a period of three months from written notification of the investor's decision to refer the dispute to international arbitration there is no agreement on one of the alternative procedures referred to in paragraph (2), the dispute shall, at the request in writing of the investor concerned, be dealt with in terms of the procedure preferred by the investor.

(4)   The decision in resolution of the dispute shall be derived by application of the domestic law, including the rules relating to conflicts of law, of the country of the Party involved in the dispute in whose territory the investment has been made, the provisions of this Agreement, the terms of the specific agreement which may have been entered into regarding the investment as well as the principles of international law.

(5) The award made by the arbitrator concerned in terms of paragraphs (2) or (3) shall be binding on the parties to the dispute. Each Party shall give effect to the award under its domestic law.

ARTICLE 8
Disputes between the Parties

(1)   Any dispute between the Parties concerning the interpretation or application of this Agreement should, if possible, be settled through negotiations between the Governments of the two Parties.

(2)   If the dispute cannot thus be settled within a period of sixth months, following the date on which such negotiations were requested by either Party, it shall upon the request of either Party be submitted to an arbitral tribunal.

(3)   Such an arbitral tribunal shall be constituted for each individual case in the following way. Within two months of the receipt of the request for arbitration, each Party shall appoint one member of the tribunal. Those two members shall then select a national of a third State who on approval by the two Parties shall be appointed Chairman of the tribunal. The Chairman shall be appointed within two months from the date of appointment of the other two members.

(4)   If within the periods specified in paragraph (3) of this Article the necessary appointments have not been made, either Party may, in the absence of any other agreement, invite the President of the International Court of Justice to make any necessary appointments. If the President is a national of either Party or is otherwise prevented from discharging the said function, the Vice-President shall be invited to make the necessary appointments. If the Vice-President is a national of either Party or also is prevented from discharging the said function, the Member of the International Court of Justice next in seniority who is not a national of either Party shall be invited to make the necessary appointments.

(5)   The arbitral tribunal shall decide the dispute according to this Agreement and the principles of international law. The arbitral tribunal shall reach its decision by a majority of votes. Such decision shall be binding on both Parties. Each Party shall bear the cost of its own member of the tribunal and of its representation in the arbitral proceedings; the cost of the Chairman and the remaining cost shall be borne in equal parts by the Parties. The tribunal may, however, in its decision direct that a higher proportion of costs shall be borne by one of the two Parties. The tribunal shall determine its own procedures, unless the Parties agree otherwise.

ARTICLE 9
Subrogation

If a Party or its designated Agency makes a payment to its own investor under a guarantee it has given in respect of an investment in the territory of the other Party, the latter Party shall recognise the assignment, whether by law or by legal transaction, to the former Party of all the rights and claims of the indemnified investor, and shall recognize that the former Party or its designate agency is entitled to exercise such rights and enforce such claims by virtue of subrogation, to the same extent as the original investor.

ARTICLE 10
Application of other Rules

(1)   If the provisions of the domestic law of the country of either Party or obligations under international law existing at present or established hereafter between the Parties in addition to the present Agreement contain rules, whether general or specific, entitling investments and returns of investors of the other Party to treatment more favourable than is provided for by the present Agreement, such rules shall to the extent that they are more favourable prevail over the present Agreement.

(2)   Each Party shall observe any other obligation it may have entered into with regard to investments of investors of the other Party.

ARTICLE 11
Scope of the Agreement

This Agreement shall apply to all investment, whether made before or after the date of entry into force of this Agreement, but shall not apply to any dispute which arose before entry into force of this Agreement.

ARTICLE 12
Final Clauses

(1)   The Parties shall notify each other when their respective constitutional requirements for entry into force of this Agreement have been fulfilled. The Agreement shall enter into force on the date of receipt of the last notification.

(2)   This Agreement shall remain in force for a period of ten years. Thereafter it shall continue in force until the expiration of twelve months from the date on which either Party shall have given written notice of termination to the other.

(3)   In respect of investments made prior to the date when the notice of termination becomes effective, the provisions of articles 1 to 11 remain in force with respect to such investments for a further period of twenty years from that date.

(4)   The terms of this agreement may be amended by negotiated agreement between the Parties. The Parties shall notify each other when their respective constitutional requirements for entry into force of such amendment have been fulfilled. Such amendment shall enter into force on the date of receipt of the last notification.

IN WITNESS WHEREOF the undersigned, being duly authorised by their respective governments, have signed and sealed this Agreement in two originals in the English language, [all/both] texts being equally authentic.

Alternative Signing Procedures

1.   Where the Signatories sign at different times and in different venues:

Done at _____, on this_____day of_____, 20__.

For the Government of the Republic of South Africa

Done at _____, on this_____day of_____, 20__.

For _____.

2. Where both signatories sign together at the same place at the same time:

Done at _____this_____day of_____20__.

FOR THE GOVERNMENT OF THE REPUBLIC OF SOUTH AFRICA

PROTOCOL

TO THE AGREEMENT BETWEEN THE GOVERNMENT OF THE REPUBLIC OF SOUTH AFRICA AND THE_____ FOR THE PROMOTION AND RECIPROCAL PROTECTION OF INVESTMENTS

On the signing of the Agreement between the Government of the Republic of South Africa and the Government of _____ for the Reciprocal Promotion and Protection of Investments, the undersigned representatives have, in addition, agreed on the following provisions, which shall constitute an integral part of the Agreement:

Ad Article 6

1.   Foreign nationals who have resided in the Republic of South Africa for more than five years and who have completed the required exchange control formalities connected with immigration to South Africa, are, in terms of South African exchange control rules, deemed to

have become permanently resident in the Republic of South Africa and the provisions for transfers of investments and returns as contemplated in Article 6 shall not apply in their favour.

2.   The exemptions to Article 6 as contemplated in paragraph 1 of this Protocol shall terminate automatically in respect of each restriction, upon removal of the relevant restriction as part of the domestic law of South Africa.

3.   The Republic of South Africa shall make every effort to remove the said restrictions from their domestic law as soon as possible.

4.   Paragraph 1 of this Protocol shall not apply to or restrict the transfer of compensation payments made pursuant to Articles 4 and 5 of this Agreement.

5.   This Protocol shall enter into force at the same time as the Agreement.

IN WITNESS WHEREOF the undersigned, being duly authorised by their respective governments, have signed and sealed this Protocol in two originals in the English language, [all/both] texts being equally authentic.

Alternative signing procedures:

1. Where the signatories sign at different times and in different venues:

Done at _____, on this_____day of_____, 20__.

For the Government of the Republic of South Africa

Done at _____, on this_____day of_____, 20__.

For _____.

2. Where both signatories sign together at the same place at the same time:

Done at_____this_____day of_____20__.

FOR THE GOVERNMENT OF THE REPUBLIC OF SOUTH AFRICA

*

Model Draft 2000

**AGREEMENT BETWEEN THE REPUBLIC OF TURKEY AND _____
CONCERNING THE RECIPROCAL PROMOTION AND PROTECTION OF
INVESTMENTS**[*]

The Republic of Turkey and_____, hereinafter called the Parties.

Desiring to promote greater economic cooperation between them, particularly with respect to investment by investors of one Party in the territory of the other Party.

Recognizing that agreement upon the treatment to be accorded such investment will stimulate the flow of capital and technology and the economic development of the Parties.

Agreeing that fair and equitable treatment of investment is desirable in order to maintain a stable framework for investment and maximum effective utilization of economic resources, and

Having resolved to conclude an agreement concerning the encouragement and reciprocal protection of investments,

Hereby agree as follows:

ARTICLE 1
Definitions

For the purpose of this Agreement;

1.   The term "investor" means:

    (a)   natural persons deriving their status as nationals of either Party according to its applicable law,

    (b)   corporations, firms or business associations incorporated or constituted under the law in force of either of the Parties and having their headquarters in the territory of that Party.

2.   The term "investment", in conformity with the hosting Party's laws and regulations, shall include every kind of asset in particular, but not exclusively:

    (a)   shares, stocks or any other form of participation in companies,

    (b)   returns reinvested, claims to money or any other rights having financial value related to an investment.

---

[*]   *Source*: The Government of Turkey, Ministry of Foreign Affairs. [Note added by the editor.]

(c)   movable and immovable property, as well as any other rights as mortgages, liens, pledges and any other similar rights as defined in conformity with the laws and regulations of the Party in whose territory the property is stuated,

(d)   industrial and intellectual property rights such as patents, industrial designs, technical processes, as well as trademarks, goodwill, know-how and other similar rights,

(e)   business concessions conferred by law or by contract,including concessions related to natural resources.

The said term shall refer to all direct investments made in accordance with the laws and regulations in the territory of the Party where the investments are made. The term "investment" covers all investments made in the territory of a Party before or after enter into force of this Agreement.

3.   The term "returns" means the amounts yielded by an investment and includes in particular, though not exclusively, profit, interest, capital gains, royalties, fees and dividends.

4.   The "territory" means; territory, territorial sea, as well as the maritime areas over which each Party has jurisdiction or sovereign rights for the purposes of exploration, exploitation and conservation of natural resources, pursuant to international law.

ARTICLE II
Promotion and Protection of Investments

1.   Each Party shall in its territory promote as far as possible investments by investors of the other Party.

2.   Investments of investors of each Party shall at all times be accorded fair and equitable treatment and shall enjoy full protection in the territory of the other Party. Neither Party shall in any way impair by unreasonable or discriminatory measures the management, maintenance, use, enjoyment, extension, or disposal of such investments.

ARTICLE III
Treatment of Investments

1.   Each Party shall permit in its territory investments, and activities associated therewith, on a basis no less favourable than that accorded in similar situations to investments of investors of any third country, within the framework of its laws and regulations.

2.   Each Party shall accord to these investments, once established, treatment no less favourable than that accorded in similar situations to investments of its investors or to investments of investors of any third country, whichever is the most favourable.

3.   The Parties shall within the framework of their national legislation give sympathetic consideration to applications for the entry and sojourn of persons of either Party who wish to enter the territory of the other Party in connection with the making and carrying through of an investment; the same shall apply to nationals of either Party who in connection with an

investment wish to enter the territory of the other Party and sojourn there to take up employment. Application for work permits shall also be given sympathetic consideration.

4.   The provisions of this Article shall have no effect in relation to following agreements entered into by either of the Parties:

(a)   relating to any existing or future customs unions, regional economic organization or similar international agreements,

(b)   relating wholly or mainly to taxation.

ARTICLE IV
Expropriation and Compensation

1.   Investments shall not be expropriated, nationalized or subject, directly or indirectly, to measures of similar effects except for a public purpose, in a non-discriminatory manner, upon payment of prompt, adequate and effective compensation, and in accordance with due process of law and the general principles of treatment provided for in Article III of this Agreement.

2.   Compensation shall be equivalent to the market value of the expropriated investment before the expropriatory action was taken or became known. Compensation shall be paid without delay and be freely transferable as described in paragraph 2 Article V.

3.   Investors of either Party whose investments suffer losses in the territory of the other Party owing to war, insurrection, civil disturbance or other similar events shall be accorded by such other Party treatment no less favourable than that accorded to its own investors or to investors of any third country, whichever is the most favourable treatment, as regards any measures it adopts in relation to such losses.

ARTICLE V
Repatriation and Transfer

1.   Each Party shall permit in good faith all transfers related to an investment to be made freely and without delay into and out of its territory. Such transfers include:

(a)   returns,

(b)   proceeds from the sale or liquidation of all or any part of an investment,

(c)   compensation pursuant to Article IV,

(d)   reimbursements and interest payments deriving from loans in connection with investments,

(e)   salaries, wages and other remunerations received by the nationals of one Party who have obtained in the territory of the other Party the corresponding work permits relative to an investment,

(f)   payments arising from an investment dispute.

2.   Transfers shall be made in the convertible currency in which the investment has been made or in any convertible currency at the rate of exchange in force at the date of transfer, unless otherwise agreed by the investor and the hosting Party.

ARTICLE VI
Subrogation

1.   If the investment of an investor of one Party is insured against non-commercial risks under a system established by law, any subrogation of the insurer which stems from the terms of the insurance agreement shall be recognized by the other Party.

2.   The insurer shall not be entitled to exercise any rights other than the rights which the investor would have been entitled to exercise.

3.   Disputes between a Party and an insurer shall be settled in accordance with the provisions of Article VIII of this Agreement.

ARTICLE VII
Settlement of Disputes Between One Party and Investors of the Other Party

1.   Disputes between one of the Parties and an investor of the other Party, in connection with his investment, shall be notified in writing, including a detailed information, by the investor to the recipient Party of the investment. As far as possible, the investor and the concerned Party shall endeavour to settle these disputes by consultations and negotiations in good faith.

2.   If these disputes, cannot be settled in this way within six months following the date of the written notification mentioned in paragraph 1, the dispute can be submitted, as the investor may choose, to:

(a)   the International Center for Settlement of Investment Disputes (ICSID) set up by the " Convention on Settlement of Investment Disputes Between States and Nationals of other States", in case both Parties become signatories of this Convention,

(b)   an ad hoc court of arbitration laid down under the Arbitration Rules of Procedure of the United Nations Commission for International Trade Law (UNCITRAL).

3.   The arbitration awards shall be final and binding for all parties in dispute. Each Party commits itself to execute the award according to its national law.

ARTICLE VIII
Settlement of Disputes Between the Parties

1.   The Parties shall seek in good faith and a spirit of cooperation a rapid and equitable solution to any dispute between them concerning the interpretation or application of this Agreement. In this regard, the Parties agree to engage in direct and meaningful negotiations to arrive at such solutions. If the Parties cannot reach an agreement within six months after the beginning of disputes between themselves through the foregoing procedure, the disputes may be submitted, upon the request of either Party, to an arbitral tribunal of three members.

2.   Within two months of receipt of a request, each Party shall appoint an arbitrator. The two arbitrators shall select a third arbitrator as Chairman, who is a national of a third State. In the event either Party fails to appoint an arbitrator within the specified time, the other Party may request the President of the International Court of Justice to make the appointment.

3.   If both arbitrators cannot reach an agreement about the choice of the Chairman within two months after their appointment, the Chairman shall be appointed upon the request of either Party by the President of the International Court of Justice.

4.   If, in the cases specified under paragraphs (2) and (3) of this Article, the President of the International Court of Justice is prevented from carrying out the said function or if he is a national of either Party, the appointment shall be made by the Vice-President, and if the Vice-President is prevented from carrying out the said function or if he is a national of either Party, the appointment shall be made by the most senior member of the Court who is not a national of either Party.

5.   The tribunal shall have three months from the date of the selection of the Chairman to agree upon rules of procedure consistent with the other provisions of this Agreement. In the absence of such agreement, the tribunal shall request the President of the International Court of Justice to designate rules of procedure, taking into account generally recognized rules of international arbitral procedure.

6.   Unless otherwise agreed, all submissions shall be made and all hearings shall be completed within eight months of the date of selection of the Chairman, and the tribunal shall render its decision within two months after the date of the final submissions or the date of the closing of thehearings, whichever is later. The arbitral tribunal shall reach its decisions, which shall be final and binding, by a majority of votes.

7.   Expenses incurred by the Chairman, the other arbitrators, and other costs of the proceedings shall be paid for equally by the Parties. The tribunal may, however, at its discretion, decide that a higher proportion of the costs be paid by one of the Parties.

8.   A dispute shall not be submitted to an international arbitration court under the provisions of this Article, if the same dispute has been brought before another international arbitration court under the provisions of Article VII and is still before the court. This will not impair the engagement in direct and meaningful negotiations between both Parties.

ARTICLE IX
Entry into Force

1.   Each Party shall notify the other in writing of the completion of the constitutional formalities required in its territory for the entry into force of this Agreement. This Agreement shall enter into force on the date of the latter of the two notifications. It shall remain in force for a period of ten years and shall continue in force unless terminated in accordance with paragraph 2 of this Article. It shall apply to investments existing at the time of entry into force as well as to investments made or acquired thereafter.

2.   Either Party may, by giving one year's written notice to the other Party, terminate this Agreement at the end of the initial ten year period or at any time thereafter.

3.   This Agreement may be amended by written agreement between the Parties. Any amendment shall enter into force when each Party has notified the other that it has completed all internal requirements for entry into force of such amendment.

4.   With respect to investments made or acquired prior to the date of termination of this Agreement and to which this Agreement otherwise applies, the provisions of all of the other Articles of this Agreement shall thereafter continue to be effective for a further period of ten years from such date of termination.

IN WITNESS WHEREOF, the respective plenipotentiaries have signed this Agreement.
DONE at _____ on the day of _____ in the _____ Turkish and English languages all of which are equally authentic.

In case of any conflict of interpretation the English text shall prevail.

FOR THE GOVERNMENT OF _____

FOR THE GOVERNMENT OF THE REPUBLIC OF TURKEY

*

Model Treaty 2001

AGREEMENT BETWEEN THE GOVERNMENT OF THE HELLENIC REPUBLIC AND THE GOVERNMENT OF_____ ON THE PROMOTION AND RECIPROCAL PROTECTION OF INVESTMENTS[*]

The Government of the Hellenic Republic and the Government of _____ Hereinafter referred to as the "Contracting Parties",

DESIRING to intensify their economic cooperation to the mutual benefit of both States on a long term basis,

HAVING as their objective to create favourable conditions for investments by investors of either Contracting Party in the territory of the other Contracting Party,

RECOGNIZING that the promotion and protection of investments, on the basis of this Agreement, will stimulate the initiative in this field,

HAVE AGREED AS FOLLOWS:

ARTICLE 1
Definitions

For the purposes of this Agreement:

1. "Investment" means every kind of asset invested by an investor of one Contracting Party in the territory of the other Contracting Party in accordance with the legislation of the latter Contracting Party, and in particular, though not exclusively, includes:

a)   movable and immovable property and any rights in rem such as servitudes, ususfructus, mortgages, liens or pledges;

b)   shares in and stock and debentures of a company and any other form of participation in a company;

c)   claims to money or to any performance under contract having an economic value, as well as loans connected to an investment;

d)   intellectual property rights;

e)   concessions under public law, including concessions to search for, cultivate, extract or exploit natural resources as well as other rights conferred by law, by contract or by decision of the authority, in accordance with the law;

---

[*]   *Source*: The Government of the Hellenic Republic, Ministry of National Economy. [Note added by the editor.]

A possible change in the form in which the investments have been made does not affect their character as investments.

2.   "Returns" means the amounts yielded by an investment and in particular, though not exclusively, includes profit, interest, capital gains, dividends, royalties and fees.

3.   "Investor" means with regard to either Contracting Party:

   a)   natural persons having the nationality of that Contracting Party in accordance with its law;

   b)   legal persons or other entities, including companies, corporations, business associations and partnerships, which are constituted or otherwise duly organised under the laws of that Contracting Party and have their effective economic activities in the territory of that same Contracting Party.

4.   "Territory" means in respect of either Contracting Party, the territory under its sovereignty including the territorial sea, as well as maritime areas over which that Contracting Party exercises, in conformity with international law, sovereign rights or jurisdiction.

ARTICLE 2
Scope of Application

This Agreement shall apply to investments in the territory of one Contracting Party, made in accordance with its legislation, by investors of the other Contracting Party, prior to as well as after its entry into force.

ARTICLE 3
Promotion and Protection of Investments

1.   Each Contracting Party promotes in its territory investments by investors of the other Contracting Party and admits such investments in accordance with its legislation.

2.   Investments and returns of investors of a Contracting Party shall, at all times, be accorded fair and equitable treatment and shall enjoy full protection and security in the territory of the other Contracting Party. In no case shall a Contracting Party accord treatment less favourable than that required by international law.

Each Contracting Party shall ensure that the management, maintenance, use, enjoyment or disposal, in its territory, of investments by investors of the other Contracting Party, is not in any way impaired by unjustifiable or discriminatory measures.

ARTICLE 4
Treatment of Investments

1.   Each Contracting Party shall accord to investments, including returns, made in its territory by investors of the other Contracting Party, treatment not less favourable than that which it accords to investments of its own investors or to investments of investors of any third State, whichever is more favourable.

2.   Each Contracting Party shall accord to investors of the other Contracting Party, as regards the management, maintenance, use, enjoyment or disposal of their investments in its territory, treatment not less favourable than that which it accords to its own investors or to investors of any third State, whichever is more favourable.

3.   The provisions of paragraphs 1 and 2 of this Article shall not be construed so as to oblige one Contracting Party to extend to the investors of the other Contracting Party the benefit of any treatment, preference or privilege resulting from:

a)   its participation in any existing or future customs union, economic union, regional economic integration agreement or similar international agreement, or

b)   any international agreement or arrangement relating wholly or mainly to taxation.

ARTICLE 5
Expropriation

1.   Investments and returns of investors of either Contracting Party in the territory of the other Contracting Party, shall not be expropriated, nationalized or subjected to any other measure the effects of which would be tantamount to expropriation or nationalization (hereinafter referred to as "expropriation"), except in the public interest, under due process of law, on a non discriminatory basis and against payment of prompt, adequate and effective compensation. Such compensation shall amount to the market value of the investment affected immediately before the actual measure was taken or became public knowledge, whichever is the earlier, it shall include interest from the date of expropriation until the date of payment at a normal commercial rate and shall be freely transferable in a freely convertible currency.

2.   The provisions of paragraph 1 of this Article shall also apply where a Contracting Party expropriates the assets of a company which is constituted under the laws in force in any part of its own territory and in which investors of the other Contracting Party own shares.

ARTICLE 6
Compensation for Losses

1.   Investors of one Contracting Party whose investments in the territory of the other Contracting Party suffer losses owing to war or other armed conflict, a state of national emergency, civil disturbance or other similar events in the territory of the other Contracting Party shall be accorded by the latter Contracting Party treatment, as regards restitution, indemnification, compensation or other settlement, no less favourable than that which the latter Contracting Party accords to its own investors or to investors of any third State, whichever is more favourable.

2.   Without prejudice to paragraph 1 of this Article, investors of one Contracting Party who, in any of the situations referred to in that paragraph suffer losses in the territory of the other Contracting Party resulting from:

a)   requisitioning of their investment or part thereof by the latter's forces or authorities, or

b)   destruction of their investment or part thereof by the latter's forces or authorities, which was not required by the necessity of the situation,

shall be accorded restitution or compensation which in either case shall be prompt, adequate and effective.

ARTICLE 7
Transfers

1.   Each Contracting Party shall permit, in respect of investments of investors of the other Contracting Party, the unrestricted transfer of all payments relating to an investment.

The transfers shall be effected without delay, in a freely convertible currency, at the market rate of exchange applicable on the date of transfer.

2.   Such transfers shall include in particular, though not exclusively:

a)   capital and additional amounts to maintain or increase the investment;

b)   returns;

c)   funds in repayment of loans;

d)   proceeds of sale or liquidation of the whole or any part of the investment;

e)   compensation under Articles 5 and 6;

f)   payments arising out of the settlement of a dispute.

ARTICLE 8
Subrogation

1.   If the investments of an investor of one Contracting Party in the territory of the other Contracting Party are insured against non-commercial risks under a legal system of guarantee, any subrogation of the insurer into the rights of the said investor pursuant to the terms of such insurance shall be recognized by the other Contracting Party, without prejudice to the rights of the investor under Article 10 of this Agreement.

2.   Disputes between a Contracting Party and an insurer shall be tried to be remedied in accordance with the provisions of Article 10 of this Agreement.

ARTICLE 9
Settlement of Disputes between the Contracting Parties

1.   Any dispute between the Contracting Parties concerning the interpretation or application of this Agreement shall, if possible, be settled by negotiations, through diplomatic channels.

2.   If the dispute cannot thus be settled within six months from the beginning of the negotiations, it shall, upon request of either Contracting Party be submitted to an arbitration tribunal.

3.   The arbitration tribunal shall be constituted ad hoc as follows: Each Contracting Party shall appoint one arbitrator and these two arbitrators shall agree upon a national of a third State as chairman. The arbitrators shall be appointed within three months, the chairman within five months from the date on which either Contracting Party has informed the other Contracting Party that it intends to submit the dispute to an arbitration tribunal.

4.   If within the periods specified in paragraph 3 of this Article the necessary appointments have not been made, either Contracting Party may, in the absence of any other agreement, invite the President of the International Court of Justice to make the necessary appointments. If the President of the Court is a national of either Contracting Party or if he is otherwise prevented from discharging the said function, the Vice-President or if he too is a national of either Contracting Party or is otherwise prevented from discharging the said function, the Member of the Court next in seniority, who is not a national of either Contracting Party, shall be invited to make the necessary appointments.

5.   The arbitration tribunal shall decide on the basis of respect of the law, including particularly this Agreement and other relevant agreements between the Contracting Parties, as well as the generally acknowledged rules and principles of international law.

6.   Unless the Contracting Parties decide otherwise, the tribunal shall determine its own procedure.

The tribunal shall reach its decision by a majority of votes. Such decision shall be final and binding on the Contracting Parties.

7.   Each Contracting Party shall bear the cost of the arbitrator appointed by itself and of its representation. The cost of the chairman as well as the other costs will be born in equal parts by the Contracting Parties. The tribunal may, however, in its decision direct that a higher proportion of costs shall be born by one of the two Contracting Parties and this award shall be binding on both Contracting Parties.

ARTICLE 10
Settlement of Disputes between an Investor and a Contracting Party

1.   Disputes between an investor of a Contracting Party and the other Contracting Party concerning an obligation of the latter under this Agreement, in relation to an investment of the former, shall, if possible, be settled by the disputing parties in an amicable way.

2.   If such disputes cannot be settled within six months from the date either party requested amicable settlement, the investor concerned may submit the dispute for resolution, either:

   a)   to the competent courts of the Contracting Party in the territory of which the investment has been made, or

   b)   in accordance with any applicable previously agreed dispute settlement procedure, or

   c)   to international arbitration.

3.   Where the dispute is referred to international arbitration the investor concerned may submit the dispute to:

a)   the International Centre for the Settlement of Investment Disputes, established under the Convention on the Settlement of Investment Disputes between States and Nationals of Other States, opened for signature at Washington D.C. on 18 March 1965, for arbitration or conciliation, or

b)   an ad hoc arbitral tribunal to be established under the arbitration rules of the United Nations Commission on International Trade Law (U.N.C.I.T.R.A.L.).

Each Contracting Party hereby consents to the submission of such dispute to international arbitration.

4.   The arbitral tribunal shall decide the dispute in accordance with the provisions of this Agreement and the applicable rules and principles of international law. The awards of arbitration shall be final and binding on both parties to the dispute. Each Contracting Party shall carry out without delay any such award and shall provide in its territory for the enforcement of such award.

5.   During arbitration proceedings or the enforcement of the award, the Contracting Party involved in the dispute shall not raise the objection that the investor of the other Contracting Party has received compensation under an insurance contract in respect of all or part of the damage.

ARTICLE 11
Application of other Rules

1.   If the provisions of law of either Contracting Party or obligations under international law existing at present or established hereafter between the Contracting Parties in addition to this Agreement, contain a regulation, whether general or specific, entitling investments by investors of the other Contracting Party to a treatment more favourable than is provided for by this Agreement, such regulation shall, to the extent that it is more favourable, prevail over this Agreement.

2.   Each Contracting Party shall observe any other obligation it may have entered into with regard to a specific investment of an investor of the other Contacting Party.

ARTICLE 12
Consultations

Representatives of the Contracting Parties shall, whenever necessary, hold consultations on any matter affecting the implementation of this Agreement. These consultations shall be held on the proposal of one of the Contracting Parties at a place and at a time to be agreed upon through diplomatic channels.

ARTICLE 13
Entry into Force - Duration - Termination

1.   This Agreement shall enter into force thirty days after the date on which the Contracting Parties have exchanged written notifications informing each other that the procedures required by their respective laws to this end have been completed. It shall remain in force for a period of ten years from that date.

2.   Unless notice of termination has been given by either Contracting Party at least one year before the date of expiry of its validity, this Agreement shall thereafter be extended tacitly for periods of ten years, each Contracting Party reserving the right to terminate the Agreement upon notice of at least one year before the date of expiry of its current period of validity.

3.   In respect of investments made prior to the date of termination of this Agreement, the foregoing Articles shall continue to be effective for a further period of ten years from that date.

Done in duplicate at........on..........in the Greek,...... and English languages, all texts being equally authentic.

In case of divergence the English text shall prevail.

FOR THE GOVERNMENT OF   **FOR THE GOVERNMENT OF**
THE HELLENIC REPUBLIC   _____

*

SELECTED UNCTAD PUBLICATIONS ON TRANSNATIONAL CORPORATIONS
AND FOREIGN DIRECT INVESTMENT
(For more information, please visit www.unctad.org/en/pub on the web.)

A. Serial publications

World Investment Report Series
http://www.unctad.org/wir

World Investment Report 2001: Promoting Linkages. 356 p. Sales No. E.01.II.D.12 $ 45.

World Investment Report 2001: Promoting Linkages: An Overview. Free of Charge [1]Available in six UN official languages and also from the web page in electronic format.

Ten Years of World Investment Reports: The Challenges Ahead. Proceedings of an UNCTAD special event on future challenges in the area of FDI.October 2000. UNCTAD/ITE/Misc.45. Free of charge also available from the web page.

World Investment Report 2000: Cross-border Mergers and Acquisitions and Development. 368 p. Sales No. E.00.II.D.20. $45.

World Investment Report 2000: Cross-border Mergers and Acquisitions and Development. An Overview. 75 p. Free-of-charge.

World Investment Report 1999: Foreign Direct Investment and the Challenge of Development. 536 p. Sales No. E.99.II.D.3. $45.

World Investment Report 1999: Foreign Direct Investment and Challenge of Development. An Overview. 75 p. Free-of-charge.

World Investment Report 1998: Trends and Determinants. 430 p. Sales No. E.98.II.D.5. $45.

World Investment Report 1998: Trends and Determinants. An Overview. 67 p. Free-of-charge.

World Investment Report 1997: Transnational Corporations, Market Structure and Competition Policy. 420 p. Sales No. E.97.II.D.10. $45.

World Investment Report 1997: Transnational Corporations, Market Structure and Competition Policy. An Overview. 70 p. Free-of-charge.

World Investment Report 1996: Investment, Trade and International Policy Arrangements. 332 p. Sales No. E.96.II.A.14. $45.

World Investment Report 1996: Investment, Trade and International Policy Arrangements. An Overview. 51 p. Free-of-charge.

---

[1] All overviews are free of charge and are available also in electronic format on the web page of the World Investment Report http://www.unctad.org/wir

World Investment Report 1995: Transnational Corporations and Competitiveness.
491 p. Sales No. E.95.II.A.9. $45.

World Investment Report 1995: Transnational Corporations and Competitiveness. An Overview. 51 p. Free-of-charge..

World Investment Report 1994: Transnational Corporations, Employment and the Workplace. 482 p. Sales No. E.94.II.A.14. $45.

World Investment Report 1994: Transnational Corporations, Employment and the Workplace. An Executive Summary. 34 p.

World Investment Report 1993: Transnational Corporations and Integrated International Production. 290 p. Sales No. E.93.II.A.14. $45.

World Investment Report 1993: Transnational Corporations and Integrated International Production. An Executive Summary. 31 p. ST/CTC/159. Free-of-charge.

World Investment Report 1992: Transnational Corporations as Engines of Growth. 356 p. Sales No. E.92.II.A.19. $45.

World Investment Report 1992: Transnational Corporations as Engines of Growth: An Executive Summary. 30 p. Sales No. E.92.II.A.24.

World Investment Report 1991: The Triad in Foreign Direct Investment. 108 p. Sales No.E.91.II.A.12. $25. Full version at http://www.unctad.org/wir/contents/wir91content.en.htm.

World Investment Directory Series:

World Investment Directory. Vol. VII (Parts I and II): Asia and the Pacific. 646 p. Sales No. E.00.II.D.11.

World Investment Directory. Vol. VI: West Asia. 192 p. Sales No. E.97.II.A.2. $35.

World Investment Directory. Vol. V: Africa. 508 p. Sales No. E.97.II.A.1. $75.

World Investment Directory. Vol. IV: Latin America and the Caribbean. 478 p. Sales No. E.94.II.A.10. $65.

World Investment Directory 1992. Vol. III: Developed Countries. 532 p. Sales No. E.93.II.A.9. $75.

World Investment Directory 1992. Vol. II: Central and Eastern Europe. 432 p. Sales No. E.93.II.A.1. $65. (Joint publication with the United Nations Economic Commission for Europe.)

World Investment Directory 1992. Vol. I: Asia and the Pacific. 356 p. Sales No. E.92.II.A.11. $65.

Investment Policy Review Series:
http://www.unctad.org/en/pub/investpolicy.en.htm

Investment and Innovation Policy Review of Ethiopia. 115 pages. UNCTAD/ITE/IPC/Misc.4. New York and Geneva 2002

Investment Policy Review of Ecuador. 117 pages. UNCTAD/ITE/IPC/Misc.2. Sales No. E.01.II D.31 $ 22. New York and Geneva 2001

Investment Policy Review of Mauritius. 84 p. Sales No. E.01.II.D.11. $22. New York and Geneva 2001

Investment Policy Review of Peru. 108 p. Sales No. E.00.II.D. 7. $22. New York and Geneva 2000 (Also available in Spanish-Tambien disponible en español)

Investment Policy Review of Uganda. 75 p. Sales No. E.99.II.D.24. $15. New York and Geneva 1999

Investment Policy Review of Egypt. 113 p. Sales No. E.99.II.D.20. $19. New York and Geneva 1999

Investment Policy Review of Uzbekistan. 64 p. UNCTAD/ITE/IIP/Misc. 13. New York and Geneva

International Investment Instruments: Compendia

International Investment Instruments: A Compendium Vol. VI 568 p. Sales No. E.01.II.D.34

International Investment Instruments: A Compendium, Vol. IV, 319 p. Sales No. E.00.II.D.13. $55, **Vol. V,** 505 p. Sales No. E.00.II.D.14. $55.

International Investment Instruments: A Compendium. Vol. I. 371 p. Sales No. E.96.II.A.9; **Vol. II.** 577 p. Sales No. E.96.II.A.10; **Vol. III.** 389 p. Sales No. E.96.II.A.11; the 3-volume set, Sales No. E.96.II.A.12. $125.

Bilateral Investment Treaties 1959-1999 143 p. UNCTAD/ITE/IIA/2, Free-of-charge. Available only in electronic version from http://www.unctad.org/en/pub/poiteiiad2.en.htm.

Bilateral Investment Treaties in the Mid-1990s, 314 p. Sales No. E.98.II.D.8. $46.

Investment Guides for LDCs Series / UNCTAD - International Chamber of Commerce
http://www.unctad.org/en/pub/investguide.en.htm

An Investment Guide to Mozambique: Opportunities and Conditions. 72.p UNCTAD/ITE/IIA/4. Geneva and New York 2002

An Investment Guide to Uganda: Opportunities and Conditions. 76 p. UNCTAD/ITE/IIT/Misc. 30. New York and Geneva 2001

An Investment Guide to Bangladesh: Opportunities and Conditions.
66 p. UNCTAD/ITE/IIT/Misc.29. New York and Geneva 2001

Guide d'investissement au Mali. 108 p. UNCTAD/ITE/IIT/Misc.24.
http://www.unctad.org/fr/docs/poiteiitm24.fr.pdf. (Joint publication with the International
Chamber of Commerce, in association with PricewaterhouseCoopers.)

An Investment Guide to Ethiopia: Opportunities and Conditions. 69 p.
UNCTAD/ITE/IIT/Misc.19. http://www.unctad.org/en/docs/poiteiitm19.en.pdf. (Joint
publication with the International Chamber of Commerce, in association with Pricewaterhouse
Coopers.)

IIA Issues Paper Series
(http://www.unctad.org/iia.)

Transfer of Technology. p 138 $18. Sales No. E.01.II.D.33

Illicit Payments. p. 108 p. Sales No. E.01.II.D.20 $ 13

Home Country Measures. p.96. Sales No.E.01.II.D.19. $12

Host Country Operational Measures. 109 p. Sales No E.01.II.D.18. $15.

Social Responsibility. 91 p. Sales No. E.01.II.D.4. $15.

Environment. 105 p. Sales No. E.01.II.D.3. $15.

Transfer of Funds. 68 p. Sales No. E.00.II.D.27. $12.

Employment. 69 p. Sales No. E.00.II.D.15. $12.

Taxation. 111 p. Sales No. E.00.II.D.5. $12.

International Investment Agreements: Flexibility for Development. 185 p. Sales No.
E.00.II.D.6. $12.

Taking of Property. 83 p. Sales No. E.00.II.D.4. $12.

Trends in International Investment Agreements: An Overview. 112 p. Sales No.
E.99.II.D.23. $ 12.

Lessons from the MAI. 31 p. Sales No. E.99.II.D.26. $ 12.

National Treatment. 104 p. Sales No. E.99.II.D.16. $12.

Fair and Equitable Treatment. 64 p. Sales No. E.99.II.D.15. $12.

Investment-Related Trade Measures. 64 p. Sales No. E.99.II.D.12. $12.

Most-Favoured-Nation Treatment. 72p. Sales No. E.99.II.D.11. $12.

Admission and Establishment. 72p. Sales No. E.99.II.D.10. $12.

Scope and Definition. 96p. Sales No. E.99.II.D.9. $12.

Transfer Pricing. 72p. Sales No. E.99.II.D.8. $12.

Foreign Direct Investment and Development. 88p. Sales No. E.98.II.D.15. $12.

B. Current Studies

Series A

No. 30.**Incentives and Foreign Direct Investment**. 98 p. Sales No. E.96.II.A.6. $30. [Out of print.]

No. 29.**Foreign Direct Investment, Trade, Aid and Migration**. 100 p. Sales No. E.96.II.A.8. $25. (Joint publication with the International Organization for Migration.)

No. 28.**Foreign Direct Investment in Africa**. 119 p. Sales No. E.95.II.A.6. $20.

No. 27.**Tradability of Banking Services: Impact and Implications**. 195 p. Sales No. E.94.II.A.12. $50.

No. 26.**Explaining and Forecasting Regional Flows of Foreign Direct Investment**. 58 p. Sales No. E.94.II.A.5. $25.

No. 25.**International Tradability in Insurance Services**. 54 p. Sales No. E.93.II.A.11. $20.

No. 24.**Intellectual Property Rights and Foreign Direct Investment**. 108 p. Sales No. .93.II.A.10.$20.

No. 23.**The Transnationalization of Service Industries: An Empirical Analysis of the Determinants of Foreign Direct Investment by Transnational Service Corporations**. 62 p. Sales No. E.93.II.A.3. $15.

No. 22.**Transnational Banks and the External Indebtedness of Developing Countries: Impact of Regulatory Changes**. 48 p. Sales No. E.92.II.A.10. $12.

No. 20.**Foreign Direct Investment, Debt and Home Country Policies**. 50 p. Sales No. E.90.II.A.16. $12.

No. 19.**New Issues in the Uruguay Round of Multilateral Trade Negotiations**. 52 p. Sales No. E.90.II.A.15. $12.50.

No. 18.**Foreign Direct Investment and Industrial Restructuring in Mexico**. 114 p. Sales No. E.92.II.A.9. $12.

No. 17. **Government Policies and Foreign Direct Investment**. 68 p. Sales No. E.91.II.A.20. $12.50.

ASIT Advisory Studies
(Formerly Current Studies, Series B)

No. 17. **The World of Investment Promotion at a Glance: A survey of investment promotion practices.** UNCTAD/ITE/IPC/3. Free of Charge

No. 16. **Tax Incentives and Foreign Direct Investment: A Global Survey.** 180p. Sales No. E.01.II.D.5. $23. Summary available from http://www.unctad.org/asit/resumé.htm

No. 15. **Investment Regimes in the Arab World: Issues and Policies**. 232p. Sales No. E/F.00.II.D.32.

No. 14. **Handbook on Outward Investment Promotion Agencies and Institutions**. 50 p. Sales No. E.99.II.D.22. $ 15.

No. 13. **Survey of Best Practices in Investment Promotion.** 71 p., Sales No. E.97.II.D.11.$ 35.

No. 12. **Comparative Analysis of Petroleum Exploration Contracts.** 80 p. Sales No. E. 96.II.A.7. $35.

No. 11. **Administration of Fiscal Regimes for Petroleum Exploration and Development.** 45 p. Sales No. E. 95.II.A.8.

No. 10. **Formulation and Implementation of Foreign Investment Policies: Selected Key Issues.** 84 p. Sales No. E. 92.II.A.21. $12.

No. 9. **Environmental Accounting: Current Issues, Abstracts and Bibliography.** 86 p. Sales No. E.92.II.A.23.

C. Individual Studies

Compendium of International Arrangements on Transfer of Technology: Selected Instruments. 308 p. Sales No. E.01.II.D.28. $ 45

FDI in Least Developed Countries at a Glance. 150 p. UNCTAD/ITE/IIA/3. Free of charge. Full version available also from http://www.unctad.org/en/pub/poiteiiad3.en.htm.

Foreign Direct Investment in Africa: Performance and Potential. 89 p. UNCTAD/ITE/IIT/Misc. 15. Free of charge. Full version available also from http://www.unctad.org/en/docs/poiteiitm15.pdf.

TNC-SME Linkages for Development: Issues-Experiences-Best Practices. Proceedings of the Special Round Table on TNCs, SMEs and Development, UNCTAD X, 15 February 2000, Bangkok, Thailand. 113 p. UNCTAD/ITE/TEB1. Free-of-charge.

Handbook on Foreign Direct Investment by Small and Medium-sized Enterprises: Lessons from Asia. 200 p. Sales No. E.98.II.D.4. $48.

Handbook on Foreign Direct Investment by Small and Medium-sized Enterprises: Lessons from Asia. Executive Summary and Report of the Kunming Conference. 74 p. Free-of-charge.

Small and Medium-sized Transnational Corporations. Executive Summary and Report of the Osaka Conference. 60 p. Free-of-charge.

Small and Medium-sized Transnational Corporations: Role, Impact and Policy Implications. 242 p. Sales No. E.93.II.A.15. $35.

Measures of the Transnationalization of Economic Activity. 93p. Sales No. E.01.II.D.2. $20.

The Competitiveness Challenge: Transnational Corporations and Industrial Restructuring in Developing Countries. 283p. Sales No. E.00.II.D.35. $42.

Integrating International and Financial Performance at the Enterprise Level. 116 p. Sales No. E.00.II.D.28. $18.

FDI Determinants and TNCs Strategies: The Case of Brazil. 195 p. Sales No. E.00.II.D.2. $35. Summary available from http://www.unctad.org/en/pub/psiteiitd14.en.htm.

The Social Responsibility of Transnational Corporations. 75 p. UNCTAD/ITE/IIT/Misc. 21. Free of charge. Out of stock. Available on http://www.unctad.org/en/docs/poiteiitm21.en.pdf.

Conclusions on Accounting and Reporting by Transnational Corporations. 47 p. Sales No. E.94.II.A.9. $25.

Accounting, Valuation and Privatization. 190 p. Sales No. E.94.II.A.3. $25.

Environmental Management in Transnational Corporations: Report on the Benchmark Corporate Environment Survey. 278 p. Sales No. E.94.II.A.2. $29.95.

Management Consulting: A Survey of the Industry and Its Largest Firms. 100 p. Sales No. E.93.II.A.17. $25.

Transnational Corporations: A Selective Bibliography, 1991-1992. 736 p. Sales No. E.93.II.A.16. $75.

Foreign Investment and Trade Linkages in Developing Countries. 108 p. Sales No. E.93.II.A.12. $18.

Transnational Corporations from Developing Countries: Impact on Their Home Countries.116 p. Sales No. E.93.II.A.8. $15.

Debt-Equity Swaps and Development. 150 p. Sales No. E.93.II.A.7. $35.

From the Common Market to EC 92: Regional Economic Integration in the European Community and Transnational Corporations. 134 p. Sales No. E.93.II.A.2. $25.

The East-West Business Directory 1991/1992. 570 p. Sales No. E.92.II.A.20. $65.
Climate Change and Transnational Corporations: Analysis and Trends.
110 p. Sales No. E.92.II.A.7. $16.50.

Foreign Direct Investment and Transfer of Technology in India.
150 p. Sales No. E.92.II.A.3. $20.

The Determinants of Foreign Direct Investment: A Survey of the Evidence.
84 p. Sales No. E.92.II.A.2. $12.50.

Transnational Corporations and Industrial Hazards Disclosure.
98 p. Sales No. E.91.II.A.18. $17.50.

Transnational Business Information: A Manual of Needs and Sources.
216 p. Sales No. E.91.II.A.13. $45.

The Financial Crisis in Asia and Foreign Direct Investment: An Assessment.
101 p. Sales No. GV.E.98.0.29. $20.

Sharing Asia's Dynamism: Asian Direct Investment in the European Union.
192 p. Sales No. E.97.II.D.1. $26.

Investing in Asia's Dynamism: European Union Direct Investment in Asia.
124 p. ISBN 92-827-7675-1. ECU 14. (Joint publication with the European Commission.)

International Investment towards the Year 2002. 166 p. Sales No. GV.E.98.0.15. $29. (Joint publication with Invest in France Mission and Arthur Andersen, in collaboration with DATAR.)

International Investment towards the Year 2001. 81 p. Sales No. GV.E.97.0.5. $35. (Joint publication with Invest in France Mission and Arthur Andersen, in collaboration with DATAR.)

Liberalizing International Transactions in Services: A Handbook.
182 p. Sales No. E.94.II.A.11. $45. (Joint publication with the World Bank.)

The Impact of Trade-Related Investment Measures on Trade and Development: Theory, Evidence and Policy Implications. 108 p. Sales No. E.91.II.A.19. $17.50. (Joint publication with the United Nations Centre on Transnational Corporations.)

Transnational Corporations and World Development. 656 p. ISBN 0-415-08560-8 (hardback), 0-415-08561-6 (paperback). £65 (hardback), £20.00 (paperback). (Published by International Thomson Business Press on behalf of UNCTAD.)

Companies without Borders: Transnational Corporations in the 1990s. 224 p. ISBN 0-415-12526-X. £47.50. (Published by International Thomson Business Press on behalf of UNCTAD.)

The New Globalism and Developing Countries.

336 p. ISBN 92-808-0944-X. $25. (Published by United Nations University Press.)

World Economic Situation and Prospects 2002. 51 p. Sales No. E.02.II.C.2. $15. (Joint publication with the United Nations Department of Economic and Social Affairs.)

World Economic Situation and Prospects 2001. 51 p. Sales No. E.01.II.C.2. $15. (Joint publication with the United Nations Department of Economic and Social Affairs.)

D. Journals

Transnational Corporations Journal (formerly **The CTC Reporter**).
Published three times a year. Annual subscription price: $45; individual issues $20.
http://www.unctad.org/en/subsites/dite/1_itncs/1_tncs.htm

United Nations publications may be obtained from bookstores and distributors throughout the world. Please consult your bookstore or write to:

For Africa, Asia and Europe to

Sales Section
United Nations Office at Geneva
Palais des Nations
CH-1211 Geneva 10
Switzerland
Tel: (41-22) 917-1234
Fax: (41-22) 917-0123
E-mail: unpubli@unog.ch

For Latin America and U.S.A to:

Sales Section
Room DC2-0853
United Nations Secretariat
New York, NY 10017
U.S.A.
Tel: (1-212) 963-8302 or (800) 253-9646
Fax: (1-212) 963-3489
E-mail: publications@un.org

All prices are quoted in United States dollars.
For further information on the work of the Division on Investment, Technology and Enterprise Development, UNCTAD, please address inquiries to:

United Nations Conference on Trade and Development
Division on Investment, Technology and Enterprise Development
Palais des Nations, Room E-10054
CH-1211 Geneva 10, Switzerland
Telephone: (41-22) 907-5651
Telefax: (41-22) 907-0498

E-mail: natalia.guerra@unctad.org
http://www.unctad.org

QUESTIONNAIRE

International Investment Instruments: A Compendium

Volume VIII

In order to improve the quality and relevance of the work of the UNCTAD Division on Investment, Technology and Enterprise Development, it would be useful to receive the views of readers on this publication. It would therefore be greatly appreciated if you could complete the following questionnaire and return it to:

Readership Survey
UNCTAD Division on Investment, Technology and Enterprise Development
United Nations Office in Geneva
Palais des Nations
Room E-9123
CH-1211 Geneva 10
Switzerland
Fax: 41-22-907-0194

1. Name and address of respondent (optional):

_____

_____

2. Which of the following best describes your area of work?

Government ○   Public enterprise ○

Private enterprise ○   Academic or research
                                          institution ○

International organization ○   Media ○

Not-for-profit organization ○   Other (specify) _____

3. In which country do you work? _____

4. What is your assessment of the contents of this publication?

Excellent ○   Adequate ○

Good ○   Poor ○

5. How useful is this publication to your work?

Very useful ○   Of some use ○   Irrelevant ○

6. Please indicate the three things you liked best about this publication:

_____

_____

_____

7. Please indicate the three things you liked least about this publication:

_____

_____

_____

8. Are you a regular recipient of **Transnational Corporations** (formerly **The CTC Reporter**), UNCTAD-DITE's tri-annual refereed journal?

Yes   ○   No   ○

If not, please check here if you would like to receive
a sample copy sent to the name and address you have
given above   ○

*